Boomers n Bitcoin

By Jerry Hutcheson

How baby boomers can protect wealth and retirement, and to actually thrive when the economy goes BOOM.

Jerry Hutcheson

Some names and identifying details have been changed to protect privacy.

Publisher: Jerry Hutcheson,
Email: jh@jerryhutcheson.com,
Website:www.jerryhutcheson.com
4210,HickoryLakeCt.
Titusville,Florida32780
-

Boomers n Bitcoin: How Baby Boomers can protect wealth and retirement, and to actually thrive when the economy goes boom. / Jerry Hutcheson.

Pages 286
Includes Table of Contents and glossary
1st Edition 2026

ISBN: 978-8-9944699-0-3 (paperback)1. Bitcoin 2. Baby Boomers 3. Investing 4. Retirement 5. Family Planning 6. Investment planning

Ordering information: Special discounts are available for corporations, associations, for details visit www.jerryhutcheson.com
call 321-244-4988
email jh@jerryhutcheson.com

Jerry Hutcheson

Table of Contents

Introduction

Think your wealth is protected? Think you are set for your retirement? Being a baby boomer has its own set of issues just like any age group or generation. Getting older. Aches and pains. Health care costs. Children growing up and moving on. Facing your limitations. I assure you that retirement and retirement savings should be on this list. I am 65 and I remember when gas was 27 cents a gallon and everyone freaked out when gas went to 36 cents a gallon. It was called the "Energy Crisis." And the days of disco and lime green leisure suits and Italian horn necklaces, and puka shells. I was young but I even remember watching the Apollo 11 go to the moon and how we all felt so proud of our achievements. Also, I will never forget the early morning my mom came into the living room to tell my dad with a serious look of anguish on her face "they killed another Kennedy." The morning after the assassination of Bobby Kennedy.

As boomers we have seen a lot. And we feel that we have been through some serious turmoil and change in the last five decades. But I believe that we are about to see changes to our lives and livelihood that are truly monumental. And we will most likely witness it in our lifetime. So, a lifetime of massive historical movement is going to actually give way to even more radical changes? How can this be? And why is it different for baby boomers? Well, that is what this book is about.

It has been said that there are too many baby boomers hitting the social security system all at once. That we are the largest generation. That is what the word 'boomer' means. It was an explosion of births, by our parents after the end of World War II. And everyone came home with the promise of continuing their education. Getting a good job and buying a home and two cars. Eventually watching grandkids grow up as they would eventually retire with a safe future, all accomplished with a single income in the family. We were secure in knowing America had the premier economy in the world. They greatest and most powerful nation the world had ever seen. We were Americans, it was our birthright. Right?

But something happened suddenly along the way. Or at least it seems to have suddenly happened. But in actuality it was brewing for a long time. And then when it is time for our generation to retire, it seems as if this simmering bubbling problem is ready to burst. And could take us down with it. There is a line from a Hemmingway Novel when asked about how bankruptcy happens. He says "gradually at first, and then suddenly." Well, we grew up in the gradually stage, and now we are getting to the suddenly part. Peter Dunworth head of The Bitcoin Advisor, says "it's a very predictable path…and that you won't retire if you don't have Bitcoin." Larry Fink the head of Blackrock the world's largest asset management firm, with a total valuation of $10 trillion. Says that Bitcoin is not a speculative asset and says that it's risky **not** to own Bitcoin. His firm BlackRock published a paper in 2024 that says you should allocate at least 84% of your portfolio in Bitcoin! These are fantastical concepts. Are you hearing this from your financial experts and advisors?

The purpose of this book is two-fold. I want to first try to help my generation head off the inevitable pain of the "crackup boom" that the great economist Ludwig Von Mises talked about. And second to ease the skids on this new transformational monetary technology that we are being exposed to called Bitcoin. Let's face it. If you have not worked in the technology field then your exposure to bitcoin is probably going to be limited.

It's too complex, it is too technical, it's too foreign to our understanding of money. And sadly, enough it has some old-fashioned values baked into it such as frugality, planning, steadiness, conservation. These values unfortunately have been squeezed out of our daily lives. These traditional American qualities have become somewhat foreign to the average American today, even though they were very common in our parents and grandparents. But these values are essential to being prepared for retirement. Bitcoin is helping to bring those back. And the cause of this lack of values is part of the issue.

My goal is to cut through the technical stuff and to help you understand the path out of this potential crisis. Learn about its reasons, and how we got here. Without going into a boring deep economic discussion. Then when you understand the challenge that is looming. I want to offer you a way out of this mess that is quite direct and revolutionary in its effect. And very doable.

But Bitcoin covers so many issues. That it would be far beyond the scope of this book to cover all of them. But we will show you how to understand Bitcoin and its essential parts. It will take a bit of learning. But you learned to drive a car, you learned how to raise children, many of you graduated from college. Many of you will be able to understand this. We of course will not be covering all of these issues. But we will certainly cover enough to get you started and on your way to safety and prosperity. And believe it or not. Understanding how to protect and grow your wealth in Bitcoin is much simpler than the current investment system that we are mired in.

I will help you to look at Bitcoin in a totally different way. A way that takes the attacks on Bitcoin and shows you the fallacy. That many of these attacks are truly advantages. And top of all of these advantages. It may just end up being a lifeline to an entire generation of Americans. To that end I am going to ask you a lot of questions along the way. These questions may be rhetorical at times in order to make you think. But there will be many questions that are literal so that you will also put you on the path to actually putting together a real plan. We say in the Bitcoin world that "you do not change Bitcoin, Bitcoin changes you." These numerous questions will be your first steps in changing the way you think.

Finally, I will actually give you concrete exercises to move you forward on this new way of thinking. So, if you participate you should get more from this book than just theory and ideas. You will gain the practical understanding how to start taking the first steps. So, keep a notepad close by. If you want to learn this clean new way of building your financial future, you will need to learn. And learning is not just navel gazing about some cool new ideas. It will take a bit of practical work. That's not too much to ask to protect your life's savings, is it?

It sounds like a lot to accomplish in one book. But I assure you the accomplishment is not mine. It is Bitcoin's accomplishment. And the fact that I am able to write this book, is proof that you can learn these new ideas and practices also. I am cataloging these practices for a specific group of people. A group of people that really need this information. This is not investment or legal advice. I am not a money manager or a formal economist. But that is one of the many advantages of Bitcoin. It is not for some secret priesthood of experts from the trading pits and boiler rooms of Wall Street and halls of academia, or the Ivory towers of the giant mega banks. Waiting to be handed down and sold to you, in tantalizing little bits like a dog begging for scraps. After the important people have had their fill at the big table. While extracting billions of fees in order to make their huge bonuses.

No this is for everyone. And I think you will find it is especially valuable for everyone in the Baby Boomer community. But the only way to know is to get started right away. You can wait and think about the changes that need to be made. But you may get passed by. I don't think there is much time left.

PART 1: THE CASE FOR BITCOIN IN RETIREMENT

If you're a Baby Boomer approaching or already in retirement, you've likely spent decades working, saving, and planning for your financial future. Yet despite your best efforts, the goalposts keep moving. Your financial security seems elusive. This book addresses a critical question that keeps many Boomers awake at night: How do you retire without losing the money you've worked so hard to earn?

Chapter 1

How Does A Boomer Retire Without Losing Money?

"Rule number 1, never lose money.... Rule number 2, don't forget rule number 1."

Warren Buffett

In 2005, my wife and I decided to move to a nicer house. Our kids were not yet in school, and we wanted them to attend good schools for their future. My business was operating very well. We felt a desire to find a bigger home, even though we already had a perfectly nice home in a decent neighborhood. Typical Americans, always searching for more.

So off we went looking for a better home. But I couldn't shake my concern about skyrocketing housing prices. I had the money for the down payment, but I was not so sure that the bank would approve the mortgage for a bigger, more expensive house. Being only in the second year of my startup, I lacked the documented income history banks typically required, despite having a strong cash flow. I had been working with banks in a business capacity since I was 18 years old. I knew the kind of meticulous scrutiny they required. And even though I've always been conservative with money, the lending process made me anxious.

But this was different, strangely, nobody else seemed worried. I even brought it up a few times to various home builders during our search, including Engle Homes, the nation's largest home builder at the time. They had a good reputation and were listed on the New York Stock Exchange. They sure weren't worried. Hell, they owned their own mortgage company to handle the loan. They offered sweet terms: low down payments, attractive interest rates, no points up front, no special appraisals, just endless upgrades and fancy fixtures.

We moved in and it was amazing. Houses sprang up all around us in our lovely new neighborhood. Still, no one seemed concerned. But something was wrong.

Four years later, we learned what had gone wrong. Lucky for me, I worked in an internet-related field called Information Technology, a *"**deflationary** industry"* (more on this important word later). So, my income was not affected by the housing bubble. But by this point, we could see something was seriously off. People started abandoning their homes. Houses suddenly stopped selling. Friends were losing their jobs. When houses did sell, prices kept falling. I distinctly remember the night when a neighbor's abandoned house was stripped of all its appliances and cabinets, including the AC unit for its copper coils. And this was in a nice, low-crime neighborhood. That kind of thing had never happened in my neighborhood before. The building boom came to a screeching halt.

11

Engle stopped returning calls. Like other home builders, they were going bankrupt. It was an awful time for a lot of people, full of fear and uncertainty. The market was in a free fall, and panic was everywhere. We were lucky. We hunkered down, kept our heads about us, and just kept paying our mortgage as it was sold to one company after another. Eventually, things leveled off. We were witnessing the Great Financial Crisis of 2008. Baby Boomers remember this well. We spiraled from great prosperity, free spending, and a record housing boom to a systemic crash that induced fear and panic. Nobody seemed to have any idea how it happened or what to do about it.

I will never forget seeing President George W. Bush on television in the early stages of the panic, declaring to the American people, "I've abandoned free market principles to save the free market system." Never has a politician so succinctly revealed just how duplicitous and bankrupt these characters truly are. One simple sentence. This was our leadership? I remember his vacuous, clueless stare coming onto my television. *Wow,* I thought, *these guys are completely lost.* And he was probably even reading this off a teleprompter!

In the midst of a genuine crisis, Bush had accidentally revealed just how incompetent and ineffective the government was at "managing" our economy. His Orwellian doublespeak foreshadowed exactly what was to come. One thing became certain. I was about to lose a lot of money. My 401(k), stocks, real estate investments, hard-earned stock options, and home value — everything plummeted into a mind-melting crash. I was terrified. I had something to lose and a young family to protect. With leadership like this, the depths of this disaster seemed unfathomable and bottomless.

Wall Street insider-turned-Treasury Secretary Hank Paulson appeared before Congress demanding $800 billion in bailout money, with no plan, no assurance of success, and no strategy to pay it back. I lost money, and so did most Americans. Recovery seemed almost impossible. He was everywhere in the media, insisting this was the only way. I didn't buy it. Boy, was I right.

But you know who didn't lose money? That's right… the banks and the large Wall Street firms. In fact, they made money. And a lot of it. They received bailouts and, worse, instead of circulating this taxpayer money through the system as promised, they hoarded it for themselves. Within a year, Wall Street elites received huge bonuses from the "profits" they were making, while everyday Americans continued to suffer. By 2011, Wall Street was thriving again. There seemed to be no escape from this rigged system. How could those of us outside the inner circle protect our hard-earned savings? One thing was obvious. With these fools in charge, we are going to lose.

Little did I know that a tiny seed of hope was germinating below the surface. Delicate, clean, and beautiful like a newborn. It was fragile and gasping for its first breaths of life. Soon, this newborn would make itself known. For now, it existed as a little 9-page white paper, a piece of visionary code gingerly getting its wobbly legs underneath it like a newborn colt on a bright, dew-covered pasture at dawn. From its beginning, it was shepherded by an eclectic collection of brilliant mathematicians, physicists, and computer scientists calling themselves cypherpunks, led by Bitcoin's pseudonymous founder, Satoshi Nakamoto. Marveled at, debated, and traded, Bitcoin began like any collectible in its early stages, think baseball cards traded by enthusiasts. Yet, this fledgling was destined for something far greater.

Savings and the American Family

Americans used to save money. It was part of our ethos. I remember being seven or eight years old when my grandmother would give me a $20 bill for Christmas and my birthday. We felt rich. Milk was 60 cents a gallon, and a pack of gum or a comic book cost 10 cents. A cup of coffee was a quarter. You could make a phone call at a corner phone booth for a dime. A pair of Converse sneakers was about $4.95, and you could get them in your school's colors.

My brother and I would go with our dad to First Federal Savings and Loan. We'd hand that money to the teller, along with our small paper passbook savings account book. She'd stamp our books, record the deposit, and we'd earn 3 ½% interest. We were told it was for college. I didn't even know what college was, but it sounded important. We didn't question it—this was just what families did in 1967. We saved.

Our parents had grown up in the Great Depression. They knew what happened if you didn't save for a rainy day. One unexpected event could wipe you out. So, they passed that lesson down: *Save your pennies. Put them in your piggy bank.* Back then, every kid had a piggy bank. Today, most don't even know what one is.

The American way of life that baby boomers grew up in encouraged savings. Savings and piggy banks were a common refrain for kids in our generation. Somewhere along the way, that mindset disappeared. No one talks about saving anymore. What happened? Why do we not save? Something changed. And it changed big.

In the early 1960s, the personal savings rate hovered around 12%. By 2019, it had dropped below 5%. This is a serious decline. It has been said that the average American household can manage only $400 in the event of an emergency. And 33% of American adults have zero savings. This is a serious problem. And there is a reason for it.

But there is more to this problem than just the numbers and the dollars. Savings means something more than just an amount of money that a family or individual has. It is more than just numbers for paying some bills. It is actually a representation of a family's ability to survive in hard times. It is a hedge against a day when things get tough, and we need to make it to the next week, month, or year.

Even more than that, savings are how we transfer the energy we have expended —the value of our hard work and innovative pursuits —into the future. Our future. When we save, we store that energy. We preserve it for our future selves, our family, our children, grandchildren, and our heirs after we die. Savings is the ability to give this energy to the future. And do with it what we please. Talking about savings might seem boring or old-fashioned, but the alternative is very exciting but not the kind of excitement you want.

We'll discuss energy, savings, and bitcoin in more detail later on. But for now, it is important to understand that something changed. It was part of our culture and part of our collective psyche to save and to prepare for the future. It taught us many valuable things. It taught us responsibility. It taught us how to plan. It taught us how to delay gratification instead of mindless hedonism in the present moment. All of these were essential values that we grew up immersed in. They formed the foundations of a strong society and helped build our country into a great place to live.

So, what happened? Something very fundamental changed how we live our lives. It wasn't a simple shift in a habit. But a deep change in the way we live our lives. And it took a really big push to make this change.

Boomers Are Booming.
It's no secret that baby boomers are hitting a peak number in retirement. And fast. Over 75 million Americans belong to this generation, and they're retiring at a staggering rate of 10,000 per day.

So, the question becomes: Who will pay for all of this? The government? Pensions? Savings? Actually, 45% of baby boomers, within 10 years of leaving work, have no savings at all for their retirement. What about their investments? Boomers have experienced the tech boom and bust, the dot-com crash, the inflation of the early 2000s, the housing collapse in 2008, and the COVID recession in 2020 brought on by the pandemic.

Each wave brought dramatic losses in investments, inflation, and economic uncertainty. Do we even know what stability looks like anymore? Today, the average baby boomer has less than $100,000 saved for retirement, far short of the estimated $1,000,000 typically needed to fund a boomer couple through their post-work years.

Let's keep going. How much does health care cost for a baby boomer? Though retired boomers make up just 13% of the population, they account for:

- 26% of all doctor visits,
- 38% of all hospital stays, and
- 34% of all prescription drug use.

Who's paying for all that? Medicare? You'd better check again. Medicare Part A routinely covers less than 80% of eligible services. And other services are not covered at all. So, it may provide essential coverage, but it is certainly incomplete. And this is only getting worse. Look at Trump's latest spending bill. And this doesn't even begin to touch quality-of-life goals, such as travel, spending time with grandkids in another city, or simply enjoying the hobbies you put off for decades. It can look pretty bleak when you think about it. And you really should think about it.

I am not here to bring you down. That is not the purpose of this book. The purpose of this book is to help you understand what you are facing as a baby boomer. If you are relying on the current system as we know it — government programs, pensions, and traditional savings vehicles — the situation may appear bleak. The depressing picture I have revealed to you is what you may face, but the reality is, you have a choice. There is an option. Something so revolutionary that when you learn about it, you will be amazed.

This option, of course, is Bitcoin. Bitcoin is possibly the greatest monetary technology innovation in the last 5,000 years. It offers a revolutionary shift that will transform our world beyond normal imagination. It is a lifeline to a drowning man. It is a shield against a coming onslaught. It is hope. It is the future.

This brings a question to mind: What does all this money really mean? The US government may act like it doesn't care about a growing money supply, but *reality* cares. And if you're a baby boomer trying to survive, maybe even thrive, through retirement, *you* should care, too. We boomers were taught that we have the most powerful military in the world. That it's there to protect us from a war. When was the last time a foreign military tried to attack the us in the USA? What we're facing now isn't an external threat. It's internal. Economic. Systemic.

And bitcoin just might be the defense we've been waiting for.

Who Saves For You?

Are you using an investment advisory service? Maybe you use a money manager? Or do you manage your money yourself? Or are you using Uncle Sam's Social Security system to save for yourself? Regardless of your approach, the results may be troubling.

The SPIVA (S&P Indices Versus Active) USA Scorecard, which tracks the performance of actively managed funds, reveals sobering results. Over a 1-year period, 68% of managed funds missed their own targets. Of the 17 categories measured, only three categories met their own benchmark index.

But it gets worse. If you extend the timeframe to 15 years, over 89% of companies underperform their own benchmarks. This does not look promising for investing your money in funds. Many reasons were cited for this, but the primary problem was a lack of accountability. Also known as trust. Trust is a huge issue in the money management industry. It's also what sets Bitcoin apart.

If your fund manager isn't held accountable for poor performance, then who is? You guessed it. You are. Because it's your money.

So, who is saving for you? You thought your fund manager was saving for you. But in the end, the responsibility falls on your shoulders. This kind of looks like the way we were brought up in the fifties and sixties. We were responsible for our savings.

Yes, having a financial planner can help. If used properly and with an educated eye. Studies suggest that working with one may boost returns by up to 3%. Sounds pretty good, and I would certainly recommend this versus doing nothing. But remember, you are paying fees. Many times, advisors put clients in products that benefit themselves or their firms more than they benefit the clients. Once you deduct fees, adjust for inflation, and factor in trust, how much are you really making? Remember what Warren Buffet said?

Remember what we said about trust and accountability? Here it is rearing its ugly head again. So, how do we deal with this trust issue? First, you need to ask yourself. Who is doing your savings for you? I see fund managers as another tool in the tool box. Not a place to dump off your responsibility for your future.

So, let's go to the last category we talked about: you are managing your own money and investments. Okay, this is good. You are saving money and taking responsibility. Now what? How is that working for you?

You may have a 401(k) at your work, and part of your pay has been going into this pretax account for several years. Good for you. You are investing in something. And you are avoiding taxes for now. At least until it's time to use the 401(k). But even more importantly, what is your company investing in? Do you have much of a choice? Are they doing the same things that money managers and personal financial planners do? Is there an issue about accountability and trust? Once again, we see the issue here.

Until you can answer that clearly, your savings may not be as secure as you think.

US Personal Savings Decline.
In 1956, a $100 paycheck was a solid weekly income. To match that same spending power today, you'd need $971. So, where did all your money go? Where is all of your money going? **Inflation.**

Take a look at this chart from the Federal Reserve. It tracks two things: the U.S. personal savings rate (in blue) and the 10-year Treasury yield (in red), going all the way back to 1960. What it shows is a decades-long downward spiral in both. In the early '80s, US Treasuries peaked around 15–16%. Today, they are near historic lows and savings rates have dropped. They are more erratic lately, but still trending down. This chart paints a grim picture that, over the years, Americans have earned less on their savings and saved less in response. Can you blame them?

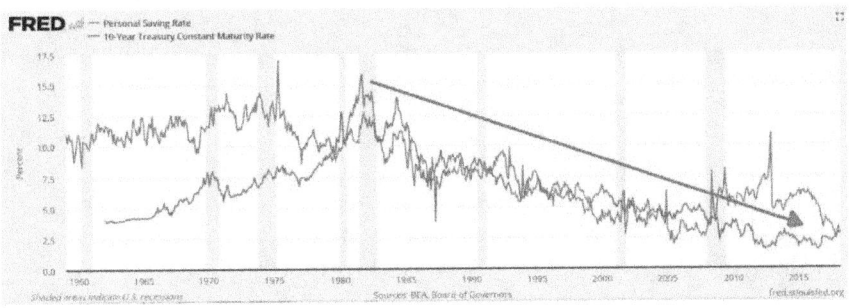

Inflation is the silent thief. A secret tax that you were not consulted on. A way of taking your money without your permission or awareness. It's like someone is sneaking into your house each night, reaching into your mattress for your savings, and taking a little bit at a time. One day, you look in this mattress and a large part of your money is gone. There is no difference.

I know this looks bleak. But it's not as bad as you might think. We will talk about solutions to all of these questions soon. First, however, we must take responsibility for our future.

Exercise 1: Do You Have A Plan?

Do you have a plan? When you have a plan, your vision will become clear. And this, in turn, will make your decisions about what to do with your family's fortune much clearer.

We've talked about investments and who you invest with. We also talked about you investing and saving on your own. If you are doing these things, my hat's off to you. You are taking your financial future into your own hands. If you are not doing these basic blocking and tackling maneuvers, you're not just falling behind, you're forfeiting the opportunity to build wealth for yourself, your family, and your heirs.

So, what does your plan look like? The average American's financial planning is almost nonexistent.

Write your goals

So let me recommend that you take a sheet of paper and actually write a plan. I don't care if you are financially literate or not. I don't care if you have nothing saved on it. Just do it anyway. This exercise will grow with you as you progress through this book.

At the top, write down your financial goal for the next year. Then write down your financial goal for five years, 10 years, and 15 years. Be specific, and make it measurable. Remember, goal setting is nothing if you cannot measure it. A vague goal, like *"I want to retire at 60,"* isn't enough. Let's reframe that into a strong goal:

> I want to have $70,000 per year in after-tax passive income by age 60, regardless of employment or active investments, and have that income last for at least 30 years.

I have done this exercise many times in my life, and it never ceases to amaze me how many things I think of once I start writing them down. The point is to get started. Get moving. Even if it's not a well-done exercise, it will move you in the right direction. And this is essential. I am not an expert in goal setting, and there are many books and systems out there to help you with this. Use them as a resource if you'd like more detailed guidance.

Make follow-up steps for each goal. Then, next to each goal, I want you to write two ideas describing how you can achieve this goal. The two ideas can overlap since some investments span a long time. So, you could put: buy gold ETFs, or corporate bonds, or a specific mutual fund. Try to be specific.

After you do this, find an online investment calculator with a compounding function to test your ideas. Beside each investment, put the amount of return you expect to receive each month or year. For example, if you have an investment of $10,000, how much will

Bitcoin Bit

The average price of a home in 2014 was $240,000, and if you bought it with Bitcoin, it would have cost you about 960 Bitcoin. The average price of a home in 2018 was $325,000 pretty nice appreciation an increase or 35% or 8% per year, almost beating inflation. However, if you bought the same house with Bitcoin, it would then cost you only 47 Bitcoin. If you have to buy a house in 2024 the average price is around $467,000 that's 31% over 2018, again another significant increase in value. If you want to buy the same house with Bitcoin it will cost you around 7 Bitcoin. I think you can see which asset is gaining in value and which is just holding on to inflation. In fact, the illusion that you are gaining value with your house or your real estate, is a curtain that hides the real bankruptcy of the system. We are believing we are getting ahead. Where in reality we are just sinking a bit slower.

you have at five years, at 10 years, etc? This will help you understand where you are and how far your plan will take you.

Once you have this plan, set it aside. We will revisit it later. This is the beginning of a plan. Add to it as you learn more. And I always encourage you to learn more. Read about money and investments. (Robert Kyosaki's book *Rich Dad Poor Dad* is an excellent resource.) Whether you are a novice or an experienced investor, keep learning and update your goals as you move forward.

This book is not about financial planning, and I am not a financial planner. And nothing I am giving you should be construed as financial advice. But I am trying to help you understand how to take control of your financial life, and at the very least, understand how money compounds. Never, ever leave your financial plan up to someone else. Also, keep this exercise available; we will use it for comparison in later chapters.

What's Your Favorite Investment?

Another important question is: **What is your favorite investment?** Now think about it more deeply. Why is it your favorite? Maybe you have several favorite investments. I know I did. And I still look at different things.

But you should be questioning these investments. You should be able to defend them and know them well. Know the good, the bad, and the ugly. Does it have a nice yield? Or maybe it gives you tax savings? Maybe it is easy to get into? Does it accomplish your goals? Or you got a tip for someone. What I want is for you to truly understand these investments and know why you selected them. I want you to know yourself. Hopefully, you can come up with an answer better than, "It makes money."

Odds are, your investment advisor or banker, if you even have a banker, has never asked you to do this before. And there is a good reason. Because no one really saves anymore. And even if they do, they hand the responsibility off to someone else — someone who may not share their goals or values.

Remember, this book isn't investment advice. But it *is* a call to responsibility. Think for yourself. Make informed decisions. And when the next economic storm hits, I want you and your family prepared, not panicked.

What if there was another way?

What if there were a way to protect your wealth? One that doesn't rely on financial planners, trust in institutions, or hope that inflation won't eat your future alive?

Because if your money just sits in cash or a low-yield account, it's **melting**. That's not an opinion. That's math.

Our current system is designed to extract value from your savings unless *you* do something different.

There *is* another way. That way is **Bitcoin**.

Bitcoin is a technology that allows you to save and protect the value of your labor over time. It can't be printed away. It doesn't rely on the whims of central bankers or corrupt institutions. And it puts **you** in control.

Bitcoin is sovereignty. If you want to reach retirement with confidence and without fear, you need to take back your autonomy. It won't be easy. But it's not impossible. Follow me down the Bitcoin rabbit hole. It will take effort. And quite a bit of soul-searching, but it might just be the most fascinating journey of your financial life.

Tech Exercise: Know Your Technology

To take control of your financial future, you'll need to understand some basic tools, starting with understanding your own devices. Here's your first tech exercise: **Write down the specs for each of your devices**

This first exercise is simple. I want you to take a minute and look at your laptop, desktop, and smartphone. Figure out what you are actually using. Write this down. This will help you gain a better understanding of how to use them. All of these exercises will only require basic tools. Nothing special, nothing fancy. Write down these specs:

- **Year of the device**
- **Model**
- **Operating System and version**
- **Storage capacity**
- **Memory**
- **Financial apps installed**
- **Bonus: List any security apps installed**

If you don't know how to get this information, that's okay. Just go on Google or DuckDuckGo or YouTube, and ask, "How do I find the specifications for my HP/Dell/ASUS laptop, or Android phone?"

This isn't just busywork. As we move deeper into the world of bitcoin and digital tools, you'll need to know what your tech can (and can't) do. All of the exercises in this book are designed to work with basic, everyday tools. No expensive gear or advanced coding knowledge required.

If anything in this exercise feels out of reach, make a note of it. This becomes your **List of Challenges**, a running list of areas where you might need help or more knowledge.

Keep this list handy. We'll come back to it later. You are going to learn how to build an entire organized plan for truly protecting and growing your hard earned wealth.

Chapter 2

No One Is Protecting You.

"...the government is a broker in pillage, and every election is sort of an advanced auction in stolen goods..."

H.L. Mencken

When it became evident that Lehman Brothers was going under during the subprime mortgage crisis, Wall Street and Washington were affected. It was like a mounting storm, coming fast. And Hank Paulson, Secretary of the Treasury; Ben Bernanke, Chairman of the Federal Reserve; and Tim Geithner, President of the New York Federal Reserve, were scheming furiously on a government-sponsored negotiation to find a buyer for Lehman Brothers, with Bank of America and Barclays Bank of London as leading candidates to rescue the company.

The three had already secured a takeover of Fannie Mae and Freddie Mac, ostensibly saving those two bloated institutions responsible for America's mortgages. These two pseudo-government agencies had precipitously overstepped their capacity to buy loans and showed no signs of stopping.

Just months before, Paulson and company had negotiated a deal where J.P. Morgan bought the failing Wall Street firm Bear Stearns. Now they were trying to do the same thing for Lehman. And while all of this was going on, they got a call from AIG, a giant insurer exposed to the housing market, which wanted a bailout, too. Are you starting to see a pattern here?

It was like a mad rush by all of these big "prestigious" Wall Street firms to be "saved" by the government. Why? Because they were too big to fail. Really? They are too big to fail (setting aside the fact that if they are so big and prestigious, why do they need to be saved?). Certainly, the government uncovered malfeasance and illegal activities on a grand scale. Was anyone arrested? Was anyone fined? No! On the contrary, they were given billions of dollars in taxpayer money. Was any company punished in any way? Not that I have ever heard of. The dirty, insider-fueled exercise of picking winners and losers was in full swing.

Isn't the government supposed to regulate these firms? Isn't it its job to protect consumers from exactly this kind of predation? Instead, under the guise of the sloppily passed Troubled Asset Relief Program (TARP), the federal government shoveled money at them as fast as they could get it out of the door, cutting lucrative backroom deals so they could go and do it again.

If your business fails and you lose money while mishandling your customers' funds, will the federal government save you? Hardly. What gives them the right to choose who gets rescued and who gets ruined? How did we ever let it get this far? Nothing that was done during the subprime crisis has been corrected. Actually, things have gotten much worse.

After TARP and the bailouts were all done, and the Wall Street banks had received close to a trillion dollars in bailouts, it appeared they'd been saved, at least for the time being. What did they do? Well, they paid themselves $18.4 billion in bonuses in 2008. The highest on record at that time. When asked about this in an interview, Paulson called the effort "cheeky," admitting that it lacked self-awareness, but emphasized that the bailouts were meant to save our economy.

Later, we'll revisit exactly what was saved, but suffice it to say, this is exactly why we do not want a centralized authority over our money. We should never concentrate this much power in one man's hands. Our grandparents understood this. Remember the old metaphor about hiding your money in your mattress? This was for a reason. Older generations had an innate distrust of banks and banking schemes, preferring to keep their money close at hand.

When the housing crisis started, Freddie Mac and Fannie Mae handled 50% of all US mortgages, and they mishandled that. The result? Instead of being held accountable, the duo was given even more power. Today, they back nearly 90% of the mortgages in the country. Since then, the intervention in the market and the centralization of monetary power have only gotten worse. Same with the big Wall Street Banks. Before the crisis, there were 10 of them. Now there are six. Similarly, centralization of banks continues to get worse.

Since it appears that every entity responsible for the great financial crisis was either rewarded or protected, what do you think will happen next time? Let's look at it this way: Imagine you walk the same route to work every day. One morning, someone jumps out, knocks you down, and steals your money. And no one stops him, including you. In fact, the next day, you bring more money. What do you think is going to happen?

What Is Fractional Reserve Banking?

"By this means [fractional reserve banking] the government may secretly and unobservedly confiscate the wealth of the people. And not one man in a million will detect the theft."
- John Maynard Keynes

That statement, from the father of modern economic theory, should disgust anyone who believes in honest money. When you look at how our financial system actually works, you realize that the theft isn't accidental. The bankers knew. The experts knew. And every step of the way, they were protected, even enabled, by the government. The line between banker and bureaucrat has all but disappeared.

This Isn't A Bug In The System. It Is The System.

The people at the US Treasury and the Federal Reserve are among the most informed and influential central bankers in the world. Their Ivy League experts, weaned on thousands of hours of Keynesian economics, specialize in fractional reserve banking.

Let me explain how it works. You go to the bank and deposit $1,000. You might assume the bank keeps that money on hand, or maybe lends it out carefully. But under fractional reserve banking, the bank is only required to keep a fraction, say 10%, of that deposit. So they set aside $100 and loan out the other $900. But it continues. That $900 loaned out gets redeposited into another bank, and now *that* bank holds it as a deposit and does the same thing, keeping 10%, lending 90%. This process repeats over and over, creating **money that didn't previously exist**. In a few steps, your original $1,000 has magically multiplied into $9,000 or more in new credit.

If you or I did this, lending the same dollar to multiple people at the same time, we would go to prison for a long time. But when registered, regulated, licensed bankers do it, they are rewarded. Not only are they rewarded, they are lauded and praised. Showered with obscene bonuses. Invited to elite conferences. Given influence over policy. They become part of the club, *the system*. This leads to a moral hazard. Let me ask you a question: If you work within a system that is built from the ground up to operate with people's money this way, what effect do you think this would have on the moral character of the people within this system? Thomas Sowell captured it best: "The first rule of economics is scarcity; the first rule of government is to ignore this rule."

It's easy to see how corrosive this would be to anyone within this system. From this corrosion rises a deep, abiding sense of cynicism that hardens into a pure, raw corruption in very short order.

As we move through these early chapters, you will see a bit of pessimism in my words. But this is necessary for you to understand the full weight of what you are up against. None of these details is superfluous.

What are those banks up to?

As you've seen, the very institutions that claim to protect your life savings are the ones rigging the game. Banks are businesses, and like any business, they seek profit. That's not inherently wrong. In fact, I don't ever begrudge the banks for engaging in fraudulent practices, such as fractional reserve banking (also known as rehypothecation) or other ridiculous schemes, including credit default swaps and other crooked practices used during the 2008 mortgage crisis. The main problem is the force they use against us regular people, those of us without money and power. That is the problem.

They literally co-opt the force and violence of the government to perpetrate this monstrous system on us. Once again, if we did this, we would go to jail. In a truly free economy, if a bank tried this, it would go out of business or maybe be run out of town as in the days of the Wild, Wild West. But what happens today is something very different.

Banks and insiders get rewarded with exclusive rights to an ever-expanding monetary system. They send their executives to Washington to run the Treasury and the Federal Reserve. In power, they write the very rules they're supposed to follow. And every few years, when the system gets unwieldy and starts to collapse, what do they do? They run to the government and cry "too big to fail," demanding bailouts. Bailouts from taxpayers, the ones scammed by the system in the first place. So, you see, Uncle Sam is not protecting you. He's the key to the grift, enabling this scam to continue year after year.

An Insider's Game.

Sadly, it's a rigged insider's game. And we're not on the inside. Every time normal Americans try to get a piece of the pie, they get rebuffed and pushed aside. Every time we get ahead, something pushes us back.

And what makes it so insidious is that there is no real way to see this. There is no real way to know it. We know down inside that something is wrong. We know that we should be able to get ahead, but we don't. We know something is broken, but we can't put our finger on it. There is no proof. There is no smoking gun, just an endless fog of jargon, complexity, and denial.

Is any of this taught in high school or college? In any college? Will you find it anywhere in the great economic textbooks of our expensive institutions? No, it's not talked about. That would spoil the grift.

These insiders work in the shadows of the backrooms of Washington and Wall Street. They join exclusive clubs where we are not allowed. They meet in secret places like Davos and within the Federal Reserve, where they have a balance sheet that we can't see. Even Congress can't fully audit its books. They shield their actions with abstract financial instruments: credit default swaps, subprime tranches, quantitative easing, rehypothecation, and collateralized debt obligations (CDOs).

Then they build web banking regulations so complex that the bankers themselves can't even understand them. And somehow, we are expected to pierce this cloud of obfuscation and come up with a working understanding of how to handle our money within this system?

Is it any wonder we cannot see what is going on? No wonder people are confused. No wonder we feel trapped. **We're not imagining it.** The system *is* broken and has been for a long time.

Crisis, Collapse, Repeat. History reveals the pattern. A financial crisis happens every few years. Always a new excuse. Always the same result:

2020: Pandemic lockdowns—mandated by our own government— shut down the economy.

2008: The mortgage crisis, triggered by predatory lending, securitization, and reckless speculation, led to trillions in losses.

2001: The dot-com bubble burst. Wall Street had taken public any company with ".com" in its name, driving a speculative frenzy. The Fed's easy-money policies fueled the fire.

1987: Black Monday. The single largest one-day drop in stock market history. Caused not just by "greed" but by Fed-induced whiplash in monetary policy.

1980s: The Savings and Loan (S&L) crisis, fueled by federal deposit insurance and deregulation, created a moral hazard so extreme that organized crime got directly involved in the S&Ls.

1970s: Runaway inflation and stagflation, caused by Nixon detaching the dollar from gold and attempting to control prices while the Vietnam War drained public funds.

Pain For The Public. Profit For The Insiders.

I could go on. But you see the pattern. The American people, individual consumers, or even the business cycle had nothing to do with these huge shocks to the economy. We were just the victims of them. We do our best to survive as the economy swerves from one major calamity after another, like a bunch of drunken clowns all packed inside a dysfunctional clown car, crashing off of each guardrail and jerking the wheel into the other guardrail again and again and again.

Maybe That Mattress Wasn't Such A Bad Idea?

But what was the result for us? We lost savings and missed opportunities. Our wealth and income eroded. Think back to the 1950s and '60s, when Baby Boomers were growing up. Families were larger, with an average of three to five kids. One income, usually the father's, was enough to support the entire household, pay the mortgage, buy a car or two, and still allow mom to stay home and care for the kids. And it wasn't considered extraordinary, simply how things worked.

Then prices started to rise. Slowly at first, then relentlessly. Moms went to work, some for fulfillment or ambition, but most out of necessity. Families shrank to reduce expenses, and both parents were stretched thin. By the 1980s, dual-income households were the norm. Kids came home to empty houses. Dinners got faster and of cheaper quality food (look at the USDA food pyramid). Even two-income families began to struggle to stay ahead. That's when consumer debt came onto the picture.

BITCOIN BIT. JACK MALLERS FAMOUSLY SAID IN RESPECT TO TAKING HIS ENTIRE SALARY IN BITCOIN. AND NO SALARY IN DOLLARS. I LIKE TO HAVE A 50% RAISE EVERY YEAR. SO, WHEN I GET PAID IN BITCOIN AND IT APPRECIATES 50% PER YEAR AGAINST THE DOLLAR THIS FEELS GOOD TO ME.

Our parents and grandparents had a healthy fear of debt. They understood it as a trap; something you could get into and never get out of. A hamster wheel of struggle, fear, and anxiety. A feeling of always being behind. But now, consumer debt is commonplace. First one credit card, then multiple credit cards. Buying cars on credit, then buying cars with extended credit terms. Mortgage terms stretched from 10 to 20 years to 30 years or more. And down payments shrank, then disappeared.

All these schemes nudged Americans further into a debt trap from which some may never escape. So, maybe we just forgo the banks altogether and just put our money in cash. Put it in your mattress. Save it ourselves. Is this possible? Technically, yes. But feasible? No. Every year, your cash loses value. Regardless of whether you trust the banks or the government, inflation eats away at your purchasing power. Your money might be safe from a fraudulent system, but it will still be eroded by it. Left in cash, your work, your time, your energy quietly dissolves.

This chart shows the negative influence of these practices by comparing the price performance of Bitcoin, the S&P 500, and gold over time. Bitcoin shows dramatically higher returns, with gains of 180% in one year, 722% over five years, and an extraordinary 66,000% over ten years, far outpacing the S&P 500 and gold in every time frame.

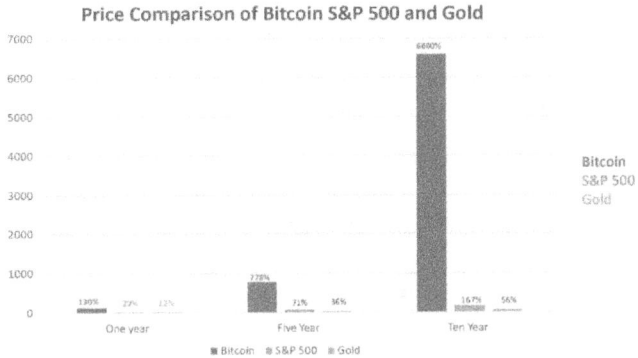

I know that we have been covering some bleak topics. But it's necessary to understand how insidious the problem is and what we're really up against. There is nothing special about the wealthy. They aren't necessarily smarter or more talented. But they tend to have one key advantage. They see the world as it really is. They question what they are told. They look, and then look again. We need to do the same.

Centralization Means Control

Anytime an institution has greater centralization, it has a greater level of control. The more centralization, the greater control.

You can see why banks fight for control, and why central banks push for even greater centralization — to give them the ultimate financial control.

Think about it for a moment. If you want to control a herd of cattle, you start by rounding them up. To control them even more, you confine them in a corral or a pen. For total control, you pack them tightly in a feedlot, preparing them for slaughter. Now you have a hundred head of cattle with infinitely more power, mass, speed, and variability than a man. Yet they can be controlled by one person. This is the power of centralization. The difference with the cattle is that you have to coerce them into the centralized space. With humans, we go willingly.

Centralization will be discussed often in this book because it is the key to the current monetary system and how it works. This is not a conspiracy theory. It's simply how systems of power evolve. Centralization is the architecture of control. It concentrates authority in the hands of a few, allowing decisions over money, markets, and lives to be made far from public view.

Today, the Federal Reserve, operating through the Treasury Department and a very small group of giant banks, exercises almost complete control of the US dollar in the USA and around the world. (An excellent book on the formation of the US Federal Reserve is *The Creature from Jekyll Island*, by G. Edward Griffith.) And, with every financial crisis, the Fed's power tightens. Governments respond with reforms, regulations, mergers, acquisitions, and bailouts that always seem to benefit the same elite players. More consolidation. More centralization. More control.

Even The Insiders Are Warning You About Your Pension.
You don't have to take my word for it. Even insiders are starting to sound the alarm, albeit quietly.

The Institutional Investor, a respected publication for traditional finance and pension fund professionals, recently published a report lamenting the risky prospects of traditional finance in the pension world. These are people who normally defend Wall Street's model, but now they're worried. Their recommendation? Consider Bitcoin. Yes—Bitcoin. That "dangerous," "unproven" digital asset they spent years dismissing. Why the change? Because, as they admit, *"in terms of returns, other assets don't hold a candle to Bitcoin."*

The key is to come up with the right strategy for allocation and risk. Many times, in the current investment environment, there is a tendency to quickly jump in and out of different assets, acting as a trader, not as an investor or saver. This is a mistake with Bitcoin. We will discuss this in more detail.

Move carefully and with a specific plan in mind. Your plan must cover allocation, risk-return requirements, and above all else, must fit with your current emotional tolerance for these variables. If you color outside these lines, there is a good chance you will encounter problems or even a possible disaster. Stick to your plan regardless of the day-to-day or even month-to-month price movements.

Warnings about your pension from mainstream organizations like *The Institutional Investor* are real. We should be listening.

So, what are we left with? What alternatives exist to this deeply flawed system? If banks, investment firms, and government institutions can't be trusted to protect your money, what can? This is where Bitcoin enters the picture. Unlike traditional financial institutions, no institution controls Bitcoin. Even better, because it operates on mathematical principles rather than human promises, holding Bitcoin doesn't require trust in any central authority. In the coming chapters, we'll explore how Bitcoin addresses many of the problems we've identified. It can't be debased through printing; it doesn't rely on intermediaries who can betray your trust; and most importantly, it puts control of your money back in your hands where it belongs.

Accounting Exercise

- Your next exercise is about your money. I want you to practice two things with this exercise. Practice your perception of reality and accounting for your money.
- So, sit down on your computer or your notebook and figure out where your wealth and your money are and what they're really worth. I suggest using tools external to the government and major institutions, where possible, to help you check your assumptions and beliefs, such as Shadowstats.com or chapwoodindex.com. It will assist you greatly. Also, look at the S&P 500 index and the US debt clock for further assistance.
- I do not mean look just online at your bank account or your ATM receipt. I mean, sit down and figure out what your total net worth is. House, assets, cars, savings, investments, precious metals, art, real estate, everything. Subtract your bills, debts, and liabilities.
- That's the accounting part. The reality part is making sure everything is really yours, and you are valuing it in a real way. The trick here is to determine if it is really yours. If your mom is supposed to give you $10,000 next year, then it's not really yours. If you have a house that you think is worth $400,000, but the last three houses in your neighborhood sold for $325,000 or less, then value it accordingly. If your money is in company stocks and the company is in financial trouble. Value it correctly. You have a beautiful sofa that you paid $7000 for a few years ago. You think you are going to even get $1000 if you had to sell it? Think again. It's highly unlikely. This is going to require you to take a long, hard look at where you are. Remember, this is for your own benefit. If this exercise is a problem, add this to your "**List of challenges**."
- The next step is to evaluate your risk for each item on the asset side. So, make a column and on the right, label it "percentage of risk." For instance, if you have a house and it's worth $500,000, and you are sure that's the value based on appraisal, assessment, or comparative valuations in your

neighborhood, give it a score of 1. If not, discount it. For cash, let's just use the government numbers. So, if you have a total of $10,000 cash in your bank account, we know the current government inflation rate is 5%. We will just use that, and score this at 0.95. So, if you use 5% then value your $10,000 at 0.95 or $9500. You get the picture. You can also use the current S&P 500 chart if you want to be more accurate. I will let you decide. Remember, this is not a precise exercise. None of us can predict the future. This is an exercise in trying to cut through the BS and see the real world. What's the probability that all your investments are going to be a success within the next year? Now see the difference between before and after the last step. How realistic do you think you were? You are grading yourself, not your net worth. Should this go on your "**List of challenges?**"

I'm sure you're asking; how does all of this affect me personally? We are now going to get into this part of the equation in the next chapters. As we link the dysfunction of the system to our own finances.

Chapter 3

This is Going to Get Personal

"Bitcoin doesn't need your intellectual acceptance. Your self-interest will force you to use it whether you like it or not."

Saifedean Ammous

A friend of mine visited the bank to send a wire transfer from one bank to another. He operated a business and occasionally had to transfer money via the US Fedwire system. It was not uncommon. Wire transfers have been around for many years, even decades. But this time proved different. The bank asked him why he needed to transfer the money. What was it for?

He told them it was none of their business. He had no criminal record of any kind and engaged in no criminal activities. But after this transfer, he received a letter from the bank requesting a meeting. He set an appointment. During the meeting, they asked him again about his wire transfers. He stood firm and was now offended that they were pressing him for details about his own money. And told them so. Soon after, the bank sent another letter. This time, they informed him that his account was being closed and asked where to send the remaining balance. This is the state of banking and privacy in the USA and other Western nations today.

Are Banks Going To Help?

Another friend's son came to me with a serious problem. Although he was young and inexperienced, he had actually amassed significant savings. He was 22 and had a part-time job, as well as some savings from gifts from his family. My friend knew that I had worked in technology and asked me to help. Using a series of phishing attacks, scammers in Africa had hacked both his bank accounts. They had taken about $5,000 of his money. He was very embarrassed and ashamed of what had happened to him. First, we filed a police report. We then contacted his credit card company and the banks, both at Chase, and his credit union to stop payment on all three. We also locked down his credit report and his social security number, deleted compromised accounts, and scrubbed all the personal data we could.

But the scammers were still at it. While we sat with the president of his credit union, his phone buzzed. It was another attempt by the scammers to lure him back in by ostensibly "fixing the problem." They just needed a little bit more information. I immediately took his phone and blocked the number.

The most shocking thing was that Chase offered zero support. They never even called us back, even after we went to the branch office. Luckily, the bulk of his savings was in the credit union, and they did recover most of his money. The credit union branch president even suggested closing the account entirely for his safety. On his sound advice, we did. The difference in the level of assistance we received between Chase and the credit union was telling. Large corporate institutions and giant banks are not there to help you. Keep this in mind.

The creeping, crawling encroachment on your personal freedoms never seems to stop. The prying eyes continue day after day, year after year. But hey. We're told, "If you have nothing to hide, you should have nothing to worry about. Right?" This is their attitude, and it is getting worse by the day. Never forget, privacy is the foundation of security. Protect your privacy like the crown jewels.

Why Do You Need Permission To Use Your Own Money?

Banks cite fraud, crime, and money laundering. But the reality is darker. What they're really doing is controlling access. They ask why you want to send your money. Demand explanations. Require documentation. You're treated like a suspect for trying to use your own assets. Yet, when fraud occurs, their questions vanish. Why does the bank have the right to question what you are going to do with your money? Here's what most people don't realize: once you deposit your money, it's no longer legally yours. It becomes the bank's. They say possession is nine-tenths of the law. Well, it's more than that. You now hold a fragile IOU. If they have it, they control it.

Privacy is critical to your banking relationship, but banking privacy is an illusion. Banks are bound by KYC (Know Your Customer) and AML (Anti-Money Laundering) laws, which require banks to act as unpaid extensions of the state.

Even your safe deposit box. You know how you have a key and the bank has a key, and they supposedly cannot enter your box without your key? Well, nothing is further from the truth. This is a fiction that gives you, the customer, the illusion of privacy. In actuality, if the police ask to access your safe deposit box. The bank will readily open it up for them, giving full access. They may not even call you to let you know they are doing it.

The moment you deposit your money in a bank, it's not really yours anymore. They hold it, and that means they control it. They take ownership and custody of it for you. And with custody goes control. We will talk more about custody in the coming chapters, custody is absolutely critical, but for now, understand this: if you don't hold it, it's not really yours. Plain and simple. You must accept this to move forward with your financial freedom.

Why Do Only Some People Seem To Have Easy Access To Money?

If you have spent any time investing as a regular, everyday person (a retail investor), you've probably felt it. Something is off. There's no shortage of investment products, financial advisors, strategies, and opportunities. The industry is enormous. But — where are all the success stories? With all of their elaborate marketing, what kind of advertisements do you get? You get pretty lifestyle ads with grandpa fishing with his grandchildren. Or a retired couple walking on a beach. If they had results, they would certainly advertise them. But they don't. So they don't even mention results in their ads.

Instead, it feels like wealth is dangled just out of reach. It's like a beautiful piece of fruit ready to be picked and eaten. Juicy and succulent with the promise of genuine happiness and contentment for our future. The end of fear and worry. The beginning of our dreams of what we would like for our future. Not a guarantee but a promise.

But when we reach for it, it always slips away. Somewhere along the way, something happens. At best, the fruit isn't as sweet as it looked. At worst, it's a rotten apple. And if we are not careful, this delicious-looking fruit will make us quite sick.

Somewhere along the way, our financial future of ease, safety, and happiness slipped away. Maybe we made a bad call. Maybe the game was rigged. Whatever the case, the result is the same: the comfortable financial future we imagined remains elusive. Meanwhile, we see others who seem to soar. They are getting richer, faster and more effortlessly. Why? What's really going on?

The Great Wealth Divide

There is a concept in economics called the Cantillon Effect. It's both simple and devastating. It says that when money printers inject money into the economy, this monetary expansion benefits the parties closest to the money printers, but has a diminishing and eventually regressive effect on the rest of society.

What does this mean in plain English? It means that the parties closest to the "money spigot" get the wealth effects of the money. The bankers, the investment banking system, Wall Street, billionaire insiders, they win. The little guy, the regular Joe Sixpack on the street, and middle-class retail investors get less and less. By the time it trickles down to the masses, the value has already been extracted. The printed money has the opposite effect of what it was intended to do. It moves regular people away from wealth preservation and towards the erosion of wealth. Over time, the effect becomes regressive. Regular people don't just miss out; they fall behind.

The data backs this up. According to Pew Research, the share of wealth held by middle-income households declined from 61% in 1971 to 51% in 2019. At the same time, upper-income households' share rose from 14% to 20%. The top 5% of earners have seen the greatest growth of all. Billionaires? Their numbers increased by 40% in just five years. By 2018, there were over 2,100 of them worldwide. The share for upper-income households has increased from 14% to 20%.

On top of this, income growth at the top 5% of families has enjoyed the greatest level of growth of all categories. This is an amazing statistic. As billionaire Stanley Druckenmiller, the great bond trader, said, "The greatest threat to equality today is the Federal Reserve system."

To be clear, I do not begrudge anyone their success, including billionaires. Actually, I encourage it. The great billionaires of the past and even the recent past produced something of real value and the little guy, received this value in the form of a higher standard of living. In the past, when someone entered the super wealthy class, they produced something of value. They invented something. They built a business or industry that employed or benefited many Americans in some way, such as developing newer and faster systems or bringing quality products to market at a cheaper price.

Before Henry Ford, automobiles existed, but only for the very wealthy. Comparable to owning a private jet today. Ford didn't invent the car, but he made it accessible to a worker making a living wage. Before Rockefeller, gasoline was expensive and difficult to find. Before Boeing and Howard Hughes, airplane travel was for the few. They helped open the skies to the masses.

These individuals built something that improved life for everyone. I'm not listing these names to idolize billionaires, but to make a simple point: we got something in return. Their innovations raised the standard of living across the board. Now we seem to have a class of billionaires who amass a whole lot of money, but there is not a lot to show for it. Not for the rest of us.

What happened to the Henry Fords, who built an automotive industry that changed the world? Or Henry Bessemer, who refined steel production. Or John D. Rockefeller, who brought order to the oil industry. Or Westinghouse and Nikola Tesla, who electrified America, or in more recent times, Andy Grove, who founded Intel, with the invention of the integrated circuit. Or Len Bosack and Sandy Lerner, who invented the Cisco router that runs the internet today. These great people-built industries that we take for granted today. Without them, our way of life would not be possible. But what do today's billionaires do for us?

They invest in things that don't seem to benefit anyone. Warren Buffett made his fortune investing in unhealthy sugary cookies, ice cream, and soda companies. Or they build an app or website, like Uber or Airbnb, that feeds off of our hard work. Or they have some online "service" — Google or Facebook — that spies on us and feeds our information to an advertising machine that we know little about and sells our attention to the highest bidder. Or they just have a lot of stock or a lot of "lucky moves" in the capital markets. Why is this? Why is it that the 1% of Americans own 40% of the nation's wealth? And the bottom 80% own only 7%? What is going on?

Is there some kind of inside game that we don't know about? Is there some preferential treatment that the super wealthy get that we are not privy to? Maybe there is.

What Our Parents And Grandparents Feared.
What did our grandparents fear most when it came to wealth and savings? Losing it. Warren Buffett said it plainly: *Rule No. 1—Don't lose money. Rule No. 2—Don't forget Rule No. 1.* And there's wisdom in that.

If you lose 33% on a $1,000 investment, you're left with $660. To return to $1,000, you now need a 50% gain, just to break even. That kind of math is unforgiving, and our grandparents understood it instinctively.

That's why so many of our grandparents did not trust intermediaries. They feared handing their money over to someone else. They shied away from banks, savings and loans, stock brokers, insurance brokers, and investment advisors. They knew the sheer terror of discovering their funds were no longer available, especially during bank runs. That fear wasn't paranoia. It was a lived experience. Look at Lebanon in 2021. The banking crisis was so severe that if you could get to the bank, the bank would limit your withdrawal to a maximum of $100 per day. Put yourself in this position for just a minute and see how it feels.

This fear may seem distant to us today. But I assure you, it is still possible. Ask your elders about the effects of living with someone impacted by the Great Depression. Ask about the trauma of finding out their money was gone, not because they spent it but because someone, they trusted lost it.

Total Military Spending $778 Billion

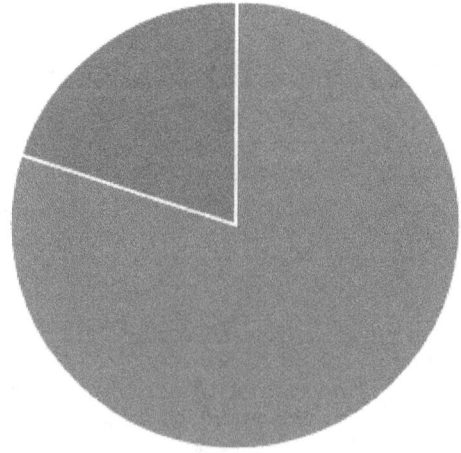

■ Accounted For $622 Billion ■ Wasted $155 Billion

Today, we operate under the illusion of a social safety net. That somehow, some way, the government will catch us if we fall. Why not? This is the United States of America. We are the preeminent power in the world. We have the largest economy the world has ever seen. It is said that we are the world's only remaining superpower, backed by seven aircraft carriers.

But this is all a fallacy. Who pays for this power? Just fueling the US military costs over $50 million per day, $19 billion per year. Just the fuel bill! It seems more like a liability than a guarantee of economic sovereignty. Those seven aircraft carriers swimming around in circles are nothing but a drain on the actual productive and honest part of our great economy. A good economy is built on sound economic principles of productivity and sound money. Not on expensive ships driving around aimlessly, waiting for a war that's not likely to happen. Are they being used for anything productive? Are they a force for good or a tool of intimidation? Are they even actually useful as a kinetic power, or are they a target?

And for what? To fight a war? No. To protect us against some unseen enemy coming to get us? Who? Where was the US military, with all its expenses and fantastic protective technology, on 9/11? Or, are they there to protect something else or someone else?

So, let me ask you, if you had $1 million and gave your child $1,000 a day, how long would it last? About 3.5 years. But a billion dollars at that same pace would last 2,739 years. Now consider this: The US national debt is nearly $37 trillion. If we repaid it at $1 million per hour, it would take until the year **6047** to pay it off. Our minds struggle to grasp numbers that large. But you must begin to understand exponential growth because it's at the heart of both the problem and the solution.

Be Your Own Bank

What if there were a way to be your own bank? What if we could do what the bankers do but for ourselves? And without hurting anyone in the process. We could actually benefit the economy as a whole.

That's the promise of Bitcoin. Not just as an investment, but as a *revolution* in financial sovereignty.

We are going to talk about how to be your own bank. How to have your money and keep it rather than watching it melt away like an ice cube. The central bankers and the financial industry want you to think that they have some special power. Only they have a special knowledge that can keep you safe and secure. Well, if they do, they are keeping it for themselves. To quote the late, great George Carlin, "It's a big club, and you're not in it." The quicker you realize this, the quicker you start to take your security and your wealth into your own hands. The better you will be.

We have a saying in Bitcoin: "You get Bitcoin at the price you deserve." If you wait, it will be more difficult and much, much more expensive. I believe it will still be available. But it won't be as easy as it is now. The rush for Bitcoin by the insiders has already started. As they move in, they'll try to pull up the ladder behind them. Why? Because of the nature of their system, the one I have been describing, is a system of greed and graft, a system of insider's vs the outsiders. They assume Bitcoin is just another asset to be captured. Another tool for the same corrupt system of insiders and outsiders. But Bitcoin isn't built that way. Bitcoin, at its very nature, is a new, honest system. It represents hope and fairness. We will return to that later. But for now, know that taking control of your wealth is not a fantasy. It's entirely possible. It's already happening. And you don't need permission. Bitcoin allows you to be your own bank, to transfer value without permission, and to protect your wealth from the erosion we've discussed. As we continue through this book, you'll see how Bitcoin addresses these personal finance challenges in ways that no traditional financial instrument can.

Centralization Is Discrimination.

Centralization, by its very nature, is anathema to how the founding fathers built this country. The founders designed a federalist system specifically to *distribute* massive power to the states. Authority was meant to reside with the states. Even at the federal level, power was divided among three branches to keep any one group from becoming too dominant. For the first 140 years, the United States had no central bank, no Federal Reserve. And what was the result? We experienced the greatest explosion of wealth, innovation, and prosperity in the history of man. The surge in technological and

Bitcoin Bit.

Did you know that the Bitcoin white paper is only 9 pages long and is available for free to anyone anywhere to read. It completely defines Bitcoin for everyone to read and to criticize and to scrutinize. In the world of our opaque and confounding financial system this is a beautiful simplicity that serves all 8 billion humans on earth. I challenge anyone to accurately explain our entire financial system in 9 pages. So, the next time someone tells you that Bitcoin is complex. Please remember this.

financial growth resulted in the Gilded Age, a period of transformation unmatched in scale or speed.

Sure, there were many deep problems — slavery, war, the shameful treatment of Native Americans— but many of these were the product of centralization, not a failure of decentralization itself. When settlers invoked the power of the US military to displace native tribes, or when American corporations like United Fruit exploited poor Latin American nations under the protection of the State Department, they were leveraging the power of a centralized

47

authority structured to victimize the weak. After World War II, the USA weaponized centralized banking cartels like the IMF and the World Bank as economic hit men to exploit developing countries around the world. Today, under the pretext of climate change and globalization, those same institutions continue to impose top-down control under the guise of progress, harvesting people's genuine desire for a clean environment to create more centralization. This is the nature of centralized systems. They discriminate. They concentrate power. And that power is inevitably used to benefit the few at the expense of the many.

Freedom Demands Responsibility.

We all enjoy a bit of convenience and simplicity in our lives. But certain things require responsibility and the freedom to act. None more than your money. The ability to decide where your money goes and what you can do with it is at the very heart of freedom. Money represents your energy, your sacrifice, your hard work, and your innovative capability. It is literally a claim on the energy that you have expended. And before you can grow it, spend it, or pass it on, you have to *keep* it. As a Baby Boomer, you know this. You have lived a life with ups and downs and learned a few hard lessons along the way. You've earned your wisdom.

Now is the time to apply it. Because when the system starts to wobble and it will then it'll be too late to prepare. You need to act *before* the moment of crisis. Are you ready to take on the responsibility?

Understanding My Optimism

I want you to understand where my optimism comes from, and why I'm sharing these stories with you. We are living through a rare and very special moment in history. But to appreciate it, we have to understand how the real world works. And that includes acknowledging how ugly and cruel the world can be. If we can't face that reality, then we can't see the path forward. We won't be able to see that there is another way. Please don't think I am telling you these stories as a way to bring you down. I'm most certainly not. On the contrary. I cherish these experiences in my life. They moved me forward to the place I am now in the world.

It gave me the ability to understand where I needed to be and how to get there. Maybe I could have taken a shorter route. Maybe I could have done it in an easier way at times. But I wouldn't trade one moment of these difficult times mixed in with plenty of good times. It made me able to be here today. To have taken the road that leads to Bitcoin. I am not sure I would have made it here any other way. So, I am grateful for every moment. It's the way it had to be.

Also, you need to understand something else, too. It's not enough to just say, "the system is broken and Bitcoin is the fix." It doesn't work that way. People are swimming in this system and don't even know they're wet.

There's a story about two fish swimming along. One says to the other, "Wow, the water's cold today." And the other fish replies, "What's water?"

This is the problem. We are in it. We are surrounded by it. We swim in a system so pervasive, so all-encompassing, we don't even realize it's there. We don't question it, even though it shapes every part of our financial reality.

As Jeff Booth discerns: *"You cannot understand the system from inside the system."* I didn't understand it either. I took it for granted like everyone else. Until one day, I *needed* Bitcoin. When asked why he criticized Bitcoin in 2014 but now is one of its biggest advocates, Michael Saylor shared, "In 2014, I didn't need Bitcoin, but in 2020, I needed it. And because I needed it, I took the time to learn about it."

That's exactly what happened to me. And, the more I learned about it, the more it made sense. The deeper I went, the more it felt like I was seeing reality for the first time. That moment of clarity turned into conviction and then into something stronger... *optimism*. It's the kind of optimism that comes from knowing there's solid ground beneath your feet. That in a world full of lies and noise, there exists a system, a mathematical, immutable, and incorruptible system, that you can trust.

I became enamored with it. It became a foundation for me. It gave me a sense of order in chaos. A sense of truth in a world full of narratives, bullshit, and propaganda. It gave me the confidence to say, 'This is real.' Not because someone told me so, but because I can verify it. Today, tomorrow, and a decade from now.

No hype. Just peace of mind.

The more I learned, the more I understood. The more I understood, the more I wanted to learn. The light glimmered, then flashed. Now it burns bright within me. To discover the truth, and to know that truth is something you can rely on, is powerful. It's a truth based in mathematics, never changing, never altering, always there for you. That gives me the foundation to stand on. A place of certainty to do whatever I need to do in the physical world. Knowing that the edifice of monetary energy, this huge, consistent, immovable wall, backs me up.

It whispers, *"Things are going to be okay."* Look at this. See reality. It's right in front of you and all the proof you will ever need. Not sure? Look again in ten minutes for more proof. Still not sure? Give it another ten minutes or the next day, next month, ten years from now? Still moving along inexorably onward, forward, omnipotent.

Wow, what a feeling to know this. And when you take the time to learn, you will feel it also. You, too, will get that look in your eyes, the look of confidence and optimism, that tomorrow will be a better day.

But first, I had to learn about it.

Tech Exercise

If you completed the exercise in the last chapter, you now have a bit more understanding of your technology in your own home. Now we want to take it a little further. You should take some actions to improve your security. These are very basic, but essential steps if you are going to start taking control of your finances and build your financial sovereignty. It will take a little time and cost a little. But, how much do you want to invest in your financial future and that of your family's?

1. If you don't have one already, please install a VPN on both your laptop and your phone. More importantly, do not install a free VPN. Make sure it's a paid VPN. Free VPNs are worse than nothing. They capture and sell your information. Remember, if it's free, then you are the product. Two brands worth looking into are Mulvad and NORD.

2. If you don't have one installed, also get a Password Manager. You can find many good ones out there. This will increase your security immensely. LastPass is a good one. NORD also has one in its suite of products.

3. Install a multifactor authentication app such as Google Authenticator or Aegis. These are free and take minutes to install and set up. Next, set up some accounts with your new authenticator, with existing apps you already have, such as your banking or brokerage app.

-   Try to do the install yourself first. Don't just ask your friend or a younger person to set it up for you. Do it yourself, if you can. There are many YouTube videos to help you.

-   If you have trouble, ask for help. Be patient, take your time, and don't get frustrated. None of these items should take a significant amount of time. But if it does, that's okay. The items you need to pay for don't cost that much money.

-   The idea is to not only increase your security and harden your systems, but to gain practice on how to use these simple tools. This, in turn, will harden your resolve and confidence for future steps.

- As always, keep adding to your "**List of challenges**."

Chapter 4

Do You Think You Know What Money Is?

"Not an ocean of tears or all the guns in the world can transform those pieces of paper in your wallet into the bread you will need to survive tomorrow."

Ayn Rand

To fully understand why Bitcoin is a revolutionary solution for Baby Boomers, we need to first define: **What exactly is money?**

This question might seem simple. Money is what we use to buy things. It's what we earn from work. It's what we save for retirement. But that's just the surface. Money is actually a technology that has evolved alongside human history. Money shapes how we interact with each other, how we store the value of our labor, and ultimately, how we secure our future.

Old Money

During the Napoleonic Wars, there was a very wealthy banking family in Europe. They weren't the biggest yet, but they were about to get a lot wealthier. And much more famous. They had been expanding into different parts of Europe, growing their banking empire. One of them was particularly aggressive and creative in his ability to exploit the world around him to make more money. During this time, in the late 18th and early 19th centuries, if you bet on the winning side of a war, your investment would rise. Lose the bet, and you'd be ruined. The Napoleonic Wars were the big action of the day, and the Battle of Waterloo was the biggest show of them all.

We now reach the climax of the Napoleonic Wars and the Battle of Waterloo. If you are familiar with these wars, you know that Napoleon won almost all of his battles. And he was winning the battle of Waterloo early on. With no internet and no instant news, battlefield updates travelled by courier on horseback, then by boat across the English Channel, and again by horse to London. The entire journey could take days. Investors would gather at the London Stock Exchange, waiting for official news to arrive. Stock prices in England and France would fluctuate, depending on who was winning or losing.

But this one aggressive banker changed the game using carrier pigeons, a little-known communication technology at the time. Flying at an average speed of about 50 mph, a carrier pigeon could deliver a message to this banker in under fifteen hours. And this devious banker had other tricks up his sleeve to further lock-in his advantage. He added lots of drinks for the courier when he stopped to change horses or to rest, and then gambling designed to let the courier win, and the attention of women at stopping posts along the way, all designed to slow the human message carrier.

True to form, early word from the battlefield suggested that Napoleon would win. But the banker's pigeons told him the truth: the British had won. Not content to make millions, he wanted to make billions. He lied. He told everyone France had won. Furious trading ensued. English stocks plummeted, while the banker quietly bought them up at bargain prices. Then, when the *real* news arrived, the market flipped again. English stocks surged. French stocks plummeted. And the banker sold, making a second fortune. His manipulation was so despised, and his profits so vast, that the family had to flee England for Switzerland. The message was clear: Money is more than currency. It's information. It's a technology.

This story reveals something we often overlook. Money is a form of communication. It's a message we send to each other about value. It shows how we store it, exchange it, and measure it. Like any message, its meaning depends on the quality of the information. When that quality degrades, through lies, manipulation, or corruption, our ability to preserve our labor and secure our future things breaks down.

The banker in this story had exploited early communications technologies. Today, those distortions are more advanced and pervasive, but the patterns remain the same. Lyn Alden, a respected macroeconomist, divides monetary innovation into two categories:

> 1. Technological innovation - These are long-lasting, global changes. They increase efficiency, transparency, and accessibility, as seen in the invention of double-entry accounting, the telegraph, and the internet.

> 2. Government Innovation - These are short-term, local changes, usually made to maintain control. Think central banks, price controls, regulations against your competitors, or capital restrictions.

Technological innovations in money typically push us forward. Government innovation often holds us back. As we go forward, keep an eye out for these patterns as we discuss both types of monetary innovations.

What is money, really?
Money is more than what we use to buy things. It's a communication technology, a tool humans created to solve problems, coordinate value, and store economic energy across time and space. But what makes something *good* money?

Money Is A Store Of Value.

The first test of any form of money is this: *Can it preserve value across time and space?*

- Can I take it with me wherever I go?
- Can I send it anywhere in the world?
- Will it still be there in 10 years?
- Can I pass it on to my children?

Most forms of money today fail this test. They may work for daily purchases but decay in value over time. Others may store value reasonably well but are difficult to move or transfer. *Good money must do both* preserve purchasing power over decades and be portable across borders.

- **Money Is A Medium Of Exchange**.
  Money must also function as a *bridge*, a way to exchange goods and services.

  If you can buy a meal but not a home with it, it's limited. In many developing countries, local currencies are accepted for small purchases like food or phone minutes, but aren't trusted for large transactions like property or vehicles. People don't trust the money, so they avoid using it for anything that matters.

  Good money works at any scale, from buying a pencil to purchasing a farm.

- **Money Is A Unit Of Account**.
- Money is also a measuring stick. It's a *unit of account*. It lets us understand the value of goods and services relative to each other.

  You likely think in dollars. You know the price of a car, a meal, or your monthly rent off the top of your head. But if I told you my car costs 12.4 ounces of gold and my salary is 22.8 ounces a year, you'd be lost. That's because gold, despite being valuable, isn't widely used as a unit of account anymore. *Good money allows intuitive, consistent valuation.*

- **Money As A System Of Control**.

- This is the part they don't teach in school.

Money isn't just a neutral tool. It's also a system of power. Those who control the money supply often control the people who use it. Central banks, governments, and financial institutions have used money to influence behavior, limit access, and enforce control.

Think of this as **economic power**, and it's why centralized money systems are so attractive to those in power. On the other hand, decentralized money, like cash or bitcoin, is *resistant* to control. That makes it threatening to those who benefit from the existing system.

Where Did Money Come From?

We are not going to dive into a long history about gold and money, but there are a few core principles you should understand before you can fully appreciate how bitcoin fits into the story of money. Knowing where money came from helps you understand your investments, your retirement, and the real-world forces shaping your future.

Before dollars, credit cards, and bank accounts, humans **bartered** (exchanged) with each other. This caused them to come together in civilized societies and to increase their wealth and specializations. A farmer might raise cows, milk them, and trade that milk for wheat, chickens, tools, or whatever else he needed. This advancement was known as barter.

But there was a problem called the **coincidence of wants**. If you had milk and I had wheat, but I didn't want milk, the trade broke down. To solve this, societies developed **tradable items** — things that could represent value more consistently and reliably. Early forms of tradable items included shells, beads, clay tokens, and metal coins. This was the beginning of money.

They tried many items: shells, beads, clay coins, tally sticks, and metal coins. Every one of these items was insufficient. Eventually, civilizations independently arrived at the same answer: **gold and silver**. These metals had the properties necessary to make trade easier and more reliable. They were scarce, divisible, durable, and universally accepted.

The Gold Standard

Gold stood out as especially strong money. It was **divisible**. It could be broken down into smaller amounts or combined into larger amounts, and you could measure it in grams or ounces. Gold was **durable**. It does not corrode or decay over time. Gold was **fungible**. An ounce of gold was the same anywhere on Earth. An ounce of gold in Rome was the same as an ounce in Egypt or China. Most importantly, Gold was **scarce and** held its **value over time,** no matter where you went or how long you held it. It took a lot to get more gold. You couldn't just go out and get more gold. You had to work hard for it. You had to dig deeper or go farther afield to find it. In fact, throughout history, the amount of new gold being added to the system has consistently been about 2% per year. That's very consistent and reliable. And with money, you want both. Why do you want this? Because money is your measuring stick when communicating value from one person to the next. And you never want your measuring stick to change. This is a very important point in understanding money and where money problems come from, even today. In addition to this reliability, it was also consistent. An ounce of gold today and an ounce of gold in Roman times would buy you one man's fine suit. This reliability is essential to trade and commerce. So, everyone valued it equally.

But gold had problems, also. It was not very transportable. It was highly valued, so many people would steal a man's gold. This meant it was dangerous to carry or to use freely. If you were on the road with a herd of cows, it was difficult for a robber to steal the cows, but easy to steal a sack of gold coins off your belt. It was also **difficult to verify.** People mixed it with lesser metals, changing the purity, or shaved off bits, changing the weight. Assaying gold required skill and equipment.

Many people were afraid to store their gold. So, they would put it in secure places with safe, reliable gold dealers. They would keep this gold in a secure warehouse, and when you needed it, you could come and get it. These gold warehouses could also assay your gold and weigh it to ensure it was correct and that you weren't getting ripped off.

Then the gold warehouse would give you a paper receipt for your gold when you needed to come pick it up. You would take this receipt and be secure in your knowledge that the gold was safe. The warehouses built their reputations on trust so that they could attract more gold deposits. They didn't need FINRA or FDIC or regulators. Before long, people realized that instead of trading in the metal physical gold, it was easier to just hand the seller your gold receipts. Saving the trouble and danger of going all the way to the gold warehouse, picking up the gold, transporting it, and risking robbery. The seller would accept the receipts because he trusted the warehouse, too. This was the beginning of banking. It was based on a valuable service with trust and reliability.

Now we have a new technology, the invention of paper money. These gold receipts were your way of claiming your hard-earned gold, your wealth, at any time. This was completely private and offered a workable, reliable solution to gold's weaknesses. The weakness of poor transportability. The government wasn't involved in any way at first. As with all technological innovations, over time, the government observes the new technology, ignorant and clueless about its potential. Later sees an opportunity to steal and exploit it. This system was based on trust and voluntary associations between individuals. Force or fraud was not the primary driver at this point.

Lending And Greed

The next step in the evolution of lending is when the gold warehouser or banker started thinking about how to make more profits. How can he use this valuable tool to really boost his income? He thinks, "The gold just sits there, and no one is coming for most of it." In fact, he can predict how much will be taken out or deposited per year. So, he started lending out a portion of the gold. But not the actual gold. He just lends out more of the gold receipts, the paper money.

This worked great. The money was lent, it was paid back with interest, and more business was built. The bank made money, and the economy grew.

But greed crept in. Banks started issuing more receipts than they could possibly cover. Recurring booms and busts followed. And then the government took notice.

Then the government starts to get involved. They smelled money and lots of it. And they want their piece. That's how it always starts. The government told bankers how they needed to protect them since the gold was so valuable. They pressured the banks to pay taxes to the kings and borrowed money to finance their never-ending wars of conquest and hubris. And slowly, over time, banks and the governments became intertwined, partners in power. Because the government had the police power, the banks had to bend to its will, at first. But eventually, the bankers learned to use this power and co-opt it. Over time, their roles blurred, two arms of the same machine. Ultimately, the banks emerged as the true power.

The Horror Of Fractional Reserve Banking

Eventually, banks became just as corrupt as the governments and churches that exerted power over them. This cozy partnership led to **fractional reserve banking, a system so dishonest and opaque that most people still don't fully grasp how insidious it actually is.**

As a reminder, this is how fractional reserve banking functions:

> You deposit $100,000 into your bank. Later, someone borrows $90,000. You might assume that money came from your deposit, but it didn't. The

bank only keeps 10% of your funds in reserve and **creates** the rest out of thin air.

That loan becomes someone else's deposit, which the bank uses to issue another loan—this time $81,000—keeping just 10% again. This cycle repeats, multiplying your original deposit into far more money than the bank actually holds.

This is **fractional reserve banking**, a system built on promises, not actual reserves. Your deposit isn't really sitting in a vault. It's being lent out again and again, while the bank hopes you never ask for it all back.

And this is rarely taught in school. But it's the foundation of the modern financial system.

This cycle repeats, creating far more money on paper than exists in reality. This is the root of systemic risk. If everyone tries to withdraw at once, the money isn't there. That's called a bank run. And when it happens, banks shut their doors. You don't get your money back, not because you did anything wrong, but because the system was never honest to begin with.

But it's worse than this. Because when you deposit this money in your bank account, and into your reliable, honest, decent bank, this is not your money anymore. It is the bank's money. And if push comes to shove, they may not give you your money back. It's called a run on the bank or a *bank run*. This is when the bank cannot give depositors their money back. Because they simply don't have it. And what do they do to stop a bank run? They close the door to the bank, refusing to pay you back your own money.

What is so nasty about this is how deceptive it is. No one is telling you this. It's not in any contract. Yes, they do tell you that the money is not yours. But the deception is deeply hidden. It is not explained in the loan discussion. No one is even teaching this in finance classes in college. But this is how modern banking works, and it's why trust in money, banking, and government is breaking down. The system is designed to work *as long as you don't look too closely*.

But when you understand this it changes your perspective forever.

Gold As Money

The late J.P. Morgan, one of the most successful bankers of all time, famously said, "Gold is money. Everything else is credit." This is so true. He knew exactly what he was talking about. After all, his business, like all bankers, was getting people to accept those IOUs instead of gold.

That's what the modern financial system does. It separates you from your money. It started with gold dealers issuing paper receipts in exchange for storing your gold and charging a fee. Over time, more layers were added: banks, brokers, payment platforms, government agencies, and central banks. Each step added convenience, yes, but also increased control and separation.

Why does this matter? Because your money is more than just paper. It is your energy. The energy you expended to work hard, scrimp, save, innovate, to do something better, or to offer a service or product no one else had ever seen. This is all energy. Your honesty, your hard work, your talent or skill, and your reliability. This is the value you add to the world. Money is how society rewards that effort. And for thousands of years, gold was the best tool for storing that value because it couldn't be printed, inflated, or easily corrupted. Or at least we thought.

Is Gold Really The Best?

But as good as gold is, it has some issues that we need to understand. Gold was a fantastic monetary technology 5,000 years ago when it was first used. Even up to about 100 years ago, it had value. It was revolutionary, and it moved mankind forward in a huge way. It started a huge, slow march towards independence and property rights. But it was like any technology, imperfect, and systems evolved to augment its weaknesses.

Let us look at gold's performance across key monetary properties in our current system.

Divisibility Gold is divisible, yes, but not easily. And, compared to what? Gold can be divided, but how easy is this? Well, we can take a gold bar and melt it down into smaller amounts, or we can take a gold coin and exchange it for smaller coins. But neither is very easy to do. How about small amounts? Try dividing a gold coin into a value of $1, or $5, or $0.25. Divisibility is a problem in the modern world.

Usability

Gold is bulky, heavy, slow, cumbersome, and very difficult to use in a world of electronic payments and instantaneous systems. So not very good for this. Try buying a cup of coffee with gold. Or ordering something on Amazon. Or a business making a $500,000 order to a Chinese supplier with gold. How about security? Gold can be a form of security if you have the money and the means to save, protect, and assay it. Otherwise, it's not very practical. How about portability? Gold is not very portable; it's heavy and attracts a lot of interest. Try taking $200,000 of gold through an airport. You'll get a lot of attention, and most likely, your gold will not make it with you.

Store of Value Well, gold is considered a very good store of value. But compared to what? In the last ten years, gold has been running about $2000 per ounce measured in dollars. If this is the case, what was the dollar ten years ago? According to Yahoo Finance, which is a conservative estimate, the dollar has lost 25% of its value in the last 10 years. So, this means gold would need to be worth at least $2,500 today just to keep up with conservative inflation statistics. Just beating the inflationary debasement of the US dollar, it is doing very well. It does not appear to be a good storage of value either. (You can see by the chat below that Bitcoin is a superior store of value.)

Confiscation Risk: Unfortunately, gold is highly confiscatable. With the stroke of one man's pen, not even a vote, Executive Order 6102 required all persons to deliver on or before May 1, 1933, all but a small amount of gold coin, gold bullion, and gold certificates owned by them to the Federal Reserve in exchange for $20.67 paper money per troy ounce. In an instant, President Roosevelt forced Americans to hand over their gold to the Federal Reserve, a private banking cartel ostensibly not part of the government.

Eventually, the order was rescinded. But, ask yourself, what would it take to do it again? We saw extraordinary overreach during COVID. So, imagine what the government might do during a financial panic. It is estimated that the world's central banks own about one-fifth of all gold that has ever been mined. How do you think they got most of that? You think they paid for it fair and square?

What About A Different Kind Of Money?

As flawed as the current fiat monetary system is, it does have distinct advantages. It is built on important technological innovations that have brought about speed, convenience, and global reach to everyday transactions.

Today, we can take a piece of plastic out of our pockets and pay for just about anything, even if we don't have the funds in our accounts. We can send money across the country in seconds and across the world in about a week. We can order and pay for things on our computer or our phone, and as Americans, we have a reasonable expectation that we will get it. Although it may be a decent store of value, gold cannot do these types of transactions. It doesn't function in a modern, digital economy; it's too slow, too physical, and too impractical.

But as useful as all of these new systems are, we have to ask: Why do we use them? Is it because they're so convenient, or have we been conditioned to *trust* them? We trust the current system with our paychecks, savings, personal data, and retirement. But is this trust deserved? Maybe we stay in the system because it's what everyone else is doing. Maybe we believe there is no alternative. But what if there were a system where trust is not required? A system that works even if you don't trust the other party. Would that be valuable to you?

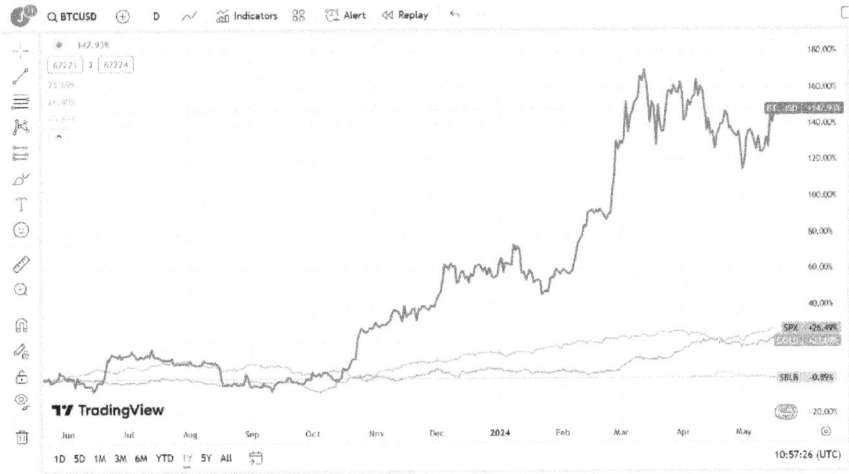

(Take a look at this chart. This is a comparison of different asset classes to Bitcoin. Bitcoin is the blue line, the turquoise line is the S&P index, orange is gold, and yellow is bonds. It's not difficult to see the difference in performance over just one year.)

Let's look at the trust layers in a typical house purchase transaction.

- You must prove to a lender that you're creditworthy.

- You give the seller a deposit and a down payment, both held by an escrow agent.
- A title company insures that the seller actually owns the property.
- Lawyers draft legal documents and file them with local governments.
- Every step requires signatures, notaries, and licensed professionals.
- Each intermediary must be authorized, regulated, and paid for.

This expensive, multi-billion-dollar structure exists to solve one problem. We can't transact directly without trust. But what if we could? What if you could transfer money, or value, to anyone, anywhere in the world, with no trusted third parties? No banks. No brokers. No letters of credit. No credit checks. No paperwork. Just a pure, direct exchange between two people, powered by math, code, and a decentralized network.

That's exactly what Bitcoin does.

Bitcoin Is A Monetary Technology.
Bitcoin is more than just digital money. It is a breakthrough in monetary technology. A next-generation system designed to solve the very problems that gold, fiat, and the banking systems could never fix. A new technology designed to serve the needs of money. It is an order of magnitude or many orders of magnitude advancement in technology. By combining multiple existing technologies with even newer and better technologies, such as immutability, decentralization, cryptographic security, and programmability, Bitcoin becomes even more usable and more valuable.

But even more important, it wrests control from the central authority to the safety and security of the individual, where it belongs. That alone marks a huge step change in the advancement of mankind. Just like any new revolutionary technology, it will create advancements over time and around the world.

Bitcoin combines the best properties of previous forms of money while eliminating their weaknesses. Like gold, it is scarce and cannot be arbitrarily created. But unlike gold, it is divisible down to eight decimal places, portable, and instantly transferable worldwide. Like fiat currency, it works seamlessly for global electronic transactions. But unlike fiat, it cannot be debased through printing and central manipulation. Most importantly, Bitcoin puts **control back in your hands.** It's about sovereignty, allowing you to store and transmit our energy - your life's work - without requiring anyone's permission. No bank, no government, no gatekeeper.

Bitcoin Bit

Did you know that Bitcoin has been the highest performing asset in 12 of the last 15 years? It has outperformed stocks, gold, real estate, bonds, and all other commodities. Sure, you can find some short-term hotshot that went up quicker than Bitcoin in the short term. But as far as annual returns or long-term Bitcoin consistently wins. Maybe this could be a good savings vehicle?

As Jack Mallers, founder of Strike, said, "In the morning, I wake up with a certain amount of money. At the end of the day, when I go to bed, I want to still have this money. So, when someone tells you that Bitcoin does not have a use case, ask yourself, *What use case is more important than keeping your own money?*

Pretty simple, huh?

Historical Exercise: Learning From Your Financial Past

- I want you to try to recall how many times in your past you have had to deal with an economic crisis. If so, what kind of crisis? How did it affect you personally? What were the intermediaries? And how did you deal with it? What would you do differently now? Rich people who manage their money successfully anticipate and prepare for financial events. They see the world clearly.

- How about older relatives, parents, or grandparents? How about relatives in a foreign country? How did they deal with currency events? Did anyone live through a currency crisis or a devaluation? What are their thoughts? These are much more common abroad. The purpose of this is to help you understand your own resilience and adaptability. I think you will see that you are a lot better at this issue of dealing with financial adversity than you think. And you are going to get even more adept.

- Now, try to list the potential historical events that are occurring in your world and the wider world right now. Don't make the list too long. Just the top five. What's the percentage likelihood of each? Think about how they could affect your financial well-being, good or bad. This is not a random exercise; this is a legitimate effort. Would a shutdown of the system, like the recent pandemic, be dealt with in the same way as the great financial crisis? Would you have known this if you hadn't lived through both? I wouldn't have.

Chapter 5

Where Did it All Go?

"I sincerely believe that banking establishments are more dangerous than standing armies, and that the principles of spending money to be paid by posterity under the name of funding is but swindling futurity on a large scale."

Thomas Jefferson

Now that we've established what money is, you may be wondering, *where has all our money gone?* Despite decades of working, saving, and investing, many Baby Boomers find themselves with far less purchasing power than expected. The dollars we earned in the 1970s and 1980s have mysteriously diminished in value.

Shockingly, this disappearing act is no accident. It's the inevitable result of our current monetary system. In this chapter, we'll explore how inflation, central banking policies, and government actions systematically erode your savings. By understanding this process, you will appreciate why traditional retirement strategies are increasingly inadequate and why Bitcoin represents such a revolutionary alternative.

Let's take a historical detour. Remember that while today's circumstances differ in degree, they share disturbing similarities. Same principles, just more gradually and less visibly.

Weimar Republic

After World War I, Germany owed massive reparations. They simply didn't have the money to pay the demands, so instead of paying them with real productivity, they just printed more money, as many governments do. In 1923, there were 10,000 printing presses running 24 hours a day. The Reich printed 400 quintillion Deutschmarks in August 1923. By November 1923, unemployment had soared to 28%. That year, one egg cost 500 billion marks. A half-pound of apples? 300 billion. Did eggs or apples all of a sudden become better to justify this value? No, they did not.

It was madness. Money lost all meaning. Middle-class families saw their savings wiped out. One of the wealthiest countries in the world rapidly descended into poverty. Now, our situation may not be as extreme, but the mechanism is the same. Just slower. Same disease, different speed.

Try to imagine yourself in their position. Have you ever had money trouble? Maybe when you were young and couldn't pay the bills? Remember the stress? The knot in your stomach when you had to borrow from your parents or a friend? The embarrassment of telling your girlfriend you couldn't take her out, or the awkwardness of asking your boss for an advance? You certainly weren't worried about who would win the football game or the next episode of your favorite television show. You were sliding quickly down "Maslow's Hierarchy of Needs." And that kind of thing sticks with a man. It stings. There's shame in it. You remember.

Now multiply this feeling times a thousand. And then make it permanent. Make it systemic. Imagine being 45 or 50, having done everything right. You worked. You saved. You provided. And now, you still can't afford to feed your family or heat your home. Worse, no one around you can either.

But people don't think about the hidden damage. It's not just the financial pressure; it's what it does to your identity. The way a father starts to feel less like a man. The way couples start fighting over bills they can't control. The way a family's warmth turns to cold silence over a dinner table. It's the dignity you lose — not all at once, but day by day. The desperation, the anxiety. People you once knew and trusted are now potential enemies to compete with to fill that grinding hunger in your belly. This is the part that doesn't show up in the headlines. The part that ruins people quietly.

Can you feel that dread? This is real fear. Something the American Baby Boomer generation has never felt.

People were suffering from food shortages and the cold. It was devastating. It created terror and panic. People were totally demoralized and desperate. Thousands of aimless, jobless young men flocked to the fledgling NAZI party. Powerless, they began to feel a tie to the radical National Socialist ideas. It seemed that the NAZI party was going to provide the strong leadership that would be required to counter the weak Weimar government. In November, the government printed a one trillion-mark paper currency note. Then, all of a sudden, the head of the central bank died. And his successor stepped in. He immediately stopped monetizing the German debt and intervened to stabilize the currency. The hyperinflation stopped, but the damage had been done. And it would not easily be reversed. By this time, fear had pushed the entire country to lean dangerously closer to the insane poison of centralization and collectivism, radical nationalism, and to its logical conclusion, National Socialism, more commonly known as the NAZI party.

Why Is Money A Mystery?

For something so central to everyday life, why do we never get clear answers about money? Why is this rarely discussed in the media or taught in schools? Where are the in-depth academic treatises defining money, analyzing its importance, and framing its use? It almost seems like there is some kind of effort to hide this.

I have a degree in finance from a good university. And an in-depth discussion of a definition of money was never had. Even in my "Money and Banking" class, it was never discussed. I have talked to many people, some educated and some very educated, and this subject wasn't taught to them either. What gives? I challenge the folks reading this to tell me of a good definition of money, and then think of where you got it. I venture to guess it was not from a traditional educational institution.

Here Is How The American Heritage Dictionary Defines Money:

1. A medium that can be exchanged for goods and services and is used as a measure of their values on the market, including among its forms a commodity such as gold, an officially issued coin or note, or a deposit in a checking account or other readily liquefiable account.

2. The official currency, coins, and negotiable paper notes issued by a government.

3. Assets and property considered in terms of monetary value; wealth.

You will notice that the first two definitions emphasize an official or government-issued currency. When in reality, that is fiat money, or money by decree. A very important distinction and part of the overall problem. Definition 3 is the most accurate, and yet it is ranked at the bottom. I would say 1 and 2 define "fiat currency," but not really money because they don't incorporate the properties of money. More obfuscation and control. Control of the money, and as a result, control of us.

So let me ask you, if we cannot define money, how will we know good money from bad? How will we recognize real value? How can we even recognize money at all? Because someone told you that it's money? Because of a decree? Because of **FIAT** money? That's what the folks in power want. Is that what you want?

Money is a technology, just like an airplane. If I decree by fiat that airplanes must be constructed of paper instead of aluminum, then people will die. And the same is true with fiat money. When the government decrees *what is money*, people die. Endless wars and suffering worldwide are caused by fiat money.

Here's a definition I prefer: "Money is a tool that helps you do the things you want in life." Having said this, is money allowing you to do the things you want in your life? Is it giving you this freedom to decide? Or is it a source of consternation and worry and suffering? If it's not fulfilling this definition, why is that?

Properties Of Money

Scarcity: Money, first and foremost, must be scarce. If it's not scarce, then its energy bleeds away over time. It must be able to move energy through space and time. Scarcity allows money to hold its value. To contain and preserve the energy that you put into it. Scarcity does this by its value. Bitcoin is extremely scarce. There will only ever be 21 million Bitcoin. This cannot change. Whereas gold is relatively scarce, its supply can increase when there is a higher demand for gold. And, fiat money has no scarcity at all; it is printed out of thin air at the whim of governments.

Durability: Money must be durable. It needs to be able to move its value through time and space. Durability also helps with this function. Bitcoin is highly durable. It is digital, so it cannot erode, fade, or go away for any reason. Bitcoin has tens of thousands of miners and tens of thousands of full nodes worldwide. Each of them stores the Bitcoin ledger and protects it from change for time immemorial. Fiat changes at the whim of the government in charge, never knowing when it will change. Gold is very durable; almost all the gold that has ever been mined is still being used or stored.

Acceptability: For money to function, it must have widespread acceptance. Gold is relatively widely accepted, but for the reasons we've discussed, many places will not accept gold in the modern economy. Currently, fiat currencies like the dollar have the broadest level of global acceptance. However, superior forms of money will eventually overtake outdated monetary systems. That shift is already underway and accelerating rapidly. Bitcoin, as a new form of money, is still in its early stages of adoption. It's not widely accepted today, but it is already being used on every continent for both small and large transactions. And its adoption curve is growing exponentially every year.

Portability: Money must always be portable. That's what allows it to hold value as it moves across space. Digital fiat currencies are highly portable but are subject to permission, which becomes more challenging as restrictions, surveillance, and geopolitical friction increase each year.. Gold, however, has almost no practical portability. Try traveling with a significant amount of gold in your possession. It's heavy, risky, and draws attention. Bitcoin is the most portable money ever invented. In April 2020, a transaction of $1.1 billion was sent across the globe in about 25 minutes. The fee? Just 68 cents. This was done with no permission from anyone and no jurisdictional restrictions. Nothing is more portable than Bitcoin.

Divisibility: Money gains greater value as it is more divisible. The ability to exchange for different items, large and small, is critical. Fiat money is highly divisible. Gold, by contrast, is not. It is hard to break up into small units. Even small gold coins are expensive, easy to lose, and difficult to verify. A tenth-ounce of gold is worth about $200. That's not exactly pocket change. Bitcoin is the most divisible form of money ever invented. There are 100 million Satoshis within each Bitcoin. At today's rate of $105,000 per Bitcoin, this means one Satoshi is worth a mere .00105 cents. Many people think they can't get into Bitcoin because they need $105,000 in order to buy a whole Bitcoin. However, this is not true. You can buy very small amounts and start saving today. Much easier than other investments.

Fungibility: Fungibility means that each unit of money is interchangeable with another. So, a dollar bill is the same everywhere. Fiat money is very fungible; gold is also very fungible. Fungibility is 100% with Bitcoin. A Bitcoin is a Bitcoin worldwide. There is no dispute about this.

Immutability: Immutability refers to the inability to alter money through coercion, manipulation, or corruption. Fiat money fails this test completely. Over time, governments have quietly shifted the definitions of money, a subtle and insidious process. Money became so mutable that today, governments just print money at will. In older days, governments like Spain and Rome clipped the coins to capture some of the gold. Even in the USA, a dime once contained silver in its alloy, and a nickel contained nickel. Now, who knows what's in there? Nothing of value, that's for sure. Bitcoin is the most immutable form of money; it cannot be changed or debased by anyone. Fiat is eternally mutable, with its value constantly eroding.

Every time you are looking at money, think about these definitions and how superior Bitcoin is as money. Once you see this, it becomes obvious why so many traditional financial institutions criticize Bitcoin so vociferously. And maybe a good reason why you should be looking seriously at it.

The Scourge Of Inflation.

There are many economic difficulties that people can encounter. From deficits to trade problems, to unemployment and low productivity, nothing can devastate and demoralize a people like inflation. In minor measurements, like most countries experience, it is just a nagging fear and an insidious theft of people's hard-earned wealth. In the case of countries like Zimbabwe, Venezuela, or Lebanon, it is absolutely terrifying. It can create panic and a complete change of behavior.

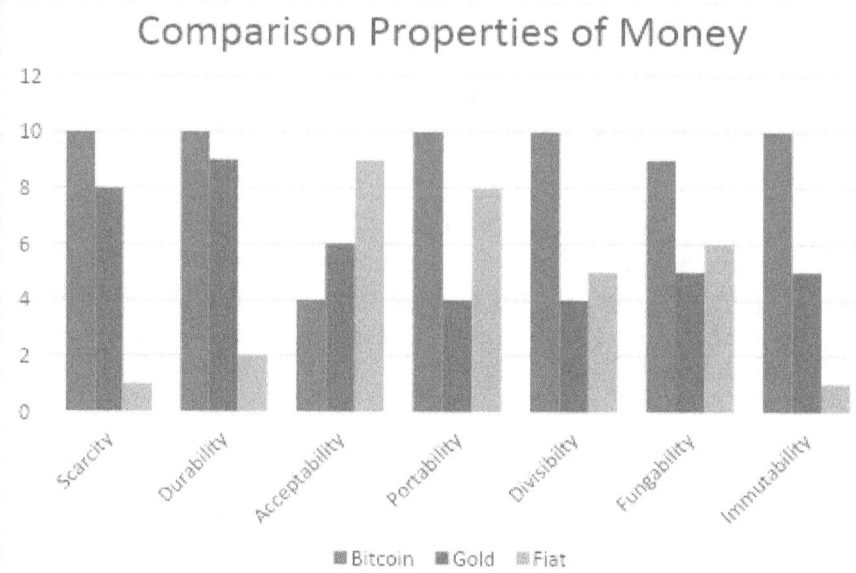

Comparison Properties of Money

Bitcoin ▪ Gold ▪ Fiat

Scarcity · Durability · Acceptability · Portability · Divisibility · Fungability · Immutability

The above chart illustrates a comparison of money on a scale of 1 to 10, showing how effective three primary forms of money fulfill these properties.

As Americans, we have been lucky. We have not experienced times of high inflation. And so, we don't feel the fear and panic of other places around the world. And then when we do, much of it gets exported to other countries through our ability to exert our fiscal dominance and use of the dollar as the world's reserve currency. This helps prop up our system and keep us free from some of its vagaries, limping along like some kind of beaten dog. But eventually, like all monetary problems, this too will come due. And unfortunately, the people in charge will run out of tricks and games they can play.

Once inflation gets out of control, it is hard to put the genie back into the bottle. The incentives to keep printing are just too strong. Look at what is happening to our own economy. Every year, the government spends more. And every year, the central bankers devise more temporary schemes to perpetuate the insanity. And no one, not the blue team or the red team, lifts a finger to try to reverse or even slow down the steady decline in our system.

Remember when you were a kid in the fifties or sixties, how much did a McDonald's cheeseburger cost? That's right, 10 cents. A cool, new Mustang ran $3,200. Today, a McDonald's Big Mac meal costs a staggering $11.64, and pickup trucks in America sell for over $100,000! Are pickups that much better?

I remember seeing my mom's school librarian paycheck: $75 a week. A fair wage. One day, I was riding with Mom and Dad in the family pickup truck, which cost $2,900 new. And they kept talking about a "gas war." It was on every corner. It was in our town. It was in every town. I couldn't figure out what they were talking about. Eventually, they explained to me what a "gas war" was. The price of gasoline was dropping so rapidly that gas stations were competing ruthlessly to sell us gasoline below market rates. There used to be four gas stations on each street corner, even in our small town. And they were going out of business as fast as the big oil companies could convince another poor sucker to open a new one. Gas prices were down to about 27 cents a gallon. And many times, it even dipped as low as 23 cents. The government had a cure for low prices, and it wasn't very pretty.

As a young boy in 1971, I injured my hand. My mother actually had the doctor's phone number. She called him on a Sunday, and he said to meet at his office. He examined my hand, did a quick X-ray, and put a splint on it. It was not very serious, after all. Then my mother handed him $7.00 in cash for the entire visit. That's it, on a Sunday! Compare that to healthcare today. It's impossible to compare this experience to anything happening in the USA today. I thought service was supposed to get better when you paid more? Something serious happened to our country.

Example of Real World Inflation

If you've visited Latin America, you've probably noticed how far your dollar goes. But if you've traveled to Argentina, you can see that taken to extremes. Inflation is more than a headline; it is a way of life. It is not hard for local Argentinians to identify tourists in Buenos Aires. They just go to the local tourist sites and observe their slightly different behavior. And if you are one of these tourists, you will notice something very different from other countries you visit. You will be approached many times by local Argentinians asking you to exchange dollars for their local pesos. This is not common in other Latin American countries. Why is this? Because inflation in Argentina is so extreme that the local folks are desperate for relief from the constant theft of their purchasing power by their own government, theft that's baked into their monetary system.

Argentina was once a powerhouse, the jewel of South America. Buenos Aires was called the "Paris of Latin America." Now it is a declining victim. Constantly trying to outrun the shadow of inflation, chasing everyone every day.

When Javier Mieli took office, inflation was running at 211%. Recently, it has come down, but only because of a massive currency devaluation, which is just inflation all at once. This economic shock has impoverished millions, slashing their ability to buy even simple goods and services.

Closer To Home. Let's look at conditions closer to home to gain a deeper understanding. The official Consumer Price Index (CPI) claims inflation is just 2.4%. But of course, we know better. The government has every reason to downplay the numbers, and they've spent decades changing how inflation is measured to make it seem smaller than it is, with the hope we don't notice that the price of cars, insurance, food, and housing are skyrocketing.

We are interested in the *real world*, so we will use a better measure, a tool we have talked about before called ShadowStats.com. And the current rate of inflation using the government's own measurement standards from the 1990s, when they were a bit more honest, would be 9%. Well, that sounds like a lot. But let's see what it means to you and me, regular people who don't have any control over how our money is debased. If I have a savings of $100,000 and the inflation rate is 9%, meaning it's losing 9% of its value per year, how long will it take for it to be worth half?

There is a simple formula for this called the **Rule of 72.** To figure out how long it will take, all you do is divide 72 by the inflation rate. $72 \div 9 = $ **8 years**. So, in eight short years, your $100,000 will be worth half. As you can see, inflation affects us all. Even we Americans with the almighty dollar. And it is getting worse.

Put another way. Let's say you have a nice nest egg of $1 million, you retire at 60, and you want to live off the interest. If you use the same calculation when you are 68, it will have half the value. And when you are 84, the same million dollars will be worth $100,000, or one-tenth of its value. It's important that we take inflation seriously and use the correct tools to measure it. Otherwise, we may find ourselves, one day, in an Argentine's shoes... asking travelers if they'll trade dollars for Bitcoin.

Money As A Weapon.
If you still don't believe how important money can be and how damaging the wrong money can be? In *War and Peace*, Leo Tolstoy—through Prince Andrew's description of Napoleon's destruction of Russia—wrote: "They plunder other people's houses, **issue false paper money,** and, worst of all, they **kill my children.**" As you can see, he is classifying the issuing of false paper money right up there with the worst things about a conquering army.

Or here is Copernicus' writing in 1525 as he studied the decline of the Prussian and Polish economies under foreign and internal pressures: "Although they are causing countless maladies...the following four are the most serious: civil discord, a high death rate, sterilization of the soil, and *debasement of the coinage*...the first three are obvious...the last operates in a *hidden and insidious way*."

See why governments want to keep inflation a secret? It cannot be overstated how damaging the destruction of a society's money can be. We do not want to be part of the next wave. But how can we avoid this?

The degeneration of our moral principles and the modern life we lead is very hard to see. We may not see this collapse play out in a dramatic flash. But it occurs to each of us. Savers are forced to degenerate into investors, investors are forced to degenerate into speculators, and speculators are forced to degenerate into gamblers. Everyone is pushed down one rung of the morality ladder. Thereby eroding our personal fiber and our ability to survive in the real world.

Central Banks And Economists.

Surely the intelligent people in the government can solve these problems. We've got brilliant economists with massive research departments. They can see the damage. So where's the fix?
We're waiting.
Prices keep rising. The government tells us how great things are. Shrinkflation continues, smaller packages, higher prices. And we're left wondering whether the banks and the government actually want to fix the problem.
But what about the US dollar is good? Right? It's the world's reserve currency. We are the cornerstone of the world's financial system. The United States banking system is the bedrock of the capitalist system. The engine of the economy. That's one of the biggest narratives we are told, right?

Crack open any freshman year macroeconomics textbook, and you'll see this claim: all assets have risk — except one. US Treasury securities are said to be "risk-free." Why is this? Well, it's simple, we are told. The US government can just make more money, borrow more money, or tax the American people to get more money. So they say there's no risk. In the financial world, a "risk-free rate of return."

Or is it? Is it true that the US government will not default on its obligations? Are they truly better than gold itself? That all they must do is print more or borrow more or tax more. That its resources are infinite? Has the US government ever defaulted on its obligations? What about those powerful institutions like the Federal Reserve Bank?

So, if the Federal Reserve and the US Treasury are the bedrock of financial capitalism, surely, they must be backed by something of value, right? If we call this "risk-free," there must be something behind all of this? Well, evidently, the US Federal Reserve does not think so. Ben Bernanke, former Chairman of the Federal Reserve, once said: "The US government has a technology, called a printing press (or today, its electronic equivalent), that allows it to produce as many U.S. dollars as it wishes at no cost."

Does this sound like it's backed by something of real value?

Neel Kashkari, President of the Minneapolis Fed, said in a *60 Minutes* interview: "There's an infinite amount of cash at the Federal Reserve." "There is no end to our ability to print money…we create it electronically." He said they could even loan money at *negative* interest rates if they wanted. Other central banks have done it," he shrugged. You can't make this stuff up. With guys like these protecting you, you don't need enemies.

Let's pause. Is cash what we need? Will a magic button that prints infinite dollars solve our problems, or will it make them worse? Can printed money replace your hard work, your ingenuity, your thrift? It didn't work in Weimar Germany, in Zimbabwe, in Argentina, in Venezuela, in Lebanon. Why would it work here?

I remember going to a friend who is a very talented financial planner. He is very successful and certified and keeps up with the latest economic, business, and market trends. He has numerous certifications and tons of wealthy clients. I turned to him when I was deeply concerned about the viability of the market during the COVID-19 crisis, as President Trump was dumping trillions of dollars into the system. My highly acclaimed friend's reply was simple: "The US dollar is backed by 11 aircraft carrier battle groups. That's what backs the US dollar. Military power." In other words, proof of war. Well, let's set aside the fact that only six of those carriers are seaworthy at any given time. That's another issue. The real issue is this: we are relying on a system built on **fiat,** money created by decree, backed by nothing but authority and the threat of force. (Recall that fiat is an old term that simply means "let it be done," basically, "because I said so.")

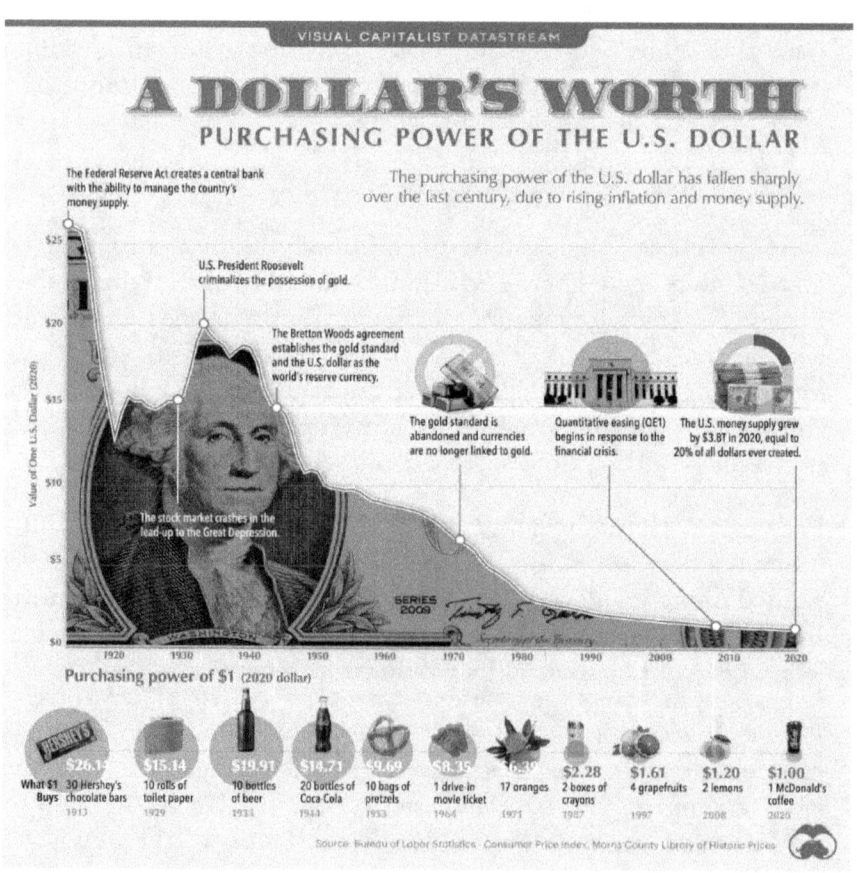

Is this what we have come to? There is nothing backing our monetary system but America's willingness to wage war. How do you feel about bombing and killing brown people in some faraway land? Did we learn anything from Vietnam or Iraq or Afghanistan or Libya or Syria?

That's it? That's all? Maybe this is why they never use the actual name for the type of money we have. They want you to think that it is backed by something. Something bigger and more important than what we are. But it's not.

Every fiat currency in history except the dollar and the British pound has gone to zero and ended up worthless. And, frankly, it doesn't look good for these two either. We've replaced gold with IOUs, IOUs with printing, and printing with military intimidation. But let me ask: When was the last time that model worked for the people?

The Assault On Integrity

The problem with all of these systems, agencies, and oversight organizations is that they actually disarm the average American consumer into thinking he is protected. Imagine that you live in a bad neighborhood. You stay alert. You check your locks, teach your kids how to be safe, and talk to your neighbors to stay informed. You're vigilant.

And then, one day, you hire someone to build a high wall around your house to protect you and your family. But unbeknownst to you, the wall is full of holes and has several ways around it. It was poorly constructed, but you feel comfortable because you assume it is providing protection and security. You put your family in this house, thinking it is safe. You are not looking for any protection. You stop trying to protect your family. You have a great wall to protect you. You drop your guard. You stop checking the locks and scanning the streets. But, in reality, it can be exploited easily. And although you feel safe, you are exposed. Even more dangerous, you don't even know it.

Once again, you can see what I talk about when I discuss the real world. Seeing the world for what it is. How important this is. To be able to see this fictional wall as an ineffective way to protect your family and safety. It disarms you. It takes away your ability to even know you are not protected after a while. You become oblivious; you become blind.

One of the best-known and most celebrated Federal Reserve Chairmen actually wrote about this phenomenon in an essay years ago, when he was a much more interesting and honest man. In 1963, Alan Greenspan published an essay titled "An Assault on Integrity." In it, he describes how the government disarms you from protecting yourself with its myriads of regulations, protections, agencies, rules, and restrictions.

In effect, they shield you from the one very thing you need to keep you alive. The truth. What is integrity? It is truth. What is truth? Truth is reality. Plain and simple. But the system, and its institutions that prop it up, have put up a smokescreen of lies to shield you from seeing the real world. How are you ever going to see the world for what it is? Well, it's going to take some work, but it can be done.

When you have a house built, and the building contractors are shoddy, you don't know this until the house is built, and it's too late. What are you going to do, buy another $500,000 house and default on your mortgage? Ruin your credit? So what do people do? They pay again. This time for private house inspectors. There is an entire industry built around mistrust. If we are going to hire house inspectors to make sure our house is safe and well-built, then maybe we should get rid of building code inspectors and use our own vigilance.

How about food safety? The government assures us it inspects our food to protect our health and safety. Does this work? The US food supply is the most expensive and at the same time the worst and unhealthiest of all 38 industrialized economies. We are tormented by a food pyramid that comes from the government, when actually, it comes from the food companies trying to sell us as much junk and GMO food as possible. Over 1,000 chemicals banned in Europe are still allowed in American food. What is the health of the average American? Americans have sky-high rates of cancer, heart disease, Alzheimer's, obesity, diabetes, and metabolic disorders. One hundred years ago, these diseases were a rare phenomenon in America. It used to be that a doctor would see only one or two cancer cases in his entire career. Alzheimer's was unheard of before the 1930s.

Now, consider financial fraud. Bernie Madoff ran a Ponzi scheme for over two decades, ballooning his fund to $50 million. Multiple people pleaded with the SEC to investigate him. The SEC even visited him, but never seemed to be able to find anything wrong. How much do we pay the SEC for this "protection?" He operated under their noses. No one was protected. In the end, his sons turned him in. That's when it caved in on him. The government wasn't protecting anyone.

I could go on, but you get the picture. If you think Uncle Sam is protecting you. Check again. See the real world for what it is. Governments are not here to protect you. They are here for power. Take a look at another valuable website called opensecrets.org and keep it close. This site will help you understand how money flows into politics. It's a good tool for helping you see through the BS. Back to Greenspan. In 1965 he wrote:

> "It is argued, the Pure Food and Drug Administration, the Securities and Exchange Commission, and the numerous building regulatory agencies are indispensable if the consumer is to be protected from the "greed" of the businessman. But it is precisely the 'greed' of the businessman or, more appropriately, his profit-seeking, which is the unexcelled protector of the consumer."

His point? When businesses are accountable to customers, not to government bureaucrats, they have the strongest incentive to deliver value. Not because they're noble, but because they want to stay in business. He goes on to explain that not only do the government protective agencies and their numerous regulations and rules not protect us. They go further. They do something more insidious. They disarm us. They make us weak and ineffective. They try to create a 'Barbie marshmallow world' where magically the world **appears** stable and orderly because our big brother government **protects you**.

But the reality is, you are not being protected by these entities. You are being first deceived, then weakened, and ultimately infantilized. One day, you wake up and not only can't you protect yourself, your wealth, and your family, but you don't even know what the problem is anymore. There are so many false agendas and lies being told on a daily basis, all in the form of a crisis that demands you follow the next government prescription to save you from calamity. They layer lie upon lie, and then other lies to cover it up. Then they feed us a crisis with more lies to keep us afraid, worried, and focused on the latest debacle. Hell, how could any of us make sense of this mess? But here's the good news. We can rearm ourselves. We can learn to see clearly again. It won't be easy. It took seventy-five years of incremental, corrosive damage to get us to this point. These problems won't just vanish overnight. The road back requires effort and discipline.

We need to relearn what our grandparents knew, about self-reliance, about money, about survival. And we must combine that wisdom with new tools. One of those tools is Bitcoin. But you have to learn how to use it.

What About Our Pensions

If you have a pension, when was your last benefit increase? How about those Social Security increases? What was the last one, 3%? Meanwhile, even conservative estimates of real inflation are close to 10%. That means in ten years, your benefits will be worth just 10% of what they are today. And many people will be retired for 20 or 30 years. It's time to face the facts and start seeing the real world for what it is.

The Idea Of Hard Money.

"I have directed Secretary (of Treasury) Connolly to **'temporarily'** *suspend the convertibility of the dollar into gold or other reserve assets…your dollar will be worth just as much tomorrow as it is today"*

President Richard Nixon, August 15, 1971 (Emphasis added.)

When President Nixon uttered these words in 1971, the world changed. And it has never been the same. Government officials have done many things to damage our economy over the years, but few decisions were as devastating and far-reaching as that one "temporary" decree in August 1971.

Let's rewind. If you are a Boomer like me, you probably remember the general atmosphere. But let's lay out the facts.

During World War II, many countries feared the scourge of Nazi invasions and the theft of their gold reserves, a common tactic in all wars. So, they sent their gold to the United States for safekeeping. After the war, the USA emerged economically unscathed while Europe and Asia lay in ruins. America was the clear victor, with an intact industrial base, a booming economy, and most of the world's gold.

After the war was over, the USA was the undisputed greatest beneficiary of the victory. Its economy was booming, the country had not suffered horrendous mass casualties like Russia or China, and the country wasn't structurally damaged like England and France. You could say that if any country benefited from this terrible war, it was the USA. So, there was a meeting of all countries after the war in 1948 to discuss recovery from the war. The USA summoned the countries to a meeting in Bretton Woods, New Hampshire, to come up with a new system. And since the USA was the top dog and creditor to all of these countries, it offered a solution. It essentially said, instead of us returning your gold, we will first help you rebuild your country, and second, and most important, we will continue to help you hold and protect your gold. You don't need to repatriate it. It is safe with us. In return, instead of using gold, you can use dollars as your reserve asset. We will peg an ounce of gold at $35, and you can just use dollars. They are as good as gold. Besides, if you need your gold, you can just come and get it. We will happily return your gold to you. We are just like a bank, except we are a bank for your country's gold.

In essence, the USA said, "Don't worry. We are a safe harbor for your gold." To make it worse, these countries were all on their knees already. They were devastated, and their economies were in shambles. In some cases, an entire generation had almost been wiped out. Who was going to say no?

Imagine you are the leader of one of these countries at this time. What would you do? You knew that your only chance of getting out of this mess — for England, France, Belgium, or Italy — was

Bitcoin Bit

Every commodity, every investment and every form of money is losing value compared to Bitcoin. Bitcoin is sometimes called volatile. Which it can be over the short term this is true. But I don't believe in trading. And certainly not trading long term assets such as Bitcoin. Why would I do that? What purpose does it serve?

to play ball. You certainly didn't have any economic might at the moment, and besides, the USA had your gold. Worse, if you were a country like Japan or Germany, you were in no position to bargain about anything. Hundreds of millions of people are dead, economies were devastated, and cities were completely flattened. No one wanted a confrontation with the biggest kid on the block. It was a hard bargain. But it was the best deal anyone was going to get at the time. Remember our discussion of intermediaries in the last chapter? Remember, I talked about looking for intermediaries in your financial transactions. This is a massive, powerful, nuclear-armed intermediary at the nation-state level. This is an intermediary with a strong standing military, and they were willing to use it. The people at that table in Bretton Woods knew what the USA was capable of. They had all seen the films of Hiroshima and Nagasaki.

This wasn't the pie-in-the-sky false "we're the good guys" image of Hollywood. This was the real world once again. And these people knew the real USA. They were exhausted; they just wanted to get on with their lives. Nationalism and the resulting two World Wars had sucked the energy and many lives out of them. Now there was a new sheriff in town, and he was going to flex his muscles with the biggest muscles he had. His financial muscles, his muscles of Wall Street, and his big banks.

We started operating the world economy under the Bretton Woods system. This didn't last too long. Just long enough for us Baby Boomers to start growing up. You see, the US government wasn't just going along, minding its own business. It was fighting wars and interfering in the affairs of other countries all over the world. Then Vietnam came, and the USA got hold of a real war. An expensive war. A war that really hurt the USA. And US politicians, not really good at admitting they were wrong, kept spending lots of money. At the same time, Lyndon Johnson's "Great Society" programs like Medicare and Medicaid added enormous domestic spending. It was called "guns and butter." It should have been called "your money and more of your money." The government was spending far more than it had, and the dollar began to weaken.

Other countries took notice. They saw the inflation. They saw the USA losing in Vietnam. They saw the bullying, assassinations, regime changes, and dirty little wars. (Americans didn't really see this. We were the good guys, we were told.) But the leaders of other countries did. And they got nervous. Gold was still $35 an ounce on paper, but the real value of the dollar was falling fast. So countries started asking for their gold back. Famously, France sent a battleship to New York to retrieve its gold reserves. What happened next is called the Nixon Shock. With the world watching, the president went on TV and announced to the world that he was temporarily suspending the convertibility of countries that had US dollars in reserve back into the gold that the USA was ostensibly holding. Remember what the USA had promised at Bretton Woods two decades earlier? If you want your gold back, we will give it to you.

The US had defaulted on its debt again. And the world would never be the same. Nixon's obscure, tyrannical move shocked the entire world economic system. A shock we still feel today. I invite you to take a look at a website called **WTFhappenedin1971.com**. You will see graph after graph of rising inequality, skyrocketing debt, declining wages, unaffordable housing, and a gradual decay of the American middle class.

Nobel laureate Milton Friedman once famously said, "Nothing so permanent as a 'temporary' government program." This rewired the global economy, and the American economy is still shuddering and slowly dying from this effect. Remember what economists tell us about the American dollar being a "risk-free" rate of return, we discussed earlier? Another question. If they are going to default on gold deposits to their own biggest allies, powerful nation-states, with standing armies, what makes you think they won't default on you? What makes you think you are safer than the countries of Britain or France or Germany? What chance do you have?

Seizability Of Gold

The problem, you see, is not whether governments will confiscate your gold or some other government's gold. It is a certainty that if they get the chance eventually, they will try. And if they don't have a chance, they will still try many other ways to get it. You see, gold is not only confiscatable, it is easily confiscatable. Think about it. Are you going to keep a significant amount of gold safe? It's unlikely. You have to hide it and protect it, all of the time. And you'd better come with some very good physical security. Can't do that? Then the next would be to hire someone who is trusted to hold it and protect it for you. However, this comes with something called **centralization**. This means that your asset, gold in this case, sits in one central location, with one central facility, with one central management or legal entity (registered with the state) to protect it. This means that if someone wants to get at it, a nation-state, for instance, knows precisely where it is. It knows the right place to go. The centralized firm holding your gold has a board of directors, a corporate charter, and employees, all vulnerable to the coercion of the government. Centralization is really bad for security. Maybe they don't want to confiscate all of the facilities' gold. Maybe they just want yours. Then they get a subpoena, and they come and get your gold. No CEO will protect you more than any other stranger on the street. In fact, there is a good chance they may give up your gold without a subpoena. Not very safe.

We are going to hear a lot about this concept of centralization in this book. So please understand this concept carefully. If you see centralization, you are seeing one of the keys to the lack of security of your assets or your money, gold, or any other asset. The more centralized something is, the more vulnerable it is to theft, larceny, confiscation, scams, embezzlement, and other forms of exploitation. In fact, when you hear the word centralization, you should think of vulnerability or fragility. When you hear decentralization, you should hear antifragile and invulnerable.

Bitcoin Is A Dream Come True.

Now, imagine a system where no one—not a government, not a corporation—could confiscate or steal your gold. What if there was a system with no CEO, no management team, no physical location, no employees, and no trace of your gold was visible to anyone? It is safe and secure. It gives you peace of mind, rather than worrying at night. That's Bitcoin.

Bitcoin doesn't require trust. It replaces trust with verification. No digging holes in your backyard. No banks. No vaults. No mattress stuffing. Just math and code that's accessible, secure, and impossible to counterfeit.

For those of us who lived through the Great Inflation, the oil shocks, the tech bubbles, and the Great Recession, this is redemption. It's what our parents hoped gold would be.

But now, we have something even better. And this time, it's ours to protect.

How many of us Baby Boomers had older relatives who didn't trust banks? It is a foreign concept to us nowadays. But if you knew what they went through in the Great Depression, you would understand this mentality.

Security Exercise

- I want you to think about what kind of security you have in place for your assets.
- Then, I want you to assess the effectiveness of this security. Just make a list of your assets and then give it a score of 1 to 10 next to each item. With a score of 1 being not safe at all, like cash in your pocket on vacation, 5 being reasonably safe, and 10 being completely safe, you will sleep well at night. No matter what happens.
- Be honest now. Judge your investments harshly. How many intermediaries are there between you and your money? We need to live in the real world from now on. People who do this get to keep most of their money.
- Once you do this, set this list aside. You will need it later when you assess the security of these assets versus Bitcoin. And the risk of each asset. As well as when you are putting together your security plan in the Chapter 7 exercise.

Part II: UNDERSTANDING BITCOIN FUNDAMENTALS

Now we turn to the solution. Together, we'll explore what Bitcoin is, how it works, why it's secure, and most importantly, why it offers unprecedented protection for your life's savings. We'll move from theoretical concepts to practical understanding, laying the foundation you'll need to incorporate Bitcoin into your retirement strategy.

What if you could protect your life savings from inflation without complex investment strategies? What if you could transfer value across the globe instantly without permission from banks? What if you owned your money in a way that no government could confiscate it?

Chapter 6
Imagine a Different World

"Imagine there's no countries; it isn't hard to do. Nothing to kill or die for, and no religion, too. Imagine all the people living life in peace."

John Lennon

When I was working in the technology industry during the 1990s and the 2000s, I had the good fortune of working for many of the major technology innovators of the time. I was an engineer who worked with the biggest computer networks in the world. I was among the highest technical level of the industry, studiously gaining prestigious technical certifications every year or two. I watched the rise of the internet economy first-hand and up close, while I worked alongside early builders of the internet at major companies.

It was a fun time. It was exciting to see and experience the innovations, dazzling us with new ideas. And challenging us with brutal learning curves, filled with treacherous mistakes and failures along the way. Sometimes spectacular failures. It was interesting to see people and companies come and go as fast as the changing seasons.

I was traveling all the time, all over the USA. I used to leave on Monday morning and come home on Thursday night. It was a grueling schedule. My peers and I used to trade stock tips and recommendations about different companies, hoping to profit from all of these changes, while the outsiders, the normal people, just relied on stock analysts and magazine articles. Not sure if any of this was ever very good information. A highly risky and fruitless endeavor at best. Disastrous at worst.

One day, during the peak of this time, I was at JFK airport. It was late on a cold, snowy, and wet night, and I could not find a taxi to carry me to my hotel in midtown Manhattan, so I could go to bed to rest my weary bones before giving a big presentation the next day. Lucky for me, a genteel, well-dressed elderly couple appeared to have ordered a car service that was just pulling up. A nice, big Mercedes. It was obvious they were not from New York. But I stepped up and offered to split the car with them if they were going the same direction. Not something you normally do in New York. But they happily agreed, and we were on our way. We got into a deep conversation. I found out that their car had been arranged by a local investment group that they were a part of, and they were in town for an "exclusive" investment conference based on the "hot tech stock market." I learned that they owned a small chain of organic grocery stores in the Midwest. These are the individuals referred to as whales, or "fully qualified investors." These folks are a registered investment advisor's (RIA) dream. They have made a considerable amount of money, and now they are going through the challenging process of figuring out where to invest this money. Not as easy as you might think. In fact, this process results in great disappointment for many wealthy people.

They asked me what I did, and I told them, naming the companies I had worked for and consulted with. Instantly, the entire tone of our conversation shifted from a friendly encounter to a very serious affair. They suddenly looked at me as if I were Galileo, and they wanted to look through my telescope. I had their complete and enraptured attention. Every word was a new nugget of wisdom. It was as if they were at Delphi, and I was the oracle. At least, that is how it seemed to them. They leaned in, desperate for any scrap of what they saw as inside information. The questions came fast and furious, and I answered them as best I could. They were so excited, practically giddy, with the feeling that they were accessing special "inside" information, which I didn't have. But it seemed like I did to them. Because they are so far outside the investment or tech community, their level of separation was considerable. And mine was a bit further up the chain. Wall Street is so distant from Main Street that they might as well be living on separate continents. The financial world is filled with liars, cheats, and scam artists, and it's guarded by jargon, intermediaries, and gatekeepers whose job is to keep ordinary people out. You see, they were in Manhattan to spend serious money, seven or eight figures worth. The conference they were going to promised to give them top-tier information. Most of it for free. Yet they believed their access was growing, just because I happened to be in their cab. It was almost comical to me. But it struck me how important this information was to them. Layers and layers of this information, meted out carefully and for a fee to only the wealthiest and most well-connected.

This story illustrates the need to follow the ebb and flow of a changing world. And how important it was to have specialized information when these changes were happening. But what if you were in a different world? A world where you didn't need this privileged and specialized information.

What We All Really Want.

Everyone wants basically the same thing: prosperity, peace, acknowledgement, happiness, safety for themselves and their family, and stability. Why is this so hard to achieve? Why do we have to go through all of these issues? Wars, economic crises, pandemics, political crises, terrorism, one thing after another. It seems that there is a constant series of panics and crises going on. One after another.

Don't people just want to live in peace and harmony? Don't you just want to do your work, earn enough money to enjoy the simple things in life, and retire with security and a bit of prosperity? We all basically want the same thing.

Bitcoin is the path to prosperity. It is simple, really, what the path is. Yes, we have to do some study. And, yes, we have to learn some new concepts. But more difficult is to unlearn some bankrupt, manipulative concepts that don't actually serve us but serve those in power. Bitcoin is the easy part.

A Clean, Beautiful Environment.

Humans love the environment. They believe in a clean, beautiful, natural environment. I have yet to meet anyone who doesn't. So why are there so many environmental problems?

There are two reasons. The first is a series of contrived environmental problems. These problems go part and parcel with the Nixon Gold Shock, when the USA defaulted on its debt. When this occurred, the government, which already had a growing stranglehold on the scientific community via the money spigot, greatly increased its death grip on science and particularly on the sciences that serve the environmental agenda. And we will get into this further, but you will see how Bitcoin is far from causing environmental problems; rather, it is actually a solution to environmental issues.

Let's look at this from another angle.

Take a subsistence farmer in Africa or Asia, trapped in the daily struggle of survival. Every day is about scraping together enough to feed his family, trying to keep his children alive, and burying far too many of them. In this state, desperation rules. He will abuse the land, the animals, and the waters around him with no thought for the future because he has no other choice.

Take that same farmer and move his economic situation up a few notches. Make it so his kids can get a good education. So that he can see his future years as relatively prosperous. And you will see a man who thinks just like us. He starts to move up Maslow's hierarchy of needs and gets out of the subsistence cycle trap he is in. He will start to be concerned about the environment around him as he keeps moving up. Maybe within a generation or two, he will start to care about the environment of his country and his continent. He will invest in his future in a far different way.

But keep him trapped in this living hell of just trying to survive, striving not to watch another one of his children suffer the same way he did. He's going to easily take advantage of the lands, the animals, and the waters around him. And all of the rules or regulations or admonitions to the contrary are not going to do any good.

The second reason is more insidious: the institutions that claim to care about the environment don't. Governments, central banks, and certain corporations love to wear green while funding wars and pollution. No entity pollutes more than a military-industrial complex. The West, for all its talk of sustainability, is also the biggest destroyer of the natural world. The very nations that preach environmentalism from podiums are often the ones dropping bombs, poisoning rivers, and destabilizing entire regions. Why? Because they're incentivized to do it. Its hard for us to see because it is hidden from us.

Upton Sinclair said, "It's difficult to get someone to understand something when his salary depends on not understanding it." The current system rewards destruction. Bureaucrats, NGO's, huge banks, multinational corporations, and their employees make their living off complexity, waste, and illusion. They write the rules, control the science, and manage narratives. They pat themselves on the back and give each other awards for "green initiatives" that never touch the root of the problem. They won't change because change threatens their power.

Bitcoin can help with these issues. Why? Because it realigns incentives. As Charlie Munger's quote about incentives reveals, people follow what they are incentivized to do. Bitcoiners have an incentive to protect the environment. As stated earlier, when you move up Maslow's hierarchy, you become increasingly aware and concerned for your environment. So, the more Bitcoiners we have, the more protectors of the environment we have. Not people just wanting a clean environment, but actual protectors of the environment.

Simply put, Bitcoin also defunds war. When did these massive, worldwide wars or 'forever wars' of industrial scale begin? In the 20th century, immediately after the advent of central banking.

It is no coincidence. It was the uncoupling of a limited monetary system from a nation's war-making capacity. From this point on, governments were able to continuously wage bigger and more expensive wars. In the past, kings and governments had to raise money or borrow money to fund their wars and raise and pay the armies. The kings would send their armies off to war, and they would fight and fight until they were exhausted or ran out of money. Then they would quit and negotiate some kind of peace until they could raise some more money for the next war.

With central banking, all of this changed because they could now print more money, facilitating bigger and more terrible wars.

Bitcoin And Energy Waste: A Win-Win

One of the most common misconceptions about Bitcoin is that it's environmentally harmful. In reality, Bitcoin mining is driving environmental innovation in energy efficiency and sustainability. Unlike traditional financial systems that consume vast resources while providing marginal benefits, Bitcoin's energy use secures the most powerful monetary network in history.

More importantly, Bitcoin mining is uniquely positioned to utilize energy sources that would otherwise be wasted.

Flared Gas

When oil is pumped from the ground, it also brings up water, dirt, and gases, including methane. Natural gas is a pollutant and what's called a greenhouse gas. This greenhouse gas is a problem for most states and their local pollution regulations. The oil company has to do something with this gas. They can capture it and sell it. But usually, it is not economical to transport and do this. What most people won't tell you is that there is a whole lot of this natural gas in the ground. What are they going to do?

They can burn the gas at the well, this is called flaring. This reduces its greenhouse gas content, but they still incur fines and restrictions.

An enterprising group of Bitcoin miners came up with a solution: a mobile mining unit. They loaded a shipping container with Bitcoin miners (basically, just computer servers) and an electric generator that runs on natural gas. They move the container to the remote oil well location. Placing the container right next to the oil well on the concrete well pad. Connect the generator to the previously flared natural gas, and start mining Bitcoin on-site.

Now the gas is captured and used instead of being wasted. The greenhouse gases and flared exhaust are no longer released into the atmosphere, creating a new way to mitigate pollution and reduce greenhouse gas emissions. The oil company makes some money off the deal, which reduces the cost of energy production. They also avoid environmental fines and the Bitcoin miners clean the environment and make money from the Bitcoin that they are mining, while getting cheap electricity. It's a win-win-win for everyone.

Flared-gas mining is one of many examples of how Bitcoin is a solution to environmental problems. This has been so successful that bitcoin mining is becoming common in the oil production industry. In fact, bitcoin miners scour the globe looking for cheap and wasted energy.

There is a whole lot of this wasted energy, especially electricity. Energy is not produced and then consumed in perfect balance. It is overproduced. Some is consumed, but much of it is wasted, particularly electricity. This waste shows up in a variety of ways, from excess power generation that is just squandered. Too much production to ensure the grid stays up, causing prices to be higher than they need to be. Electric utilities are unable to bring power to impoverished areas because the waste is too great of a cost. All of these problems can and are being mitigated by Bitcoin mining.

Methane Gas And Landfills

Another concern of the climate change agenda is the rise of greenhouse gases and carbon dioxide emissions. Of all the greenhouse gases, methane is the most destructive to the Earth's upper atmosphere. So, particular attention is paid to how to control methane at its source. In addition to this, every city or community in the Western world has landfills where they bury their garbage and waste. From this buried garbage, the materials of our highly consumerist and fiat system produce methane, a lot of it.

The fiat system demands that we continue to produce and waste over and over again. This causes the landfills to grow and grow to contain all of the waste that comes out of the other end. Landfill waste has almost doubled from 1960 to 2018. And when this landfill waste breaks down, it produces the unwanted byproduct of methane gas in massive quantities.

But there is a solution that costs municipalities nothing, while greatly reducing methane emissions. These giant mounds of trash have to flare their methane gas, just like oil wells do. And this is still a huge pollutant. But that gas can be captured and used to power mobile Bitcoin mining rigs, at no cost to the municipality. The result? Less methane in the air. Cleaner environment. Stronger Bitcoin network. Another wonderful win-win-win for everyone.

In fact, it has been estimated that one methane-mining operation for a small city's landfill, running for one year, is the equivalent of planting 50,000 trees and growing them for ten years. That's what real environmental action looks like. And Bitcoin is making it possible.

Balancing The Grid

Many people believe in green energy, and they think it will help moderate the temperature of the climate. Two popular green energy initiatives are wind power and solar power. However, in the power generation industry, these two forms of energy generation have some serious problems. They are extremely inefficient and costly to implement. Another problem is that they produce energy inconsistently. And in order to produce energy for the power grid, we need lots of consistency. Because the users of the energy grid are inconsistent, the generator systems need to be as predictable as possible.

In fact, the less consistent the energy grid is, the more it costs the users. Now, you might say that's great. I don't mind paying an extra $50 or $100 a month to help the planet. But that's what is called a "first-world problem." Most electric users worldwide are poorer than us and can't withstand a mere $10 increase in their electric bill, assuming they can afford electricity at all.

If consumption goes down, power plants cannot just turn off their generators. They have to do something with the electricity. And what they do is ground the electricity. They send it to the ground, wasting it. Wasted energy.

We are paying to produce energy, and then dumping it if no one can use it. But Bitcoin miners help with this problem. Miners go into a market and make a deal with the power company: "We will take your off peak production at a discount so you don't have to waste it." And then you can make some money from this arrangement while providing a good service to its users.

When the opposite occurs, when a market is short on electricity, such as when a blizzard comes through, the miners agree to shut off their mining machines so they don't put a strain on the power grid when it is needed by consumers.

This relationship stabilizes the grid, lowers costs, and makes green energy more viable by smoothing out inconsistencies. Another win-win-win for consumers, the miners, and the environment. The cost of electricity is mitigated in a market; the service is more predictable for the power company and the consumer. Green energy projects are enabled where they would normally be unfeasible.

A World Living In Peace.

Where are all of these people who want war? I can't seem to find them. Everyone I talk to just wants to live their life in peace. And yet, somehow, we are always at war, with someone, somewhere, in multiple countries at once. And it only seems to get worse.

In his farewell address, President Eisenhower urged us to beware of the US military-industrial complex. We, of course, did not or could not heed his warning. It was already too late. The machinery had been set in motion, and we were being marched into another violent, immoral, unnecessary, and tragic war — Vietnam.

What the war did to the people of Vietnam, and to our own citizens, was obscene. The damage was immense. And yet, it didn't stop us. After a brief pause during the Carter administration, the war cycle resumed. Dirty wars in Latin America, the Middle East, and parts of Asia and Africa. Governments overthrown. Civil wars stoked from the outside. All the while, mega corporations and banks profited, and the American public, largely unaware, footed the bill through quiet tax increases and rising inflation.

Today, the United States operates over 800 US military bases worldwide, that we know of. How many bases does our ostensible enemy, Russia, have? She has one. China has none. Sadly, America has become the most warlike country in the world.

But why? Like the answer to almost all questions, it is money.

We like to think Congress declares war and controls the purse strings. Most of the financing for these wars and other incursions is not funded by overt taxes. We don't necessarily see our taxes go up, per se. But we feel something. We feel this strange sensation of prices going up in a steady drip, with an occasional market bubble bursting to accent the economic cycle. And we feel it in the erosion of the value of our money, the debasement.

This is what happens when the Federal Reserve can print money. They don't need our votes to start a war. They don't need our consent. They just need the Federal Reserve to fire up the presses.

The government fight wars around the world to maintain its global hegemony. It's about power and coercion. And it's all being done in our name and with our money, all under the guise of freedom, security, and economic order. I don't know about you. But I would prefer them not to do this. But they aren't asking me.

With a stable, **immutable** monetary system, the government cannot do these things. They have to come to the citizenry to ask for taxes to pay for a war. And that's difficult when they need our vote. Eventually, when taxes get too high, people start asking questions. Why are you doing this? And governments would have to come up with good answers, which they cannot do. Ultimately, they will stop getting voted into office, and the wars and foreign adventurism might actually come to an end.

Bitcoin is that immutable form of money. It can't change, and its value or properties can't be altered at the whim of a government bureaucrat. You can't change it by fiat. As you will see, they can't just print more of it. No one, not even a superpower, can just print more Bitcoin.

Remember one of the properties of hard money that we discussed earlier? Gold had value because someone couldn't just come along and make more gold. They used other solutions before gold. Stones, beads, shells, copper. But cheaters would just make more.

Then gold came along, and no one could easily make more of it. But eventually, they got around the gold standard by introducing a fiat monetary system. It is said that "All wars are bankers' wars." When you control the money, you control the war machine. Bitcoin takes that power away.

The Illusion Of Fairness

Do you ever wonder why some groups seem to be getting richer, while we seem to stay the same or get poorer? Just like we have all experienced in the corporate world. We have all seen examples of uneven treatment. But at the level of global wealth and central banking, they have a much more lucrative and powerful inside track. In addition to all of that, it cannot be taken down very easily. The late, great George Carlin famously said, "It's a big club, and you're not in it."

A Special Protected Class

Wall Street caters to a special class of investors called the *Fully Qualified Investor*. Are you familiar with this? This rule allows large banks and hedge funds to limit the sharing of investment opportunities to only the wealthiest people. The requirements include earned income of a minimum of $200,000 and a net worth of $1 million plus!

Can you imagine that there is a legally specified class of investors that is specifically designed to keep you out? This is a literal system with a special class enforced by the federal government. The story at the beginning of this chapter was about these kinds of folks. It's part of the sales funnel that Wall Street companies use to identify the most lucrative clients.

But they will tell you this is for your protection. You are not sophisticated enough. We don't want you to risk your money. But they happily let you buy as many lottery tickets as you like and go to casinos all over the USA and waste your money until you are destitute.

You're also welcome to wade through a baffling array of thousands of companies and investment products so complex it would take a full-time job just to sort through the options. No one stops you from making bad investments, but when a good investment with a greater opportunity for success comes along, suddenly you're not "qualified." (To be fair, these fully qualified investors aren't either. They just have more to spend.)

Anyone can buy Bitcoin. Anyone of any age who can get an account on a Bitcoin exchange can buy Bitcoin. Anyone who wants to can buy Bitcoin at a Bitcoin ATM. Anyone who can't get a Bitcoin exchange account can buy it peer-to-peer from another person or earn it in their job. Or they can run their own mining rigs and get paid in Bitcoin. No special class. No special knowledge. No permission from anyone. Refreshing, isn't it?

Cantillon Effect: The Root Of Inequality

But it goes further, much further, and much larger. There is an economic concept called "the Cantillon Effect." What happens if the central bank or Federal Reserve inflates the money supply? They inject more and more fiat currency into the system. But this doesn't enter the monetary system neutrally. Think about it. Billions and billions of dollars are printed every year. Do you receive any of it? Are you getting a check every year for this inflation. Is a share of it fairly distributed to you?

Let's take just the deficit, not the entire federal budget—say, $1 trillion. Divide that by the US population, and every man, woman, and child would receive over $30,000 a year. Are you getting an extra $30,000 in value from the government? Of course not. But the money *is* going somewhere.

In the 1950s and 1960s, when we were kids, you could see a more even distribution of income. And it wasn't distributed by the government. It was distributed mostly by your ability to convince an investor or a real main street banker. They would loan you money for a money-making project, with collateral that would provide a return.

It was possible to get ahead. Start a business if you want to, come up with a new idea, product, or service. There is less and less possibility of this today. The ultra-rich percentage of ownership of the US stock market has grown from 40% in 2002 to 54% today; the rest of the stock ownership goes to large institutions that "hold" the stock for us, such as ETFs and pension funds, while extracting fees along the way. Meanwhile, the richest 5% of Americans now own two-thirds of the nation's wealth.

Income taxes are paid by income earners. Not wealth holders. This means, as you struggle to support your family and pay your taxes every year, the super wealthy pay less and less in taxes and get richer. I don't begrudge anyone going out into the market and earning as much and as high as their ability can take them. But the system we have now is hardly this.

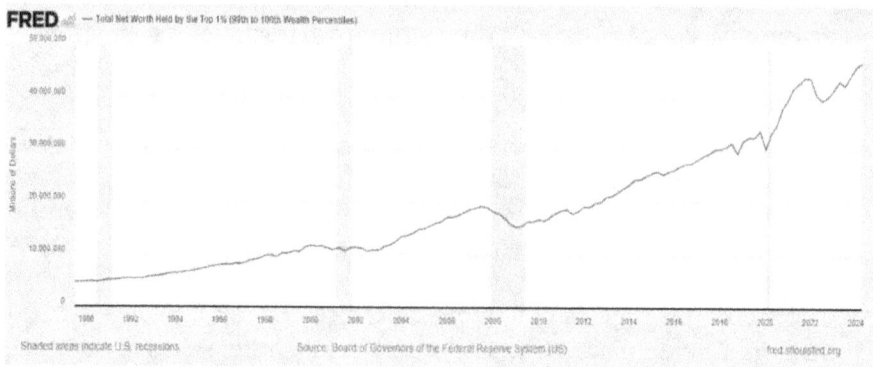

As you can see in the chart above. Ninety percent of all wealth is owned by the top 1%. How did this happen?

From Producers To Rent-Seekers

In the days of the "Robber Barons," we had some very unpopular guys making a whole lot of money. They were ruthless. But at least they built things. Rockefeller standardized oil exploration, refinement, and production. Carnegie made the US the world's steel powerhouse, helping to build heavy industries and massive construction projects. Jay Gould created a railroad empire by consolidating hundreds of separate, failing, corrupt, rent-seeking (scammy) railroads into a transcontinental system and network that benefited everyone. He provided reasonable and affordable transportation for a nation. But what do billionaires provide for us today? What is Warren Buffett producing? Investing in junk food companies that make us sicker. What about Bill Gates? He's living off a monopoly on PC software. And the list goes on. Most are rent seekers or living off the magical government spigot. Please name one major corporation that produces something of value today, some new innovation or world-changing technology.

Yes, there are some small companies that still build things. But most major corporations aren't providing anything of value. Take Apple. Yes, they make elegant laptops and Phones. But real innovation at Apple? Apple hasn't done any major innovation since Steve Jobs died.

In fact, Apple just seems to figure out ways to limit users' access, rather than expand it. Netflix? Amazon? Google? Are they providing value or just monetizing attention and data? Trapping us in monthly contracts that constantly creep up. Never seeming to offer any added value. There are some companies doing good work, but most of these companies are overseas now. This is the financialization of the American economy. CEOs just chase stock prices so they can get their bonuses.

The 2 And 20 Racket.

In the financial services industry, there is a compensation system referred to as "2 and 20." Firms charge a 2% annual fee on assets under management, plus a 20% "performance fee" on profits above a certain benchmark. And very few "retail investors," that means investors like you and me, have even heard of this. Did you even know they refer to us as "retail investors?" As Investopedia notes, this model has made fund managers very wealthy.

The funds become wealthy from your investments, not you. This means that once you're "allowed" to invest with them, they charge their fees, and you pay them. You can see how this can get out of control quickly and completely destroy any gains you may have made. And when you check their track record after fees, you'll find it's pretty dismal.

Bitcoin Return With Fees

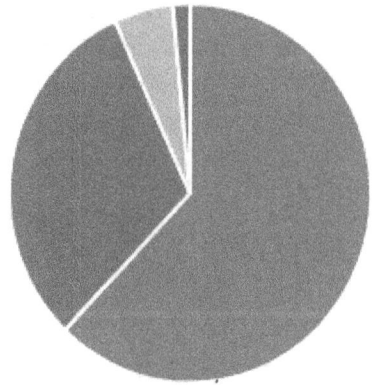

- Principle $10,000
- First Year Return $5000
- Exchange Comission $850
- Custody Fee $250

S&P500 With 2 and 20

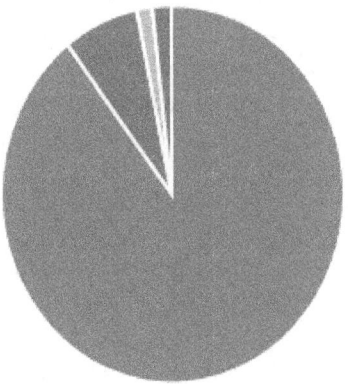

- Principle $10,000
- First Year Gain $800
- Twenty Per-cent on gain $160
- Two Per-cent on Principle $200

(Total return in the first year after fees is $3650. That's $5000 gross return minus $850 exchange fee and $250 custody fee. Total return on the S&P 500 with 2 and 20 is $440. That's $800 gross return, minus $160 on the gain and $200 on the principal. The difference is quite dramatic.)

As you can see, the current system is not fair. It is heavily stacked against the regular Baby Boomer investor. Are you relying on and forgetting about savings? Even if you have a good income and have saved your money.

Go anywhere in the world where there is poverty, and you will see very quickly that the biggest concern is their economic situation. Other freedoms are usually secondary. When you are starving, nothing else matters. Our parents and grandparents knew this because they lived through these times. There is nothing fair about this system. And as the system progresses, it gets less fair and more skewed in favor of the Cantillon class. And against us.

Front-Running And IPOs: First In Line.

Want to know how insiders really make money? They're **first in line.** They have some way, some edge, some sneaky government advantage, or a rapid computer program to make sure they are the first to the table. Then they "dump it on retail" (their words, not mine) for a quick profit.

We Baby Boomers remember well the wild and exciting times of the tech stock boom of the 1990s, referred to in my story earlier, and we may have even been in on a few really good deals, such as Microsoft, Apple, or Cisco Systems.

We remember how cool it was to get in on this and possibly latch on to a big one and ride it up 20% or 50% or maybe even more. But what most of us don't know is that for each of these actual winning companies, there were 100 other losers that lost money, but actually made money for the Wall Street insiders. These were the IPO initial public offerings, famous on Wall Street at that time.

Wall Street didn't care if the stock succeeded. They got in early, hyped it up, then dumped it on the market. This is called **front-running**. And when they know it's a "dog with fleas"? Even better. They pump it, dump it, and walk away with a profit. You're left holding the bag.

These are the same people who tell you investing is fair. That the markets are equal. That the system rewards merit. That the SEC protects you.

They don't mention that they're always first in line, and you're the exit liquidity. There's no fairness in a system where one class prints the money, gets the best deals, takes the least risk, and still gets bailed out when they fail.

Bitcoin doesn't promise utopia. But it does offer a *level playing field*. No Cantillon effect. No insider access. No "2 and 20" club. Just hard money with fixed rules, open to anyone, anywhere.

The beauty is you don't need to be rich to own Bitcoin. Just choose to opt out.

Fairness For All

With Bitcoin, for the first time in history, normal everyday people and regular retail investors have the opportunity to front-run Wall Street. And we are doing it. It is estimated that there are over 200 million Bitcoin wallets already, and most wallets, about 194 million, have less than 0.1 Bitcoin in them. This means that wealthy people only have about 6 million of the wallets.

Bitcoin Bit
The first time that Bitcoin was ever monetized was the purchase of two pizzas for 10,000 Bitcoin in May 22, 2010. Bitcoin had not experienced any price discovery and this was the first critical step in taking Bitcoin from a collectible to an actual medium of exchange. The natural progression of all real money. It was a momentous day.

But the important point is that you can front-run Wall Street now. Most big Wall Street firms and major investors are late to the game. So, all of those years you struggled to get to the front of the line in the next big IPO are not a problem. Now you have the opportunity to gain the most valuable and most pristine asset ever created before the rich Wall Street crowd does. An opportunity like this has never been seen before. This is a beautiful thing, a gift from the universe. We couldn't have designed a fairer system.

Look at it another way, there are about 59.4 millionaires in the world. And there are only about 2 million Bitcoin left in circulating supply. Meaning the supply of Bitcoin available for sale and not in cold storage. Even if they wanted to, these millionaires can't all own a whole Bitcoin. It only takes 0.73 of a Bitcoin to be considered in the top .001% of Bitcoin owners. That's not just scarcity. That's fair. Bitcoin is a radically democratic asset.

Bitcoin Is Always There for You.

Bitcoin is always there for you. It cannot be debased. If protected with good custodial habits, which I will teach you, it cannot be stolen. It can't be changed or altered; it is immutable. It is very difficult to manipulate, and if it is manipulated, it is visible to everyone via a transparent public ledger that anyone can audit any time they want.

It is secure. It secures your wealth. It is always verifiable on the Bitcoin network. It is safe and ready to protect your family's wealth. There are no takeovers or stock splits or bankruptcies or other drama. No scandals or monetary debasements, no fraud, or lies. Bitcoin doesn't care about games. It gives you peace of mind. It frees you to do what you want with your life. Currently, it is the highest-performing asset over one year, five years, ten years, and fifteen years. There has never been an asset like this in the history of mankind. Sure, you can cherry-pick a specific point in time when some short-term Bitcoin crash has occurred, or some highly speculative investment beats Bitcoin. That will always be so. But take any four-year contiguous period of time, and you will be profitable.

Bitcoin was launched during the debacle of the 2008 global financial crisis. When Satoshi Nakamoto mined the first bitcoin block, the Genesis Block, he included a headline from *The Times* of London that read, 'Chancellor on the brink of second bailout.' It is quite clear what the purpose of Bitcoin was.

When COVID hit, governments around the world shut down the economy. Markets went into a free fall, and the world panicked. What happened to Bitcoin? Absolutely nothing. It just kept churning out a new block every ten minutes, day and night, just like it has for fifteen years nonstop. And it still does. It's always there for us; it's there for everyone.

The Ticket To Admission

The price of admission into the wonderful gains and benefits of Bitcoin is knowledge and information. You need to understand a bit about money. Economics and banking knowledge. And you need to understand how Bitcoin works. You must have the confidence to apply this knowledge.

This knowledge can be gained in a variety of ways. Through the study of Bitcoin in books like this one, listening to podcasts and videos, or talking with your financial advisors. But make no mistake, you need to have some knowledge. You don't intend to become a Bitcoin expert. You don't need a master's degree in finance or engineering, but you still need a baseline of knowledge.

How do rich people do it? Just like this. They get educated; they learn from their family members. They have trusted advisors, and they use their own experience based on fundamental principles they have developed over time. They do not just turn it over to someone or some institution and forget about it. That's a good way to lose your shirt, or, at the very least, make that institution rich while you slowly get poor. The important thing is to understand that this is not a passive process. It is an active, intimate, involved process that will never completely end. Never ever turn over the decision-making of your money to anyone. No matter how much help you get or how many advisors you have.

Your Bitcoin education is not a passive process. You must pay this price of admission, or you will wake up one day wondering what happened.

Financial Exercise

- Go to a site called tradingview.com or your favorite charting site and do a comparison between Bitcoin and your favorite investment.

- Using these charting tools, compare the one-year, the five-year, and the ten-year performance. Then do this with each of your investments.
- Study these charts, record this information, and keep it handy. Notice the dominance of Bitcoin over all of these asset classes. Can you find a short-term investment where Bitcoin is not superior? Sure, you can. It is possible if you look hard enough. You can cherry-pick some special time frame with a special asset. But you have to try to find this.
- Remember, we are looking to protect **generational wealth**. Bitcoin is about saving, it's about long-term wealth, not some get-rich-quick scheme. That is part of our goals and our strategy. We are not looking for trading secrets here.

Chapter 7

Are You Going To Be Safe Or Sorry?

"Imagine if gold turned to lead when stolen?"

Satoshi Nakamoto

"Is it safe?" This question sits heavily on every Baby Boomer's mind. After decades of experience with traditional financial institutions — banks, investment firms, brokerages — the idea of a purely digital asset will naturally raise concerns about security.

* * *

Many years ago, when I was much younger, early in my adventure in the business world, pumped full of naivety, I used to believe that if I studied hard, got my college degree, got a good career, and followed the rules, I would prosper. I would rely on my intelligence and wit. My resourcefulness and bright ideas, I was a smart guy, and I would demonstrate this to everyone, showing my hard work and reliability. These values would propel me into a successful career and financial prosperity. The first lesson that I learned was that it didn't necessarily work that way. I mean, I did okay. I made some money. I worked really hard at a professional job at a very 'good' company for a few years. A large Fortune 50 corporation in the defense and aerospace industry. At the time, this was the primary industry driving new technology in the world. And it did lead to a good engineering career at innovative companies over the years.

But what really happened was far different from what I figured. I just thought the people in power would notice me. They would see what a great guy I was. How hard I was working. Give me

115

promotions and raises, and recognition. They would certainly know how innovative I was, how honest and reliable I could be. That I could do the job better. I demonstrated techniques that showed better ways to do the job. I was respected and well-liked by my peers. I had many good professional relationships. Surely, they would want to reward me for this. Right?

I mean, I had my college degree. Followed the rules and contributed to innovation. I had not caused any trouble. I knew the technology, as well as or better than my peers. It was a technology-oriented company, building high-tech weapons systems for the military, focused on engineering. I was a technically sophisticated employee, more so than most of my peers. Surely, they would recognize me as a technically savvy and innovative person? What was the result of this? Not much. At least not much for me. No promotions, no raises, other than compulsory annual salary increases that everyone got. I worked 60 or 70 hours a week. Paid off my student loans. And continued to get the same thing or less than the lowest performing employee would get.

I was young and naïve. I had been with the company for about three or four years, toiling away. Then things changed. You see, there was a vice president in another division, who was upstream of my division, and he had a daughter. And she was pregnant. And she had just married a guy from Chicago who knocked her up, and they had both moved down to our city. Her new baby daddy needed a job. He had driven a delivery truck in Chicago. Nothing wrong with driving a truck, but it was quite a different skill set from the IT and engineering world I worked in. The environment in which I struggled to gain and maintain my competence. Doing the things I thought this company ostensibly said they wanted.

This truck driver knew nothing about IT infrastructure and nothing about engineering. He never did, and he never would. In fact, as far as I can tell, he knew little of anything. I saw no indication that he had even finished high school. He was arrogant, abrasive, boorish, and puerile. He had no professional skills and no particular skills that I could see. He didn't study or learn anything that I could see.

Within a year, he was my boss. And he wasn't very good at management either. He never attempted to improve himself, learn technology, or go to night school to get a GED or perhaps a college degree or professional training. None of this. But it was okay. There were no consequences for him.

About two years later. He was caught and prosecuted for grand theft for starting and running a major computer larceny ring within the very company that had taken him in. He had been stealing literally millions of dollars of computer equipment. Evidently, he did have some skills. Luckily for me, I had moved to another department. Away from that train wreck. The funny thing is, the vice president/father-in-law never experienced any blowback from this. Reality was being carefully hidden and under wraps.

The point of this story is not to complain about my personal situation. Things happen to all of us. It's for you to recognize the inherent systemic issues that pervade our current economic world. A place where connections matter more than competence. Where gatekeepers don't reward skill, they reward allegiance. We must learn to see the real world as it is. Where the system is, at its core, built on a different set of values than the ones they tell you to live by. Risks like this don't show up on your investment statements, but they are everywhere. They are entirely absent from Bitcoin. Bitcoin doesn't care about your résumé, your connections, or who you married. It doesn't promote fraud. It doesn't reward nepotism. It doesn't look the other way. Bitcoin runs on math, not politics.

Security First
Nowadays, it's a common assumption that if you deposit your money in an institution, it will be there when you need it. All you have to do is ask for it, and you will get it. But this is no longer a guarantee, if it really ever was, and it is becoming less so every day.

So, what can we do to keep ourselves safe? How do we preserve our wealth, grow it, and hand it down to our progeny? Because if

117

we don't figure this out, there is a good chance that everything we've saved and sacrificed could be taken from us.

In the Great Financial Crisis of 2008, when cracks in the mortgage industry were exposed, people were stunned by what they saw. Every part of the system was corrupted, top to bottom, with lies, fraud, and perverse incentives. An intricate web of dishonesty and bad incentives, it was as if the housing market was a giant, dying animal, its carcass picked apart by the jackals and hyenas of Wall Street, Washington, and the banking industry. They gorged themselves on the decay, insatiable, unable to stop, like some giant orgy of consumption and excess that was beyond imagination. Normal people who were a part of this system saw how the others were eating. They wanted to eat, too. So, what should they do? Should they starve or join in? Or even worse, compete to be more corrupt and devious. When the system is corrupt at its core, how can regular people change it?

Deception and brinkmanship were rampant. Wall Street banks were packaging loans in Collateralized Debt Obligations (CDOs), which were supposed to blend good and bad mortgages in a way that reduced overall risk. In reality, they were dumping toxic debt into shiny wrappers and selling it as gold. This essentially removed the obligations and loosened the collateral, lying to the investors who didn't care as long as they were earning money through fees and bonuses. Mortgage companies were supposed to carefully assess the viability of homeowners to borrow and pay back loans. Instead, they simply approved the loans without any verification. There was actually a phrase in the business at the time called a "no-doc loan." These mortgage companies would quickly sell the mortgages in the secondary market to investors and remove them from their own dirty books.

The ratings agencies gave everyone on Wall Street a pass because they were afraid of losing business to the other ratings agencies. Mortgages were traded like poker chips at a cheap casino. And the government agencies designed to provide oversight of these companies did absolutely nothing. We all know about the great housing crisis. We are Boomers. We all lived through it. We saw fantastic movies like *The Wolf of Wall Street*, *The Big Short*, and *Margin Call*. If you haven't seen them, I recommend all three.

But what does it have to do with security? Everything.

As Bastiat warned, "When plunder becomes a way of life, men create for themselves a legal system that authorizes it, and a moral code that **glorifies** it."

When push comes to shove and the system comes down, I assure you it will fail. It always does. The folks in power are going to need money. And they are going to need a lot of it. And where do you think, they are going to get this money when printing doesn't cut it anymore, and there is nothing left to tax? Where do they go? I will let you fill in the blank. Remember what they used to call economic depressions before they changed the name to make it sound a little better? They called it a panic. And that's what it is. People panic because all of a sudden, everything they ever worked for is drying up right before their eyes. And everyone around you who used to be your friend is now a competitor, trying to protect their dwindling share of their money. Think back to that scene in *It's a Wonderful Life*, where there is a bank run on the Savings and Loan. Everyone scrambling in front of the bank teller to get their money out of that bank knew each other. They weren't strangers. It was a small town where people knew and talked with their neighbors. They didn't seem very neighborly to me. Now imagine this scenario times a thousand, and you don't know anyone you are competing with to get your money.

We are deeply ensconced in a world of disintegration and graft. A world governed by corruption and protected by illusion. Security is a façade. The institutions that offer protection are the same ones profiting from your exposure to the downfall.

One of the fundamental building blocks of any monetary system is security. If there is no foundation of security, then the money cannot be hardened. If it cannot be hardened, it will eventually lead to theft and corruption. This impairment of basic security will eventually lead to outright sabotage. And the actors in it will then become a part of this endemic corruption, out of sheer necessity and survival, until it fails completely. This is what we are seeing with our monetary system now. And the other monetary systems around the world. It is a predictable part of a fiat monetary system. It always happens. It always will.

There have been around 300 different fiat currencies throughout history. All have failed, except the British pound and the US dollar, but in actuality, there were defaults with those two also. They have been able to recover so far. So, the question is, what do we do about it? How do we ensure that we have safety and security in our wealth and our family's wealth? How do we make sure that when we do business, send money, or receive money, it will be there? How do we make sure the money that stores our energy, our hard work, our productivity, our very survival, will not wash away like the sand on a seashore?

Your Security Is Your Responsibility.
Never forget that security is your responsibility. The moment you abdicate this critical responsibility; you become a victim. A victim of every scammer and con artist out there. Those are harsh words, but once again, we must see the world in a realistic way and not give up our protection to anyone else.

Think about a place where you trust everyone in your circle of friends and family. Now, imagine for a moment that you are in a distressed position and all of a sudden you have to take $100,000 cash and entrust it to someone in this close circle. This $100,000 is all of your liquid wealth that you and your immediate family have in the world. You may have a car or two, a house, and some other stuff, but this is your future. All the cash you can get your hands on. And it is under threat. What will you do? Who will you hand it off to?

Now think of that same circle of close friends and family. Do you select the same people with the $100,000 in the mix? Or is the number of people smaller? I certainly know my circle would get much smaller. Now add another question, not about trust or responsibility, but about ability —the ability for this person to actually be able to keep this $100,000 cash safe. How will they do it? In a personal safe? A safety deposit box at the bank? With another third party? Is the circle getting smaller? Who has both skill sets?

How many people have ever thought of these? Before you answer these questions, take a very hard look at your current situation. Is that bank really safe? How much do you trust them? How big is your circle of friends and family now? It's getting really small. I have friends with whom I have had this conversation, and they could not name one person. Let alone three or four people.

If and until you take charge of your own security, you will always be at risk of a financial catastrophe. We don't like to think about this, but it's a fact. That's the real world. Freedom and sovereignty come with responsibility; there is no way around it. Yes, our system is convenient. This is one of the ways the current banking and Cantillon-based system works. It makes you feel safe, it is convenient, and this is nice. But it is not secure. This is a decision you will have to make. I cannot make it for you. But I can assure you that the current system is not safe, and the convenience you have will not protect you when the time comes.

How Deep Is Bitcoin's Security?

"Bitcoin is a swarm of cyber hornets serving the goddess of wisdom, feeding on the fire of truth, exponentially growing ever smarter, faster, and stronger behind a wall of encrypted energy." This quote comes from one of Bitcoin's largest and most influential investors: Michael Saylor. His company, Strategy (MSTR), has purchased nearly 600,000 Bitcoin. And the impact has been extraordinary on his company's success. So much so that Strategy is about to enter the S&P 500 index and is one of the most profitable stocks on Wall Street, ahead of the magnificent seven and even NVIDIA.

To understand Bitcoin's security, you must grasp the concept of exponential numbers. And since exponential numbers is a concept that is difficult for the human brain to comprehend, I will borrow an example from Jeff Booth, a principal with EgoDeath Capital and a prolific Bitcoiner. Here is an example he uses frequently:

If you take a sheet of paper and fold it in half, it doubles in width. Then you fold it in half again, and it doubles in width again. Each time it is folded, it doubles. It's impossible to fold it fifty times, but if you could, how wide would it be? An inch? Ten inches? A foot? A yard?

Bitcoin Bit

The Bitcoin network has never been hacked. In fact, it has sustained continuous cyberattack since its inception and never been hacked. You may think this is not special but virtually all other alt coins or cryptocurrencies of any value, as well as traditional finance networks, and banks, have been successfully hacked. But Bitcoin the one with the greatest value by far has never been broken.

The answer is that it would reach from the Earth to the sun!

That's right, when you double something just fifty times, you are working with exponential numbers. This is important to help comprehend the power of 256-bit encryption, which is used in the protection scheme of Bitcoin.

Bitcoin uses encryption to protect your wealth. The network has a concept called public key cryptography. And the encryption is considered military grade. This encryption works with such large numbers that no one has even come close to breaking it. The scale of this encryption scheme is hard for the human mind to comprehend. The number of possible combinations protecting your bitcoin is estimated to be around 150,000, **billion, billion,**

billion, billion, billion, billion, billion, billion, a number so vast it is nearly impossible to grasp.

To this day, the Bitcoin network has never been hacked. Yes, Bitcoin companies and Bitcoin exchanges have been hacked, or individuals have made mistakes or been robbed. But the *network itself* has never been hacked. There is talk about theoretical quantum computers that will be able to do this. And I guess anything is possible in the future. But this begs us to question the fallacy of moving in this direction: Why would anyone invest their money, time, and effort to make themselves a criminal to steal Bitcoin, when they could simply just buy some Bitcoin and make money legitimately and be safe to spend it when they wanted to?

Security isn't just about technology; it's also about incentive. Bitcoin aligns both.

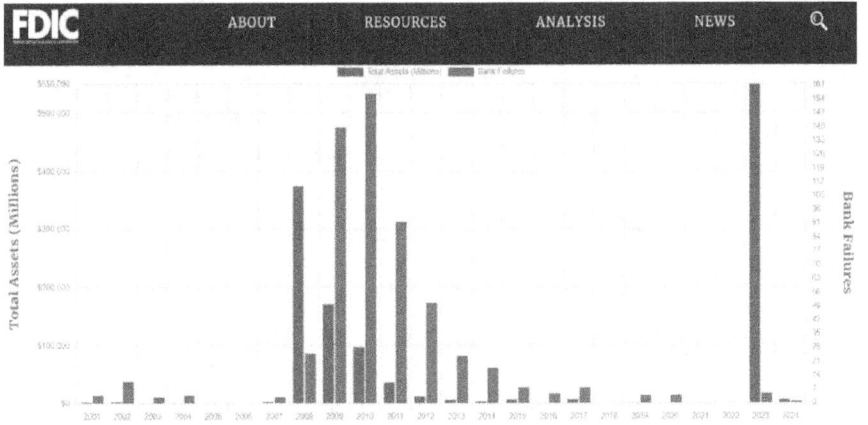

As bank failures increase, so does the risk of losing your money. Eventually, we will get to the point where the FDIC cannot cover these losses.

Basic Rules Of Security.
Okay, so you've decided to invest in Bitcoin. Before you do this, you should know how to protect your money. Security is not automatic. But it's not rocket science, either.

Let's cover some basic rules about security. Some of these are common sense, some are just basic data security, and some apply specifically to Bitcoin.

1. **Passwords**. Use complex passwords. Don't use familiar names or phrases or people or things that you are familiar with. Even better is to use a password manager such as LastPass, Nordpass, or Bitwarden. These password managers keep your passwords safe and complex but are easy for you to use and not lose.

2. **Updates**. Keep your computer, phone, and other devices up-to-date with the latest operating system (OS) improvements. Most OS updates include security patches to fix vulnerabilities. So, keeping this update keeps you safer.

3. **Practice Anonymity**. Don't talk to strangers about what you are doing with your computer or your Bitcoin. In fact, don't talk to anyone you don't trust about security related items. And even the people you do trust, don't share more details than they need to know. Your greatest protection from hackers is your anonymity. The less people know, the safer you are.

4. **Physical Security**. Keep your stuff locked up when you aren't using it. Lock your doors at home. If your computer has to be in your car, lock the doors. Put it out of sight. Even better is to keep it in the trunk of your car. When you are in a coffee shop, don't leave your computer unattended on the table for anyone to come by and steal it or extract information from it. Going to have strangers at your house, such as for a party? Lock your computer in a desk or another room.

5. **Backup Your System**. Keep current and safe backups of your system. If something happens, such as a malware or ransomware attack, it shouldn't mean a total loss. Neither should hardware failure nor theft. If you're not backing up, you're gambling with your data. As an added plus, going

through the backup process will help you better understand your computer.

6. **Get A Good Router**. Don't use those super cheap routers and firewalls that come with your ISP. Spend a few bucks and get a good router with stronger security. Some good brands are SonicWall or Ubiquiti.

7. **Get A Good VPN Provider**. Don't use the free VPN providers. Remember, if it's free, then you are the product. Meaning, they are actually capturing the data you're supposed to be keeping secret and selling it to someone else. Not good at all. Look at a good VPN provider like Mulvad or ExpressVPN.

8. **Malware And Antivirus**. Same with malware software and antivirus software, find a good, reliable one. Avoid the free versions that come pre-installed on your computer, for the same reasons as you'd avoid free VPN providers. Good brands are Bitdefender, Mulvad, and Proton.

9. **Educate Yourself.** Continue to learn and educate yourself on cybersecurity basics. Don't just rely on someone else to handle everything. I know this is annoying, and you just want it all to happen for you. But I assure you that you will sleep better at night as your understanding of both physical and cybersecurity grows.

10. **Start A Succession Plan.** You should have a person or two picked out whom you can trust and give selected information to. Start teaching them and sharing your knowledge in case something happens to you. The simple act of training another person will help you tremendously. Confucius said that "we teach best what we need to learn the most."

11. **Find A Good Maintenance Provider**. Proper maintenance on your technology, primarily your computers, is essential. You cannot have a secure system if it is poorly maintained. Security and maintenance go hand in hand. Updates, cleaning of the system, a second set of eyes periodically are essential. And you should have this

maintenance provider scan your system twice a year to keep it running in tip-top condition.

Talk About Risk.

We also need to address risk from a financial viewpoint. If you are serious about improving your understanding of Bitcoin, you must first fully understand the risk of your current investments, and then compare this to the risk of owning and holding Bitcoin. When looking at your wealth, consider two different risk categories. Security risk, which is the risk of someone outright taking your wealth, such as a burglar or a pickpocket. And the other type of risk is financial risk. The risk to your investment in whatever investment vehicle you are working in.

Once you look at both categories, you'll begin to see there is a huge difference between traditional finance and Bitcoin. Bitcoin has been called a "risk on" asset, meaning it is risky. But I beg to differ. Let's look at Bitcoin compared to some major risk categories found in traditional finance.

1. **Currency Risk**. Whatever investment you make, stocks, bonds, or real estate, you have the risk of that item being priced in a currency that is losing value. This means your investment is losing value. And since we have learned that all fiat currencies are losing value, your investment will have to overcome this risk. This is not a problem with Bitcoin. **Bitcoin is money** — the **hardest, most secure** money ever invented. So instead of investing in something that may make money but is denominated in a melting ice cube, invest in the asset that is hard money already.

2. **Government Risk**. Governments can and will confiscate your assets, particularly if they are tracking what you are doing. So far, governments have not paid much attention to Bitcoin unless it was used in a crime. And when governments try to ban Bitcoin, nothing happens because Bitcoin is so **decentralized**. Even China, the most powerful surveillance state in the world, may be worse than

the USA. They banned Bitcoin two years ago, and nothing happened. In fact, now the Chinese government is allowing more and more Bitcoin operations within the country again.

3. **Risk Of Theft**. Many assets can be stolen easily, such as gold or jewelry theft, real estate swindling, or securities fraud. But Bitcoin is very difficult to steal. It isn't impossible to steal, but practicing the security principles I teach makes it very hard to steal. Nick Szabo said it best: "Every third party is a security hole," or what hackers call a honeypot. What does this mean? Well, you remember the famous saying, "Why do you rob banks? Because that's where the money is." It's the same concept. If you are a hacker, and you've got one really good shot at pulling off your hack, who are you going to target? Some random guy who you think may have a few Bitcoin? Or are you going to target a custodian like Coinbase, who you know for sure has billions in Bitcoin in custody? The answer is quite clear.

4. **Property Taxes**. Real estate and some personal properties are subject to government taxes. Bitcoin is not subject to these taxes. There is a host of taxes that are levied on valuable investments. This has been going on for centuries. Bitcoin is pseudonymous and highly portable. This means it is difficult to assess, levy, and collect taxes on it. I am not advocating not paying your taxes. But governments realize that they cannot collect taxes on Bitcoin, so they focus on other areas.

5. **Property Regulations**. There are a huge number of regulations on real estate, from easements and special assessments to maintenance requirements and tenant rights issues. With stocks and bonds, we have seen how the rich and powerful control regulatory agencies such as the SEC and the New York Stock Exchange. Unsurprisingly, the regulations always seem to fall into their favor (remember the fully qualified investor discussion, earlier?). None of these can be applied to Bitcoin. You own it, and you control

it. You don't get permission from anyone on your ownership, control, or disposal. What a novel concept.

6. **Confiscation Risk**. In certain jurisdictions, governments change, and they like to confiscate property. If, for some reason, you have to leave your jurisdiction, can you take your apartment or your house with you? Can you take $100,000 worth of gold through an airport security check? What about your stock investment account at the local financial institution? Is it accessible from other jurisdictions? If there is a change, none of these forms of wealth is going with you easily, if at all. However, with Bitcoin, you can easily transport it anywhere in the world. You can take your Bitcoin wallet. Or your backup phrase can be memorized and carried in your head. You own it, and you decide where it goes. No one gives you **permission** to take it with you.

7. **CEO Risk**. What about a change in the CEO of a company where you own stocks or bonds? This is a concept talked about in value investing called "bet on the jockey, not the horse." There could be a scandal. He could get arrested or fired. What happens to the value of the stock then? What happened to Apple computers after Steve Jobs was fired? Bitcoin has no CEO. It has no board of directors, no management team. Not a problem. Bitcoin just keeps on going.

8. **Natural Disaster Risk**. Imagine a natural disaster, such as a hurricane, destroys your apartment building rental property. It's going to take a million dollars and two years to fix it because the entire area is devastated. Or, what if a company that you own stock in has its headquarters wiped out by a flood or fire? How long will it take the company to recover? What happens to your investment in the meantime?

I used to work with large Fortune 500 companies on designing large-scale disaster recovery architectures to mitigate such issues. Bitcoin doesn't have these problems.

It is in cyberspace, and you have a backup. It is not at risk. The ledger sits on literally tens of thousands of different nodes spread across every continent and over a hundred countries. If ten, twenty, or even a thousand Bitcoin nodes go down, nothing happens to the Bitcoin network. That's **decentralization** —digital resilience built on the most powerful computer network on the planet today.

9.   **Regulation Risk**. What if there are new environmental or health regulations levied against your company or your real estate? This happens all the time. Bitcoin is not subject to this. Because of Bitcoin's decentralization, Bitcoin cannot be controlled or regulated. The network is too widespread; it is too agile, and its code is protected by encryption that cannot be pierced. And if some repressive government bureaucrat starts imposing strict regulations, Bitcoin will move jurisdictions.

10.   **Competition Risk**. Companies go out of business all the time due to competition. And usually, no one sees it coming. Remember Sears and Roebuck? How about Blockbuster Video or IBM or Xerox, or Kodak? This list is long and distinguished. What about real estate? You have a nice investment rental apartment building. It's a moderate building with a dozen units. You've invested a few million and lots of work into the project. It's starting to throw off some cash flow, and in 11 years, you will have paid off the financing. In year three, a huge real estate company builds a 100-unit high-rise complex next to you or, worse, on both sides of you? They offer modern amenities such as a spa, a doorman, and low-interest financing incentives. In addition, their dominance has created parking problems for your tenants. This is a very typical scenario. Now, you can no longer charge the rents you need to achieve those good cash flows. The competition is eating up your future. Bitcoin, however, has no real competition. Bitcoin is the beneficiary of something called the **network effect**. This means that there can only be one main top money. Winner takes all in the monetary world. And that's Bitcoin. The more people adopt it, the stronger it gets. History shows us that these monetary systems always coalesce into the one best money. This is what made the US dollar supreme for 80 years. And the British pound before that.

Comparing Financial Risks: Traditional Vs. Bitcoin

We often hear that Bitcoin is "risky," but let's compare specific risks:

Risk Type	Traditional Finance	Bitcoin
Inflation Risk	High -	None -
Confiscation Risk	High -	Low -
Counterparty Risk	High -	Low or None -
Censorship Risk	High -	None -
Security Breach Risk	Medium -	Variable -
Inheritance Risk	Medium -	Variable -

Price Volatility Risk	Low to Medium -	Medium -
Management Risk	High -	Low-
Political Risk	Medium -	Low -

This chart reveals an important point: many risks appear "normal" in traditional finance because we've lived with them our entire lives, but they are actually eliminated or reduced with Bitcoin. Meanwhile, Bitcoin's primary risk, price volatility, diminishes significantly over longer time periods, making it particularly suitable for long-term savings.

For Baby Boomers focused on retirement security, this risk profile deserves careful consideration. The short-term volatility that concerns many investors is offset, over time, by Bitcoin's protection against the slower but more certain risk of inflation that erodes traditional savings.

Exercise: Your Security Plans.

- I would like you to start putting together your security plan.

- You can take a pad and pen or use your favorite text editor and start writing. Keep this plan secret. And start to put down specifics. You already have your past exercises with goals and your current technology inventory that you have done. Once again, you can put this on your "**List of challenges**" if needed. This is not to replace the use of a security consultant or an outside security expert. This is a starting point. So you have something to give a security expert if you go in that direction.
- You've got your tech upgraded and updated to the latest good release levels. So now start adding more to it. Here are some areas to start filling out your plan. This will only be the beginning. You will add more to this as we go on. And as you learn more.

1. Security goals. Items such as the goals you want to achieve.
   a. Make all passwords on all my devices secure.
   b. Ensure I have a secure physical storage location
   c. Develop a succession plan.
   d. Name and list three successors with contacts.
   e. Name and list three trusted security team members, wife, son, daughter, etc.
   f. Set security levels.
2. Set some security events.
   a. What to do in the event of a robbery.
   b. What if my computer is hacked?
   c. How do I recover a lost password or lost data?
3. Include all of your equipment inventory.
4. Put together all of your possible risks that you are concerned about. Remember the safety of your current assets from Chapter 5? You can refer to this here.
   a. Confiscation risk.
   b. Risk while traveling.
   c. Risk of robbery.
   d. Risk of someone finding your Bitcoin Wallet.
5. Set a maintenance schedule.
   a. Times when you update the OS.
   b. Schedule for backups.

c. Schedule for upgrades.
d. Annual maintenance check with authorized service provider.
e. Annual training and review to share information with successors and security team.
f. Annual test of the security plan to find information.

A Word About Effort

The exercise above is just a rough outline. I encourage you to think about this carefully and add more to it. Think about what you would do if something happened to you. You get in a terrible accident and have a traumatic brain injury. Or heaven forbid you die. What will happen to your wealth? These are the same things we go through when preparing our inheritance for our heirs. It's not fun. It takes effort. If you leave it all up to others, such as lawyers, there's a good chance the lawyers will make plenty of money, and you will not be satisfied with the result. Or should I say, your successors will not be happy at all. There are plenty of horror stories about battles over wills and trusts, probate, and legal quagmires that last for years and eat up your wealth. Sometimes nothing is left when it's all done. Families are split apart, and the money's gone.

Is it really too difficult? Maybe you should just leave it in traditional finance for the RIAs, wealth fund managers, and lawyers? Yes, it's difficult, but what did you work for 40 years for? To have them squander it? So, they can get their 2 and 20, while you become too old and can't keep up with the latest investment trends, rules, and laws? There is a coming crash. We know this. The current system is unsustainable. When the crash comes and everyone is headed for the exit, are you going to say, "I heard about this Bitcoin thing. Maybe we should move some money into Bitcoin?" I assure you; this will be too little, too late. This is how people get hacked or taken by unscrupulous actors. During a panic is the perfect time to get taken. You are desperate; you haven't done the necessary due diligence; you are in a hurry. So now is the time to put in the work. Gain the knowledge you need, or at the very least, understand your options, and at best, actually manage and take control of your life's savings. A time to identify and work with reliable experts that you know you can trust. And not just pass on the family wealth, but to pass on the knowledge and good habits required to keep it in your family for generations. How much time do you spend on leisure or fun pursuits? A few hours each week could be diverted to this effort.

Michael Saylor said that it takes at least 100 hours of study to understand Bitcoin. I tend to agree with this. Actually, I believe it takes more, but let's set the bar at 100 hours, minimum. He also said that if this seems like too much, think of it this way: You will spend approximately 40,000 hours working, accumulating your life savings. Is 100 hours too much to invest in a method to ensure that you keep it?

Chapter 8

Who Do You Trust?

"Building trust is a process. Trust results from consistent and predictable interaction over time."

Barbara M. White

Bitcoin is unlike anything before or since. It had no development team, no company to rely on, no roadmap to follow, just an idea and a pseudonym. Satoshi Nakamoto emerged from the shadows of a loose-knit group of rebels, mathematicians, cryptographers, and coders who called themselves cypherpunks. If you saw these guys out in public, you'd probably never talk to them. They were the nerds, the super-intelligent, the unusual people. They are the brilliant characters who make our world better every day, and we never say thank you to them. Most of them are obscure. The obscurity of these giants is one of the reasons for the decline in our society. Instead, we worship musicians and criminals, and other characters of notoriety. But even with the contributions of others, Satoshi mostly worked on his own. No one has ever met Satoshi; no one has ever seen a photo of him. No one knows where he came from. Was it more than one person? He was completely anonymous, and to this day, we don't know if he is even still alive. As far as the world is concerned, he is a ghost. A made-up fiction and legend to be mythologized. The only way he could be.

Although we don't know him, we do know what his work has accomplished. And it is probably one of the most important inventions of human history. Just think for a moment about some of the accomplishments of Satoshi. He developed an online system of money that cannot be copied or counterfeited. This alone is a

135

huge innovation. When you understand that the internet and computers are electronic copy machines, you start to see the genius of Satoshi. He took a system built for duplicating information and created a way to make it impossible to falsely copy Bitcoin without the network catching it. This is absolutely critical in a money supply. For this reason alone, it's worth offering a quiet thank you to Satoshi every day you use money.

He also created a public ledger system to record and verify every transaction, a system open for the entire world to see. Right now, I can go onto a public website and find any transaction that has ever occurred on the Bitcoin network. And you can, too, for free and with very little effort. (Does your bank give you anything for free?) With this open ledger, Satoshi revolutionized accounting by creating triple-entry accounting.

This is why Bitcoin is so bad for criminals. They prefer cash that cannot be traced to Bitcoin, which is highly traceable and verifiable. If you want to sell a piece of real estate, it is much, much easier to send payment via Bitcoin than a bank wire, the SWIFT network, or a cashier's check. Those methods are easily hackable or can be counterfeited. Plus, they can take a long time, including days of phone calls and tedious verifications, hoping to dear god that your money doesn't get lost along the way. If you have ever spent days or even weeks sweating feverishly during a real estate deal, waiting for money to arrive and be confirmed by some giant gray faceless intermediary somewhere, then you know what I mean.

Satoshi created a self-building, self-replicating, and self-securing network. He didn't go out and raise billions to hire thousands of people and buy high-end equipment. He designed a system that would attract the best and brightest innovators and put them to work for their own interests to build what, within a few years, has become the largest and most secure computer network the world has ever seen. There was no management team, no government agency or regulator, no central planners. How did he do this? How is this even possible? I worked as an engineer in the field of network technology for many years for some of the biggest technology pioneers, building some of the most sophisticated computer networks. And I can assure you; it takes a lot of effort, coordination, engineering, money, and skill to build a worldwide computer network. Satoshi had none of these. But here we are. Stand back and look at that accomplishment for a second. The breadth is astounding. There is no way that anyone can even conceive of this if it hadn't been done organically by Satoshi. Someone, please show me the Satoshi Nakamoto Bitcoin networking company that was in charge of building the Bitcoin network? We talk often about the inability of humans to understand the laws of compounding, but I challenge any human being to have conceived of this achievement.

Once Satoshi released his 9-page whitepaper (freely available for anyone to read at any time), outlining how Bitcoin would work, he and his cypherpunk community friends brought the system into the world.

The Genius Of Bitcoin Mining

This brings us to the next part of Satoshi's genius: how to bring the actual Bitcoin to the world. The solution was Bitcoin mining. Simply put, he created an incentive system that essentially said, if you want Bitcoin and see value in it, I'm not going to give it to you as a favor or as a friend or family, or as some pre-IPO insider play or some other grift like airdrops or staking. If you want Bitcoin, you are going to have to work for it, just like anything else of value that you want. I am giving you the network and designing the protocol, but the Bitcoin itself, you have to work for. Money has value, and Bitcoin is money. If you want some, then you work for it. Value for value. Not value for favors, or value for insider connections. And the work involved using a computer to perform Bitcoin mining. Just like any other authentic money (the kind of money that people actually want, not government fiat money), Bitcoin requires work.

At first, there was no one to work for it. There was just Satoshi Nakamoto shortly after other cypherpunks joined in. So, he started mining Bitcoin on his own computer, by himself, earning the block rewards (the actual new Bitcoin). The incentive is simple. Miners compete to create a new block approximately every ten minutes, and within these blocks are currently requested Bitcoin transactions that will be included for a fee paid in Bitcoin to the miner. And if there is more than one miner, then they compete to service the next block. The more miners, the more competition. The reward for processing the next block is called the block reward, which started at 50 Bitcoin per 10-minute block. How is it determined who will get to service the next block? There will be a puzzle set to be solved by any prospective miners. The more miners there are, the more difficult the puzzle is, and the difficulty is adjusted every two weeks to account for the number and competitiveness of the miners. So, if there are too many miners, the level of difficulty goes up. And if there are too few miners, then the level of difficulty goes down. And all of this occurs automatically, adjusting itself to keep the block time at approximately 10 minutes. Like a living, breathing being. I still sit here in amazement at the simplicity and at the truly inspired vision it took to bring us such an elegant system.

During the first four years, when the block was complete, the network released 50 Bitcoin to the successful miner to use as he liked. He could sell it or use it however he wanted to. Of course, at first it had no defined fiat value, as price discovery had not yet begun. All real money starts this same way — as a collectible. Later, it naturally evolves into a store of value. Then, it evolves to be a medium of exchange. And finally, it becomes a unit of account. All money throughout history evolved this way.

Soon, other miners joined and started competing, a few at first and then more. Competition grew. Faster computers, more computers, special computers dedicated to just mining. Growing stronger and stronger, using more electricity. They did more and more work to get the **Bitcoin Block Reward**. This is what is known as **proof of work**. It is a critical part of the Bitcoin network. It is a self-referential system that continues to secure the Bitcoin network today.

During the first two years, as the network grew, Satoshi continued to make tweaks and updates to the system. Suddenly, he disappeared. He vanished from the face of the earth. No one knows where he is or what he is. All we know is he gave us a gift that we can never repay. And in his final act, which some say was an even greater gift than Bitcoin itself, he disappeared. There is no cult figure to worship, attack, or blame for our problems. No inventor to put on the torture rack when the government wants to villainize Bitcoin. Just the Bitcoin network, turning out a new block every ten minutes. Thus far, every attack imaginable has been leveled at Bitcoin. None of them was successful.

Before he left, Satoshi mined about 1 million Bitcoin. These 1 million Bitcoin are still sitting in the wallet from when he mined them. And they have never been moved. (Remember, we can see every transaction that was ever done.) This would make Satoshi Nakamoto one of the richest men in the world today. But it has never been touched. A true enigma.

Why Do You Trust Money?

Why do we trust the money we have? What makes it trustworthy? The simple answer is that other people trust it. So, if they trust it, then I will trust it. If it's good enough for them, then it's good enough for me. Or another reason may be that there is no other alternative. It's not like I can start using Japanese yen at the local Walmart or ask my supermarket if they will accept another form of money. It's simply not allowed.

But even deeper than that. Think back to our earlier discussion about gold, money, and trusting the banks. Over time, institutions build reputations based on trust. We live with this every day. You trust that your employer will pay you. And that they will pay you in a money that is usable, fungible, and reliable. Your employer trusts that you will show up on time and that you will do the tasks that they need. The entire economy is built on this fragile system of trust.

Over time, and through a lot of trial and error, trust solidifies. One of the things that gave America its power and preeminence in the world is the US dollar and other countries' trust in it. Among the over 100 fiat currencies in the world, none is trusted more than the dollar. This is key to making sense of the very system we live, work, and trade in every day. This trust is more than just a convenience for us to buy something at the store; it is a moral issue. It goes directly to our ability to rely on our fellow man, and in turn, for him to do the same. Like a ripple in a pond, this reliability spreads throughout the system and is verified every day, again and again.

And the system is extremely powerful. It builds power and strength over time. And this makes it very difficult to undermine or take this power away. This trust system has many parts: reputation, financial strength, government regulation, insurance systems, and reinsurance systems. There are multiple layers of rating systems and agencies. There are even media ratings and media reports. When you put all of these together, you have an interlocking trust system. And we all rely on these systems daily to know we have trust in the economic system that we so desperately need to use.

But there is even more. There are financial intermediaries. And these intermediaries are critically important. If you want to send a payment to your electric company, for instance, do you just send them cash? No, you either send them a check or maybe pay with a bank card or an electronic payment system. These financial intermediaries facilitate the payment and charge a fee.

If you want to buy a car, are you going to walk into the dealership with $45,000 in cash? No, you will most likely use a bank draft or cashier's check (intermediary), or more likely take out a loan for the car from the financial intermediary, then pay back the bank over time using credit.

The same process applies to purchasing a house or some type of real estate. You will almost certainly use credit to make the purchase. At this point, these financial intermediaries will be playing a bigger, much more lucrative game — the game of making your payments for you and charging you interest, a much higher fee than just facilitating a one-time payment. We talked about how banks use the credit system to create fiat money out of thin air in earlier chapters, and this is true. But in order for the financial intermediaries to do this, they must have something very, very important. And that is trust. Essentially, they are using all of these systems in a large interlocking dance to give you the illusion of trust.

Trust On An International Scale

Trust is not isolated to a local micro or macro scale. There is a much bigger picture to consider. It is behind the scenes to most of us. But it certainly affects our lives every day. It is a system of trust that has been built over decades of international treaties, multinational business arrangements, political arrangements, layers of contracts, court systems, commodities trading systems, and currency trading systems. In fact, it is hard to emphasize how important this system of trust is to our daily lives. We often hear about "supply chains" in our daily news, usually in the context of minor disruptions blamed on the pandemic. At least this is what we are told. But it is much more than this.

When we talk of the US dollar being the world's reserve currency, this is what we are referring to. Through a long series of complex processes, agreements, and historical events, the dollar has been chosen, not by decree but by trust, to serve as the world's reserve currency. So, there are literally over 100 currencies in the world, but only one is the world's reserve currency. Surely there are other good currencies? Well, there are a lot of bad currencies, and most of them are really bad. Fiat currency, by its very nature, is prone to being bad. It is incentivized to always corrupt and to be corrupted. But there are a few other good currencies, such as the British pound or the Swiss franc. But they are still not as good or as hard as the dollar. And this is because people, systems, and economies tend to standardize on the "best" currency. This is the network effect, in essence. Everyone gravitates to the best use. Remember, money always moves towards its highest and best use. So, of all the fiat currencies, the US dollar is the least bad. And one of the main reasons for this is trust. Trust that it will not debase. Well, that it will not debase as fast as other currencies because all currencies are debasing, including the dollar. The dollar is just the cleanest dirty shirt in the laundry.

Many people would not even support their own fiat currency if they weren't forced to by their own government's legal tender laws. Many use the dollar even if their government forbids it.

The reason for all of this is trust. And what do we mean by trust at this level? When a country wants to trade with another country, it needs to establish trust. First, maybe at a treaty level. This would ensure that people, products, and services can cross borders. Next, at a financial level, to make sure that money and funds can cross borders. This means that that when payments are required, they will be honored and exchange rates can set. And finally, trust is needed in legal systems so that when there is a dispute, the parties have an agreed-upon method to resolve these disputes quickly and fairly.

But unfortunately, at the financial level, dispute resolution is not always so easy or affordable because these same governments that want the trade to make their own economies prosperous and bring peace and wealth to their people don't always follow their own rules. They manipulate their currencies; they cheat on agreements; and they devalue their own currencies. They constantly restrict trade and commerce, but if there is a standardized currency to use, this can grease the skids a bit. But it doesn't stop all the cheating.

These are national governments, and governments always cheat and lie about just about everything. But it does help to have a stable, standardized currency issued by a third party that everyone can agree on and trust. This is where the US dollar comes in. Gold used to perform this task, but gold is too bulky and difficult to use for trade settlement in the 21st century. Gold is still a good store of value, and it has performed this task well for over 200 years. But now, it is mostly hoarded by central banks and governments.

Anatomy Of An Inferior Transaction.

So, if a company in Brazil wanted to sell cocoa to a company in Germany for $5,000,000, it wouldn't sell this cocoa in Brazilian reals, or German marks, or even euros. It sells it in dollars. It is priced in dollars based on the Chicago Mercantile Exchange located in Chicago, USA. And it goes further than this. The Brazilian company's bank in Brazil will have a deal with the German company's bank in Germany. And these two banks will have a deal with an intermediary. Remember, we discussed the need for intermediaries earlier at a micro level. Here it is again at a macro and international level. In most cases, this intermediary is a large multinational bank based in New York, like Chase, Citibank, or Bank of America. There aren't many of them. This intermediary will issue a letter of credit between the two parties' banks, which certifies cooperation between the two companies, basically stating that basically they are good for it.

Then the transaction will be broken down to make the exchange, since there are all kinds of other funny business going on all the time — cheating, debasement, manipulation. For instance, the Brazilian real has gone through an average of 87% annual inflation for the last 40-plus years. This means that 100 reals in 1981 is about 30,909,359,999,999.99. So, with that kind of utterly ridiculous chicanery going on, businesses are desperate for a currency they can trust. And in a case like this, the US dollar with 7% annualized inflation looks like a dream.

The trusted third party will then convert the payment from Euros in Germany to dollars. Those dollars are then transmitted to the bank in Brazil, where they are converted again, this time into Brazilian reals. Only then is the payment made to the Brazilian company, once shipment and receipt of the cargo are confirmed. Such a fragile system.

The System Of Trust Is Cracking. So, you can see, trust is essential. The problem is that the dollar is now losing its preeminence as a trusted vehicle to facilitate transactions. This has been a long time coming. But as of the writing of this book, it is accelerating at a harrowing pace.

There are many reasons for this. But the biggest is that the USA is doing the same type of chicanery as these other countries. It's using the US treasury and the US dollar, its biggest stick, to forward its aggressive hegemonic ambitions. Fully one-third of the entire world is under US sanctions. And it's getting worse. These sanctions are ostensibly used to try to cause foreign governments to bend to the will of the US State Department. But they only really serve to impoverish the poor people of the target country, which makes the economy weaker and more fragile here in the USA for American citizens.

Simply put, sanctions do not work. The countries with the most brutal and long-lived sanctions are Cuba and North Korea. Regardless of what you think of their leaders and how they treat their people, good or bad, sanctions do not dethrone leaders or make them change their leadership style. In fact, one of the tools despotic leaders like North Korea's Kim Jong-un use to keep their people under their thumb is poverty and starvation. Sanctions actually make this worse, playing into the hands of the dictator.

So, as more sanctions and more controls are brought to bear on more people, the system simply becomes a joke. Countries and people find ways to get around the sanctions, so much so that sanction evasion has grown into a full-blown international industry. Alternative currencies are being used, and global trade is shifting away from the massive New York-based megabanks. The large global South trade alliance called BRICS, which stands for Brazil, Russia, India, China, and South Africa, is expanding rapidly and is already larger than the G7 and on track to outgrow the G20. New members are begging to join so they can get away from the West. And it is planning on building a complete universal trading currency system between its members to avoid the US dollar.

No one can predict how this is going to work or how well it will work. But one thing is for sure, whatever they do, if it's using gold, one of their fiat currencies, or a basket of their fiat currencies, they will cheat. And they may even go back to using the fiat US dollar. But the best way to leave the US dollar would be to use the only neutral money system — one that is not being debased, is internationally recognized, easily auditable, electronically native, verifiable, and programmable. And that money, of course, is Bitcoin. It may take them some time to realize it. But it will inevitably happen. Remember, money always goes to its highest and best use.

What If You Don't Need To Trust?

You go online, and you find a car. It's a used car, and it costs $7500. You contact the seller. You go to look at the car, inspect it, and agree on the price. In the back of your mind and the seller's mind is one big elephant in the room. Who is this guy? He is some stranger; I don't know him. Is he going to rip me off? Is he going to take my money somehow? All kinds of scenarios go through your mind. What if he says I didn't pay him, accusing me of taking his car? What if he thinks my money is no good, and I'll rip him off with a bad check? What if I go to the DMV to register the car and find out that the seller did not verify the sale? How do I register the car?

A ton of nightmare scenarios go through the heads of the seller and the buyer. But you still have to make the deal. You need the car, and he wants the money. So, you use financial intermediaries. Bank checks or cashier's checks. You go down to the bank and make the exchange at the DMV or at the bank. You are both using intermediaries to enable trust.

But what if you didn't need trust? There is no need for a financial intermediary. You make the deal. The seller signs over the title to you, verifies the deposit of the funds, and it all takes about twenty to thirty minutes. Everyone can see the money was deposited, and everyone is happy. That is how Bitcoin works. Bitcoin exhibits superior simplicity.

Bitcoin Makes This System Trustless.

Our traditional financial system is based on an edifice of trust. Some of it is legitimate, and some of it is not. Many parts are obscured to hide their illegitimacy, while others have been legitimized through historical use. Today, the entire system is starting to fail, bit by bit and day by day. And when the real panic sets in, and I assure you it will, trust will be a very scarce and valuable commodity. It will be the most valuable commodity.

This brings us to another concept that needs to be discussed, and this is the concept of counterparty risk. Simply put, counterparty risk is the danger you face when you hand over your money to someone else for a period of time. This other party is usually that intermediary we talked about earlier. It can be for a few hours, like currency trading, or several years, or even decades, in the case of a loan. These all involve risk. And because you do not control this other party, you must trust them.

But in the case of Bitcoin, you do not entrust your money to another party. You maintain custody until your transaction or other business is completed. This removes counterparty risk.

A trustless system like Bitcoin is so revolutionary that we have to sit and think about it for a moment and walk through some examples to really understand the value in this. For example, let's look at the car purchase. If you use a cashier's check or a wire transfer, you are trusting a counterparty like the bank to take your money and move it to another person's account. This can take days or even weeks, sometimes. That's an uncomfortable feeling.

But with Bitcoin, you make the transfer either face-to-face or across the world in a matter of minutes. Night or day. Not waiting for the bank to open and resolve any issues. Or waiting for a phone call or verification code. You just make the transfer, and you're done. The actual verification of the transfer is being done by literally thousands of Bitcoin nodes and Bitcoin miners across the globe. Not subject to any jurisdictional rules, not a victim of a crooked banker or bankers. Or a stupid clerk somewhere. It's all done within the Bitcoin network. And the amounts can be as significant as you like, from a few dollars to literally millions or even billions of dollars.

This is unnerving to think about. Just imagine for a minute, you had to walk around with a $35,000 cashier's check for a few days or a few weeks? Walk through it in your mind. Where do you keep it? Who knows about it? How will you store it? How do you verify it's good? After all, cashier's checks and even wire transfers are hacked and counterfeited all the time.

Go through the process in your mind for a moment. Imagine the feeling. Maybe you're not a wealthy person. How does it feel knowing that the check can easily be stolen at any minute or counterfeited? How does it feel? Seller delays the deal for a week due to weather or unforeseen circumstances. What then? Do you wait? Now you have been protecting this vulnerable money for over a week. Talk about feeling exposed, naked, and a bit scared.

What about the clerk at the bank? Are they honest? Who is watching him? Who is watching the watcher? And on and on. Wells Fargo Bank has been caught repeatedly defrauding its own customers. That's just one example. Not a very pleasant experience. Now multiply this. Add a few zeros to the transaction. It gets worse. The temptation to steal or interfere with the transaction grows as the zeros grow. The temptation for some other entity or jurisdiction to interfere or capture your funds also goes up. Happens all the time. So, what counterparty do you want to trust? Think I'm being hyperbolic? According to NBC, it happens about 500,000 times per year. And if it happens, you will be the one suffering a financial loss. Not the bank.

Understanding Trust Trade-offs

As we explore Bitcoin's trustless model, it's important to understand that adopting Bitcoin doesn't eliminate trust entirely; rather, it shifts where the trust is placed. Understanding these trade-offs allows us to make informed decisions about incorporating

147

Bitcoin into our retirement strategies. Let's compare trust models for traditional finance and Bitcoin.

Traditional Finance Trust Model:

- Trust in institutions (banks, investment firms, governments)
- Trust in human judgment and integrity
- Trust in regulatory oversight
- Minimal personal responsibility for security

Bitcoin Trust Model:

- Trust in mathematical principles and open-source code
- Trust in distributed consensus rather than central authorities
- Trust in your own security practices
- Significant personal responsibility

For those of us who have spent decades in the traditional system, making this shift may seem unnatural. You're trading familiar trust relationships for a system that places more responsibility in your hands, while removing vulnerabilities inherent in human-centered systems.

This doesn't mean you need to completely abandon traditional financial services. Many Bitcoiners maintain a hybrid approach, especially in the beginning. The key is understanding the trust implications of each system so you can make choices aligned with your values and risk tolerance.

What's particularly powerful about Bitcoin's approach is that it allows you to verify trust assumptions directly. Unlike traditional finance, where you must rely on auditors, regulators, and rating agencies to verify institutional trustworthiness, Bitcoin's open system allows you (or software working on your behalf) to verify that the rules are being followed without requiring permission from anyone.

This shift from "trust but can't verify" to "don't need to trust because you can verify" is a dramatic upgrade in how we relate to our money and those who handle it.

Comparison Of A Superior Trust System

Current System	**Bitcoin Network**
Requires trust.	Trustless.
Opaque accounting system.	Completely open.
Intermediaries granting permission.	Permissionless,
Many corrupt bureaucratic layers.	Very few layers.
International problems.	Travels across borders
Ledger is changeable.	Immutable ledger.
Audits are limited and corrupt.	Openly audited
Massive counterparty risk.	No counterparty risk.
Subject to international corruption.	No international influence.
Rules change by jurisdiction.	Rules are consistent.

Bitcoin Is A Ledger.

One of the brilliant inventions of Bitcoin is its ledger system. This may sound mundane, but it is so important. Some of the first writing ever discovered in caves is a series of accounting marks about the numbers of cows and other animals. The earliest writing wasn't because someone was creative and wanted to write poetry; it was about necessity. And from this necessity came a recording of business transactions. A ledger. A simple single-entry bookkeeping ledger. You bought something for one piece of money, like one shell, one coin, or one bead. This was simple single-entry bookkeeping. It was necessary, and it moved humanity forward. The earliest known writing was Cuneiform in Mesopotamia, showing ledgers and transactions around 3400 BC.

We lived with this system for millennia. Then, with the advent of the Medici family and modern banking, we came up with a new system. A system of recording and bookkeeping called double-entry bookkeeping. This allowed the ability to credit one account and debit another account. This greatly moved record-keeping forward and made our system more efficient and verifiable.

Bitcoin Bit.

When Satoshi first mined Bitcoin. There was only his computer to do the mining. But today it has grown massively a single large mining operations can consist of thousands of individual mining servers called ASICS. This means Application Specific Integrated Circuit. An ASIC does only one thing very fast and very well. These ASICs are very fast single use computers and one can cost over $3000.

And it allowed two parties to have corresponding debit and credit entries for each other, representing a transaction. A debit for one party would be a credit for the other party. And vice versa. This is simple accounting but very important. This provided a balanced view from two sides. Many times, these two sides would be the intermediaries of this transaction. But there was a problem, as we have seen with all intermediaries. And that is trust. In this case, the transaction was visible to only the two parties, which are normally the intermediaries. And you, me, or anyone else, including the actual parties to the transaction, don't get to see these books. We are all excluded. And it's been this way for the past 500 years. Let me ask you. If you have a dispute with your bank, will you get to review their books? Can you see the actual entries or, even better, audit their books to confirm or correct the discrepancy? Of course not. This is a form of counterparty risk and goes directly to your ability to trust your intermediaries. Not a good situation.

Bitcoin, however, operates as a decentralized, transparent ledger. It has completely upended the dominance of traditional finance. This open-ledger system allows anyone to see every transaction as it happens. Each transaction is publicly visible, validated by objective third-party Bitcoin nodes, and permanently recorded, making it fully auditable, both in real-time and for posterity. In addition to all of this, we now have a system that gives you final settlement. Traditional systems based on credit cards and checking systems, bank transfers, and wire transfers can take weeks, even months, to reach final settlement. All of this is done with the Bitcoin network in a matter of minutes, making it the fastest and most scalable transaction network in history. This has been called triple-entry bookkeeping.

And then after all of this is done, the transaction now lives on the Bitcoin time chain (mistakenly referred to as the blockchain), forever and ever. These are accomplishments of immeasurable proportions. It is going to take many years for humanity to fully understand the gravity of accomplishments like triple-entry bookkeeping. What's revolutionary here is that both parties can transact directly, no intermediary required. But if you'd rather pay fees and invite interference, sure, go ahead and involve one. Meanwhile, the Bitcoin network quietly does the real work, serving as an impartial third party, recording every transaction in a permanent, tamper-proof ledger for all of posterity.

Bitcoin Exercise:
- Make a comparison of all your investments by risk and profitability.
- You have sat down, and you have a list of all your investments. You have rated them. You have a better understanding of each one.

- Maybe you are using an Excel spreadsheet or Google Sheets to keep things organized. I highly recommend this. You have assigned qualitative values to each one.
- Now, create a column next to each investment and assign it a risk score. Maybe something like a number from one to 10. One being the least risky and 10 being the riskiest. Then assign a percentage value to each risk level. For instance, set the lowest risk at a 1% risk discount, and the highest at a 50% risk discount.
- This will then be multiplied by the amount of return you expect. Of course, Bitcoin would be the least risky if you have been reading so far. You can use the previous risk factors to help you apply risk values to your investments.
- This is, of course, subjective. But the important thing is you are taking the time and the effort to figure this out. As opposed to letting someone else do it. Someone who will never know your situation. Even if they are helping you, they can never know as well as you should.

Chapter 9

Protect Your Bitcoin And It Will Protect You

"I think anyone who is interested in keeping their money safe from the criminal banking system would want silver, gold, and Bitcoin."

Max Keiser

For Baby Boomers, Bitcoin represents a new way of thinking about financial security. Throughout your life, you've been told that security comes from trusting institutions, banks with their vaults, brokerages with their insurance, and advisors with their credentials.

When I first purchased Bitcoin, it was cheap and hard to work with. I had no idea what I was doing and how to manage it, acquire it, or keep it safe. To me it was another investment, maybe there would be fantastic wealth gained. But I had no clue.

I purchased the Bitcoin on the exchange, and just left it there. And I didn't even set up a Bitcoin wallet, the step that would actually make the Bitcoin mine. By the time I finally set up my own personal wallet, some of my Bitcoin had vanished. It wasn't until about a year later, after I started to understand Bitcoin, that I really started to protect it in a real and determined way.

When Michael Saylor was once asked why he had criticized Bitcoin early on in 2014. But then went back on his earlier condemnations of Bitcoin, he explained, "I didn't need Bitcoin back then. Now I need Bitcoin, and I took the time to learn about Bitcoin."

It was the same with me. I didn't know anything about Bitcoin, either. I didn't even know that I needed it. So, I didn't take the time to learn about it. Later, after I lost some of it, and felt the pain of this lost value. And I was reading and started to understand the uniqueness of Bitcoin. Then I realized the value of what had been lost. This shook me up and showed me that this was something interesting and very important. At that point, I took it seriously and started to protect it more and more.

Protecting Bitcoin Is A Progression.

Just like my story above, you will find that Bitcoin is a progression. You will start with a little bit of Bitcoin, and then you will learn more and more about it. And the more you learn, the more you will value it, and want to protect it.

First, your security will be a simple password on your account on a Bitcoin exchange. Then you will graduate to implementing two-factor authentication on your account. You will start to hear stories about how untrustworthy Bitcoin exchanges are. You will learn that some exchanges with many alternative coins and tokens are riskier. And you will consider moving to a Bitcoin-only exchange to reduce your exposure to risk.

Next, you will install a hot wallet on your phone and move your Bitcoin off the exchange because you hear stories about how exchanges use your Bitcoin without your authorization or permission. Or, in scarier instances, the exchanges lose your Bitcoin altogether. Stories about Mt. Gox and FTX will terrify you. Then you will learn that some wallets are better than others. So, you will start to learn about wallets and move from your hot wallet to more secure wallets, such as hardware or cold wallets. This process will continue for quite a while. But this progression is very valuable to your education and your confidence. And as you move forward, you need to look at these steps in security as a progression that never ends. There will always be improvements that need to be made, like software updates and maintenance fixes. This will not only make your security better, but it will keep you fresh and confident.

Privacy Is The Cornerstone Of Security.
I knew an elderly gentleman years ago, when I was little in my hometown. He wore basic, kind of dirty clothes and spoke simply. He was very friendly and easy-going. His car was a basic old pickup truck. His house was big, but it was old and in a rural neighborhood. You would not notice this man if he walked by you. He would not gather your attention for any reason other than to notice he was not interesting.

One day, my dad told me the man was worth millions of dollars. But if you looked at him, you would never have guessed it. He quietly owned many income-producing properties and didn't talk about them very often, if at all. He was a private man. My dad knew him, and when I was nearby, and they were talking, I never heard them talk about money. Their own money or anyone else's. This man was the picture of modesty. But even more important, he was the epitome of discretion. He was a private man. He was the embodiment of discretion. But more than that, he was *private*.

He had carefully cultivated this private persona in the public world for a very specific reason. And it served him well. His reason had more to do with modesty and not being overestimated in business dealings. But it brought with it the added benefit of security. Security of his wealth and his well-being. Protection from swindlers and thieves.

This is your first and most fundamental step in Bitcoin security: **Stay Private**.

Don't talk about your Bitcoin to anyone who does not need to know about it. Possible exceptions to this would be discussions with trusted family members or friends, and maybe other like-minded Bitcoiners, with whom you are learning. But with the rest of the world, talk only about Bitcoin in the abstract, as in the ideas of Bitcoin. But never in the specifics. Do not publish your Bitcoin details and certainly not any ownership information. Keep your Bitcoin private. This alone will protect you in ways that you cannot imagine. What you do with Bitcoin stays with you. This does not mean to shy away from learning or reading about Bitcoin; on the contrary, continue to study and to read. Keep discussing Bitcoin with friends and thought leaders. Or attend Bitcoin meetups, a wonderful source of information. Just don't talk about specifics with others.

Seven Rules For Protecting Bitcoin.

1. **Learn about Bitcoin and never stop.** One of your greatest tools for protecting your Bitcoin is to understand what exactly you are dealing with. If you don't understand it, like in my story above, you will not value it, and you will not understand how to protect it.

2. **Backup your Bitcoin.** You should always keep backups of all your valuable data, and this goes double with Bitcoin. When you store your Bitcoin, you will be using a software-based or physical Bitcoin wallet (see below). This wallet will generate a seed phrase that acts as your key to your Bitcoin. This must be protected and backed up. If something happens to your wallet, then your backup seed phrase can be used to set up a new wallet and access your Bitcoin again.

3. **Get Help.** If there is something you don't understand about Bitcoin, it is okay to get professional help. However, I would be leery of free help. Professional help is more likely to give you real value and protect your personal information. Free help is more likely to see you as a commodity to be sold.

4. **Keep your stuff updated.** Technical systems, software, and hardware can contain vulnerabilities. As they evolve, their attack surfaces increase. It is important to use valid updates to keep your electronics and software protected from bugs and vulnerabilities. It's equally important to keep your legal documents, instructions, and planning systems updated, too.

5. **Get your Bitcoin off the Exchange**. Treat the crypto exchanges like a dirty public bathroom. Get in, do your business, and get out. Untold millions of dollars of Bitcoin have been lost or stolen or pilfered while sitting on crypto exchanges.

6. **Compartmentalization**. Compartmentalization is a fundamental security concept. It means separating different functions among different people or companies and even different locations. Compartmentalization includes avoiding crypto exchanges vs Bitcoin-only exchanges and avoiding crypto wallets vs Bitcoin-only wallets. When thousands of crypto products use the same exchange or wallet, each of these cryptos has the potential to be exploited or hacked, leading to contamination of your Bitcoin stash. Focusing on Bitcoin-only products limits your risk and exposure.

7. **Use open-source over proprietary**. Open-source systems and products make their source code publicly available for critique from multiple developers and bug hunters worldwide. More eyeballs mean fewer bugs and faster fixes. It's not a silver bullet, but it's a meaningful advantage. When in doubt, lean toward transparency.

Wallets, Nodes, And Custodians.
Three other details about Bitcoin should be discussed: Wallets, Nodes, and Custodians.

Wallet: A wallet is not actually a wallet containing Bitcoin. It is just a euphemism for where you keep the keys to your Bitcoin. Bitcoin, like we said earlier, is actually stored as a ledger entry on the Bitcoin blockchain network. It is kept safe on this ledger entry by a massive encryption algorithm. Your individual ownership is protected by your own personal keys. These keys are kept safe by a separate, encrypted algorithm that you control individually. This set of keys is stored inside your personal wallet. These keys are used to access your individual Bitcoin addresses and send the Bitcoin to any recipient you choose.

The wallet also contains a series of addresses known as public receive addresses. They are generated to receive Bitcoin into your wallet's account. Although an address can be reused, it's strongly recommended not to do so for privacy and security reasons. Fortunately, your wallet will easily generate a new receive address for every transaction.

Wallets come in many forms. The two primary categories are software, or hot wallets (meaning they connect to the internet), and cold wallets. Usually, hot wallets reside on your phone and should be considered less secure than a cold wallet, but more secure than the wallet on a Bitcoin exchange. Some good hot wallets are **Blue Wallet**, **Muun Wallet**, **Wallet of Satoshi**, **Samourai Wallet**, and **Sparrow Wallet** (desktop only).

Cold wallets are considered much safer than hot wallets. They do not actually connect to the internet and are much better for storing Bitcoin long-term. Cold means your Bitcoin is in cold storage. The hardware devices sometimes look like some kind of USB Key, or an old calculator, or even an old push-button cell phone. They contain specialized software and usually plug into your phone or laptop to operate. There are other types that operate using a small set of encrypted software keys on the cold wallet. Important: only order and receive hardware wallets directly from the vendor, not from third parties, and never use a second-hand wallet. In fact, if you stop using a cold wallet, you should destroy it.

When you first set up a wallet, it will generate a backup or seed phrase when you first set it up. This comes from a set of random numbers that you generate. If it already comes in the package with a set of seed phrases, this is a compromised wallet and do not use it under any circumstances. The wallets usually have a random number generator that generates the seed phrase for you. Either 12 or 24 words. Never create your own seed phrase and never, ever give this information to anyone (unless you want them to have complete access to all of your Bitcoin), including the customer service representative of the vendor. If someone asks for this seed phrase to help you with a technical problem, it's a scam. They will immediately steal your Bitcoin.

Never, ever record your seed phrase or backup phrase in any electronic form. Don't put it in any electronic document or spreadsheet, don't take a picture of it, and don't send it to yourself by email. You only record it by writing it down. And I recommend writing two copies on two separate pieces of paper and hiding them in two separate secure locations. If the locations are geographically separate, this is even better. You will not need the seed phrase for day-to-day use. It is only used as a backup in case you lose access to your wallet or in an emergency. It's not like a daily password that you need to memorize, but you will set a password or pin for daily use of your wallet. Some good cold wallets are **Cold Card**, **Blockstream Jade**, **Foundation Passport**, and **Bitkey** by Block.

You should also look at wallets as a progression, the same as your dollars. You wouldn't walk around with $100,000 in your pocket. And you wouldn't store a few dollars in a bank vault. It's the same with your Bitcoin wallet. Decide what is appropriate for you. And then stick to some simple rules. I will show you a basic chart to go by, but numbers and amounts are strictly up to you.

Spectrum of Bitcoin Custody

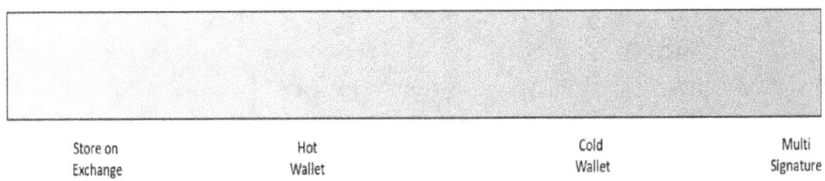

Store on Exchange	Hot Wallet	Cold Wallet	Multi Signature

This gives you an idea of the progression of Bitcoin custody. Very few people get to multi-signature or even cold wallets. Most users are concentrated on the left side of the spectrum. See possible guidelines below. You must decide your own progression.

Bitcoin Wallet Progression.

Type of Storage	Cost of Storage	Value
Hot wallet, phone.	Free	$1000 less.
Hot wallet, PC	Free	$10,000 more.
Cold Storage Wallet	Approx $150	$100,000 or less
Multi-signature 2/3	Approx $300/yr.	$500,000 or less
Multi-signature 3/5	Approx $500/yr.	$500,000 or more

This is simply a set of guidelines, but it gives you an idea of how your progression might look. You can set your own thresholds and limits. This is the same way a bank does it. They only hold so much cash on hand. When larger amounts of cash accumulate, they have it picked up and sent to a more secure facility. Beyond that, they turn it into the Federal Reserve branch and convert it to something more secure, like T-Bills. You are literally becoming your own bank. Not your own bank account, but "being" your own bank. This is a big leap in sovereignty and freedom. It requires a move up in responsibility.

And with this responsibility comes some requirements to learn and to stay alert. Sure, it's going to take more effort. But not as much effort as you might think. The most important thing is to never leave this up to someone else. It is when you abdicate this responsibility to someone else that you lose. I am not saying you have to do everything yourself. You should get help from professionals when needed. And you may need a lot of help. What I am saying is to never give away your responsibility. Never relinquish custody of your Bitcoin. Never give up your sovereignty. And absolutely never give up your wallet keys. We will soon be talking about the different options for getting help and some guidelines on getting help in another section.

Multi-Signature. Multi-signature, often shortened to *multi-sig*, is an advanced technique where you split up the signing of Bitcoin transactions amongst multiple wallets or keys. This increases your security and, at the same time, protects you from loss or theft of one of these wallets or keys. The way it works is quite straightforward.

The normal way to sign for a Bitcoin transaction is to sign it with the wallet where the Bitcoin is stored. This is **decentralization** at the Bitcoin wallet level as opposed to the monetary level.

In a **2-of-3 multi-signature** setup, you create three sets of keys, and any two of them are required to authorize a transaction, just like if you had a door that required two keys to unlock. Now it's more difficult for a government or a thief to take both sets of keys. To make it even more protective, you have a third wallet (keys), and any two of the three keys can sign for the transaction. This way, if one of the wallets (keys) is lost, stolen, or confiscated, you still have two wallets (keys) that can sign the transaction.

Multi-sig setups can be extended even further. A 3-of-5 configuration is common for large institutions and custodians of Bitcoin. And yes, you may notice that I am using the terms wallet and keys somewhat interchangeably. That's because in practical terms, your wallet is where your keys are stored and accessed.

One additional thing about multi-signature. Bitcoin as a technology allows you to set up multi-signature yourself, and it's very secure. However, it can be complicated, and I do not recommend this for most users. A better option is to employ the services of a multi-signature provider.

So, in a 2-of-3 setup, you have your two sets of keys, and your multi-signature provider has a third key. The provider can only co-sign a transaction with your authorization, typically in the case of an emergency scenario like a lost key. They do not have access to your Bitcoin. It is an elegant solution. And the provider provides a white glove service for helping you to secure your Bitcoin. Then you pay them a set fee annually for the service. They will also participate in your succession plan in case something happens to you. Some good providers to possibly help with this are **Casa** and **Unchained Capital**. I am not sponsored by either of them. It is strictly up to you to interview and research them or others. I am just giving you the starting point.

Nodes
A Bitcoin node is a small computer that sits on the network and runs a piece of software that validates transactions on the Bitcoin network. This is different from a Bitcoin miner. Bitcoin miners process transactions and bring new Bitcoin onto the network, while also protecting the Bitcoin network.

Nodes validate the transactions and keep a copy of the Bitcoin ledger in their database. Nodes are used and set up by regular Bitcoin users on the network and give the network protection from manipulation by other nefarious actors.

Nodes are completely optional and relatively easy to set up if you have some technical knowledge and time. You can use an old laptop or a small microcomputer to set one up. The hardware is your option to pay for but can usually be gathered together for around $500.

Avoid using underpowered or very old machines for this. But you don't need some high powered or new machine to build a node either. For example, if the recommendation is for 8 Gigabytes of memory, never use less than 16 Gigabytes. If one terabyte of storage is recommended, never use less than two, etc.

Stay away from tiny Raspberry Pi setups or 10-year-old, dusty laptops, unless you want a frustrating 2-month install project. If your instructions start out in the title telling you it's simple to set up, look for other instructions to verify this. There are some nicely packaged setups out there, such as Start9 and Umbrel, that make running a node easier.

The Bitcoin Core software is free. This is the node software for the Bitcoin network. There are currently over 18,000 reachable Bitcoin nodes running in nearly all countries and continents around the world. When changes or updates to Bitcoin Core are proposed, they can't be forced on the network. Approval requires consensus among the nodes, not the miners.

Miners may have money and influence, but they do not control the protocol. Their incentives are tied to their mining profits, which means as profit seeking businesses, they will always push for changes that benefit them. But nodes are independent users like you and me. Another genius move by Satoshi. Because it's very hard to get changes into the Bitcoin network. And that's the way it should be.

Because of the node consensus rules, it's not required for a Bitcoin holder to run a node. But doing so adds a layer of security. Every Bitcoin transaction is first sent to a node somewhere. If that node is yours, you gain more privacy and control.

Custodians.

Custodians are the people or institutions actually holding the keys to your Bitcoin. If you are holding your Bitcoin in your own wallet, then you have the keys. And you are the custodian. This is the most secure option.

But if you leave your Bitcoin on an exchange after purchasing it, then it is the custodian's, not yours. In that case, you do not actually own the Bitcoin. You have a claim to it, but not possession. It's just like a bank account. If you deposit your $100,000 in your bank, that money becomes the bank's asset. What you get in return is an IOU for the $100,000. The funds may be listed under your name, but you're trusting someone else to hold them.

The saying is simple: "**Not your keys, not your coins**." If you want to own your Bitcoin, then you need to be the custodian.

Now, I understand that this may not be possible. In this case, you need to look at a secure way to custody your Bitcoin. We are Baby Boomers, and it's not realistic to expect that everyone reading this will have the technical skill to become a self-custodian of their Bitcoin. One good way is a white-glove multi-signature service, as discussed above.

Two very good providers are **Unchained Capital** and **Casa**. Both have good reputations and offer strong technical support structures to walk you through the process. Some other highly recommended legitimate white glove services would be a company called **Swan**

Bitcoin Bit.

The most common attack and exploit of a cryptocurrency network is called the 51% attack. This is basically an attack that tries to take over 51% of the productive hash power of the network. If the 51% attack is successful the attacker can then start creating fictious transactions to divert funds to his own wallet. While 51% attacks are numerous and tried on all cryptocurrency networks and have been successful on most. There has never been a successful 51% attack on the Bitcoin network. 51% attacks on other crypto networks are common. That is nice peace of mind.

Bitcoin. They have an add-on service called Swan Vault to allow collaborative custody for multi-signature. Another custodian is **Kingdom Trust.** They provide Bitcoin custody through your IRA. Investigate this carefully and get third-party advice, if you can. Some good third-party organizations include **The Bitcoin Way** or **The Bitcoin Adviser**. Bitcoin services companies provide consultation and advice but not custody services.

Other custody/consultants include **CASA** and **Swan Bitcoin**, which also offers extended white glove services and even IRA

Bitcoin services and succession planning. Another excellent Bitcoin services company is **Unchained Capital,** offering multi-signature services, Bitcoin loans, IRA Bitcoin services, and succession planning. I have no affiliation with any of these companies, nor do I receive compensation from them. This is just to give you an idea of where to go for help.

Exercise

- Start researching some possible wallets.
- Find at least four wallets in both categories: hot wallet and cold wallet. Go to each wallet's site and read their features and watch at least one review on YouTube.
- Compare the wallets with your requirements.
- Then select two wallets from each category.
- Install these wallets and back them up. Watch the online tutorials on YouTube. Write down the seed phrases and keep them safe.
- You will have to spend some money to purchase cold wallets. It's a piece of hardware with built-in customized software.
- Do not fall into the habit of just looking for something for free, especially when it comes to managing your money. This is exactly how you get hacked.
- Research and review two reputable Bitcoin exchanges that are acceptable to you. I recommend Bitcoin-only exchanges such as **River, Swan Bitcoin**, and **Strike**. They are safer and have a smaller attack surface. They understand and support Bitcoin technology.
- Buy a small amount of Bitcoin from the exchanges and transfer the Bitcoin to your wallets.
- Transfer the Bitcoin between the wallets and confirm that you can use all wallets.
- Make sure you can use all four of them.

- Reset or erase each wallet and recover the small amount of Bitcoin on it. This confirms your use of the wallet as well as your backup procedure.

Chapter 10

Can Baby Boomers Avoid the Next Crisis?

"Everyone has a plan, till they get punched in the mouth."

Mike Tyson

When Victor Hugo, the great author of many classics, sat down to write, he had a problem. He suffered from a serious case of writer's block, struggling with a great conflict from within. For long stretches, he couldn't produce anything he considered worthwhile. So, he developed an extreme solution to his extreme problem.

He would hire his servant to perform a certain ritual in the evening. They would prepare a stark empty room with nothing in it but a basic chair and table. No food, no bed, no comfortable furniture, or bedding. Just his writing materials, a desk, and a chair. Then he would have the servant lock him inside his room overnight. He would specifically instruct the servant not to open the door under any circumstances until Hugo had submitted 2,000 words under the door. This deliberate discomfort was specifically designed to trap Hugo in a self-imposed prison and force him to perform the tasks he so desperately wanted to finish. And the servant would be paid to assist him with this task.

The man who gave us *Les Misérables* and *The Hunchback of Notre-Dame* overcame internal resistance by designing a system that made success inevitable. We don't need to go to such extremes, but the principle stands. If we want to survive, even thrive, we must plan. With a framework of some sort of discipline.

167

We Boomers have lived in a time of incredible prosperity and convenience. But as we've covered, this is all going to change. We need to show discipline to make changes to our habits in order to get through the coming hard times. I cannot predict that we will have truly catastrophic times. But I can say, we need to be ready if they come. I don't believe the recommended changes to our habits will be onerous. You won't need to be locked in a room overnight. But it will take effort, determination, and persistence. As we go through these issues, I will continue to introduce the basics of Bitcoin so you can start to understand this important invention called Bitcoin.

Baby Boomers Grew Up With Social Security.
We have always had a safety net. Programs like Social Security, Medicare, unemployment insurance, pension systems, and even welfare systems have formed a societal safety net that underpins our sense of security. We may not necessarily use them. But they are there for millions of people to keep us from hitting rock bottom. They are a fundamental part of what makes us feel safe. But unfortunately, these systems are based on a broken fiat system that is completely bankrupt. I am not going over the details again, and there are numerous works written about this. But we all know that nothing lasts forever, and empires all crumble. The USA is not going to be any different. If that safety net disappears, what catches us? That question is why I wrote this book.

The answer, of course, is Bitcoin. But if all these other massive, powerful systems fail, how will Bitcoin still be safe? Well, I am not a financial advisor, and this is not financial advice. I will never profess to predict the future. But let's look at what Bitcoin is. We have learned that it is an immutable ledger. It can't be inflated. It can't be hacked. It can't be manipulated behind closed doors. It's infinitely more secure than our current system, and importantly, it will always be there, making it fundamentally different from the current system.

We have talked about how money always finds its highest and best use. And from now on, that will be Bitcoin. This is simply the way it is. As our financial system grows increasingly more fragile, its failures become larger and more systemic. Money will move out of the current system and into Bitcoin. People, especially the wealthy, will seek a safer place with fewer risks for their capital. They will, of course, try gold, silver, other commodities, and assets such as real estate.

Bitcoin will stand alone as the apex asset. This takes time, of course, but it's speeding up. And one day, the rush to the exits will be closed to regular people, as prices skyrocket and on-ramps become restricted. But right now, there is still time. So we Baby Boomers need to hurry up. Yes, we are still early, but this will go away one day. And on the other side of this is our age. We only have so much time to move a portion of our wealth into a safe haven like Bitcoin. These are unique problems that other generations don't have. So we need to get going.

Hugo Stinnes

Hugo Stinnes was a German industrialist and politician during the Weimar Republic in the 1920s, and he is called the "Inflation King." Why is this? Because during this time of crisis and panic, inflation went out of control, most people were either wiped out or completely impoverished. But not Hugo Stinnes.

Stinnes noticed something else was going on. While the money was being whipsawed up and down and finally into massive debasement, he saw that commodities were actually doing well. Why was this? Simple, money was worthless, and as it became more and more worthless, something was replacing it in value. That was commodities. And the more useless the money became through fits and starts and volatile up-and-down moves, commodities got better and better.

Any commodity would be preferable to fiat money. Even at the micro level, this was evident. People were so beaten down by the massive inflation that as soon as they got paid, they would run to the store and buy something, anything to unload the worthless currency before another grinding, gut-wrenching devaluation decimated their purchasing power once again. And as throughout history, money moves to its highest and best use. And in this case, the highest and best use was commodities and hard assets. Metals, gold, grains, cotton, livestock, coal mines, factories, etc.

Stinnes saw the trend early and moved aggressively into these assets, protecting and multiplying his wealth. He became hugely rich. While others were devastated, he turned inflation into an opportunity, exploiting this terrible government money-printing circus.

Refer to the chart below about the Weimar inflation. You'll see violent, massive upward sweeps in the price of gold, which was considered the most stable and trusted asset of the time. And it was. Compare it to the red line. What do you see? You see violent percentage moves in the gold price measured against the German mark.

Maybe this is because we are looking at this chart in two different ways. The black line shows the price of gold in German marks. The red line shows the price of German marks in gold. These are two totally different things.

There are two lessons to learn from this. First, you need volatility to make money. Large money gains are not made in a straight, smooth line. Second is that the increase in the supply of the German mark dumped into the system in fits and starts due to the incongruent and haphazard moves by panicky politicians. They thought they could repair the economy and its delicate balance by throttling it with injections of fiat currency.

The same thing has happened with Bitcoin. It is a consistent and smooth progression of Bitcoin being released into the system every 10 minutes when a new block is published. There are no haphazard massive injections and then throttling. Bitcoin is predictable, mathematical, honest, and consistent. On the other hand, we can never tell what the Federal Reserve is going to do. And they certainly don't tell us, or they shamelessly lie about it. Or even worse than that, they actually don't really understand the sheer complexity of the system they are fiddling around with.

It's not like there is some brilliant, complex genius or computer system that is making these decisions. It's simply not possible. So, it goes again and again, in fits and starts and stops like some drunken sailor weaving about in a smoky bar, crashing into tables and chairs and people, never quite sure what it will hit next.

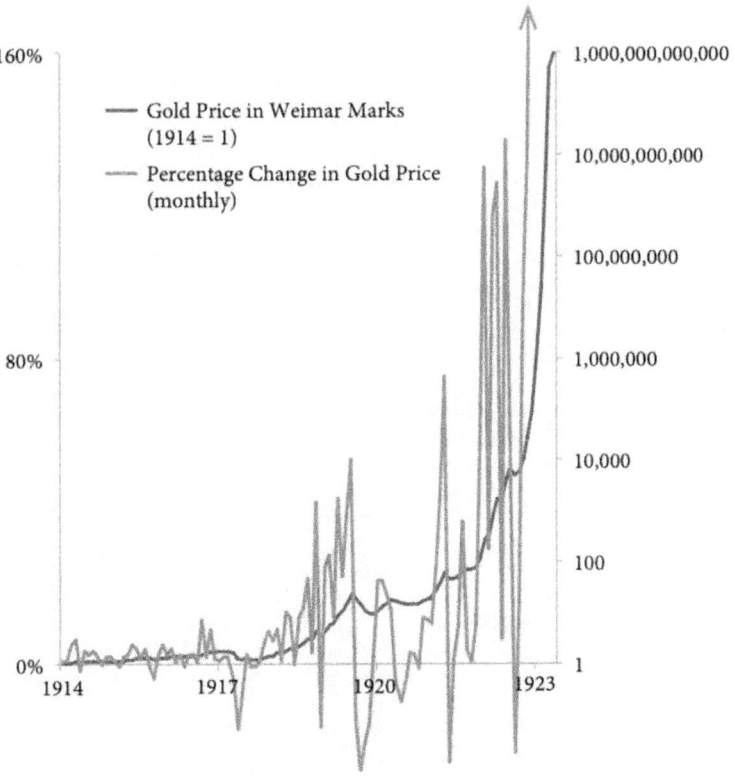

Fundamentals of Bitcoin as a Superior Asset.

The lesson here is that to protect ourselves, we must learn to recognize macroeconomic trends and act early. Bitcoin is the leading edge of this trend of debasement. It did not cause or even exacerbate the coming collapse, but it is our way out. It shows us the exit of this corrupt, chaotic system. Even the head of the European Central Bank (ECB) said the quiet part out loud: Bitcoin is the exit ramp.

Another basic lesson to learn is that economics matters, and Bitcoin follows real, unmanipulated economics. When an asset is immutable, it becomes essential in an economic crisis. Bitcoin is that asset. We are not Hugo Stinnes. We aren't going to buy a coal mine, or a granary, or gold bars and worry about storage. But we can buy Bitcoin easily, quickly, and safely. In any amount, large or small. Anytime we want, day or night, 7x24. We can also sell it anytime we want. We can trade it or send it to our friends and family. We can convert it into different currencies around the world. We don't have to ask permission from anyone. And it can be done in an emergency in a matter of seconds. Would Hugo Stinnes have used Bitcoin if it existed in Weimar Germany? Absolutely.

Bitcoin Is Highly Divisible

Bitcoin's flexibility is unmatched. At the time of writing, Bitcoin is worth around $105,000. But you don't need to buy a whole coin. Each Bitcoin is divisible into 100 million units, called Satoshi's, in honor of the inventor. A single Satoshi today is worth about .00105 Dollars, or 10 one-hundredths of one cent. For comparison, the US dollar is only divisible into 100 units. And a piece of real estate, or a coal mine, or a house, or a cow is not divisible. Even gold is not realistically divisible into units smaller than about a gram (which is over $100). I reiterate this to encourage you to think in this new way.

Other commodities have value, and many hold value well. But they are not usable as Bitcoin is. By solving the usability gap, Bitcoin bridges store of value, usability, and divisibility. This means you can buy very small micro amounts if you like, making it easy to do business with. You can use one Bitcoin to buy a car or 0.0001 Bitcoin to buy a cold beer or a sandwich.

Bitcoin Is Fungible

There is one other key feature that Bitcoin has that makes it valuable to all 8 billion people on Earth is the property of fungibility. This is the property that says Bitcoin is consistently interchangeable with other units of the same item. For instance, one Bitcoin equals one Bitcoin. Or, ten units of 0.1 Bitcoin can always be traded for one whole Bitcoin. Just as five units of twenty-dollar bills can be traded equally for one 100-dollar bill. Anywhere in the world.

Going back to Hugo Stinnes, if you have a coal mine, and you want to sell it for 1000 ounces of gold, you may be able to make the trade, or you may not. It will require expertise in multiple areas and many intermediaries. Lots of negotiation and haggling, and a considerable amount of security and lawyers on both sides. This makes it very difficult to scale.

However, if you are investing in and storing your Bitcoin in your own custody, you don't need any of this. And you get the properties of all these assets without having to be a rich oligarch. In fact, many of the owners of Bitcoin today are regular people like you and me. Sure, some are rich oligarchs, but most are not. Bitcoin is owned by 200 million people already, and is available to all 8 billion people on Earth. Meaning you can take this Bitcoin anywhere on Earth, and it will still be recognized and traded as Bitcoin. And this acceptance is growing rapidly every year.

Example Of A Crisis

Let's walk through a basic, fictitious example of economic crisis to show how Bitcoin can quietly deliver security, portability, and value, even in the midst of chaos.

173

Imagine a political crisis. The economy goes into free fall. The stock market crashes. GDP collapses. Price and wage controls are imminent. The country is plunging into a deep recession. You and people you know are losing their jobs. People are actually dying. Think of the Great Financial Crisis of 2008 times 10. This is a very likely possibility in the near future.

Did you know that with every 1% increase in unemployment, 40,000 Americans die? You can't pay your mortgage. You are having trouble generating income to buy basic items. Your house is losing value, and you don't know how you are going to pay your kids' college tuition. It's a very scary time.

You and your neighbor both lose your jobs. Countless people around you are losing their homes and can no longer afford tuition, groceries, and the things that made life normal just months before. Everyone is overwhelmed and panicked.

Your neighbor invested in several real estate properties, has a 401(k), and a stock portfolio he manages. You have a house, too, but instead of additional investment properties and a stock portfolio, two years ago you opened a Bitcoin exchange account. First, only a few thousand dollars' worth, then you began dollar cost averaging aggressively. You bought a hardware wallet, studied self-custody, and helped your family do the same. You joined a Bitcoin meetup group and went to monthly meetings with like-minded people. You read Bitcoin forums and asked educated questions. You took control of your life.

Then you set up an account with a reputable Bitcoin-only exchange to do DCA, or dollar cost averaging (automated, programmable). You added to your Bitcoin stack every week with more and more capital (store of value). So, as you invested more in Bitcoin and removed your hard-earned wealth from the government Ponzi scheme known as the US economy (a store of value), you were away from the government.

You were also learning about Bitcoin and became more proficient and confident. You joined a Bitcoin meetup group and went to monthly meetings with like-minded people. You read Bitcoin forums and asked educated questions. You took control of your life (freedom).

You were gaining the personal power of steering your financial future as you acquired an asset outside the system. This feeling is exciting and gives you a feeling of satisfaction. The feeling of sovereignty and freedom (portability, fungibility). The idea that you hold your future in your own hands (store of value). No one else. Sure, it will take work and learning. But it's worth it. You feel better and better every day. And on top of all of this, your Bitcoin stack is not only growing in size, but it's growing in value.

Over time, Bitcoin appreciates much faster than virtually every asset known (store of value). In fact, all other assets are going to zero compared to Bitcoin.

You don't check your Bitcoin stack every day. Because you know, over time, it will be safe, and it will go up (secure). Watching volatility is a stressful road. The economic crash hits. Your employer collapses like many others, and you have lost your job. Now you have bills to pay. What do you do? Well, you can be secure knowing that you have your Bitcoin to hold you and your family over and to pay your bills. You liquidate a small fraction of the Bitcoin to pay some bills and continue to save the rest (portability, fungibility).

You begin to notice that most of the time, you don't need to exchange the Bitcoin for worthless, debased dollars. People are happy to accept Bitcoin because they, too, see the benefits of it during an economic crisis. So, usually, you can securely pay them in Bitcoin. But you notice something else.

In times of economic crisis, just like during the Weimar German inflationary crisis, hard assets rapidly and massively increase in value (store of value). And so, the Bitcoin you had before is worth much, much more than it used to be. And it continues to go up in value because everyone else in the economy is leaving traditional investments in a flight to quality (secure).

They don't want to lose their money either. So, they are driving the limited supply of Bitcoin up higher and higher. This is a feeling of security and strength. This is what we are preparing for. And this is a general scenario of how to go about it from a 30,000-foot view. And you can still be involved in Bitcoin; we are still early.

Don't think a crisis can happen to you?

Remember The Savings And Loan Crisis? And How About The Great Financial Crisis Of 2008?

We've been here before. The Savings & Loan (S&L) crisis of the 1980s is an event that we Boomers remember well. This was a serious crisis, and many of us were probably directly affected by it. Perhaps we lost our homes, our jobs, or had our investments liquidated. In any case, it was bad. In fact, are there S&Ls anymore? Why? Because they were wiped out. And the industry was decimated and absorbed into the banking world.

The same happened with the Great Financial Crisis of 2008, except that it was larger and more impactful. Many more people lost their jobs. Many more homes were abandoned, and people were left on the street. And, worse, the next crisis will be bigger, still. Why is this?

Because the government, the Federal Reserve, the parties responsible for the savings and loan crisis, as well as the crisis of 2008, and the tech bubble of 2001, are causing the problem again. And when these entities ostensibly "fix" the problem, they actually don't fix the problem. They just paper it over with more government money. Money, they don't have, so what do they do? They print more debt for the American people to somehow pay off in the future, with no way to actually pay it off.

This has been referred to as kicking the can down the road. But the idea of kicking the can down the road is too generous a metaphor. Because this metaphorical can gets bigger and bigger, and if it were an accurate description, we would know that the can is so big it takes a massive bulldozer to just move the can down the road a little bit. Simply put: the next crisis will be deeper, more complex, and harder to rescue with trickery and government scams. Many believe we've never recovered from the last crisis. We are still living with the shocks.

Example Of Bitcoin Protection

We can predict that during our fictional economic crisis, the government and the Federal Reserve will rely on deeper and more invasive interventions. Let's look at some of the things they will most likely do to try to slyly trick their way out of it.

What have governments and central banks done in the past to avoid having to pay the piper for their profligate spending and debauchery? One of the things they like to do is to lie about it. Tell us the economy is better than it is. We talked about this already but expect to see much more of this. They will tell us everything is fine. No one is going to lose their job or their money in the bank. While in reality, that's exactly what we will see. Bitcoin exposes those lies.

- During a crisis, people run to safety. It's actually called "a flight to safety." As the economy worsens, you will hear this phrase more and more. Always remember that Bitcoin is the safest and most secure. They cannot lie about Bitcoin. Actually, they can lie. But everything about Bitcoin is out in the open, honest, and published. So, these lies only work for so long. Bitcoin has a publicly traded price that's continuously available 24 hours a day, 7 days a week (transparency). And it has a public triple-entry accounting ledger that faithfully gets updated every ten minutes, regardless of what is happening and what anyone says (immutability), giving anyone who is being lied to an honest and true accounting of what is happening on the

Bitcoin network. But if you are in the rest of the fiat economy, trying to figure out the truth, then it's almost impossible.

- As we enter a massive economic crisis, what happens to the economy? And what other machinations will the government try to avoid the crisis? They will tax more. So, if you have income or income from property, or income from annuities, your income will be taxed more and more. The more the government needs money, the more it will raise taxes. If you own Bitcoin, you own an immutable asset that is classified as property by the IRS. And it cannot be taxed. However, its proceeds, if sold for a gain, *can* be taxed.

- Another gambit that governments will try is to print more money. This is an inflationary activity that they engage in all of the time. And in an inflationary bubble, it will simply cause more of the same problem. The inflationary activity of printing money just keeps the problem growing and growing. But if you own Bitcoin, your Bitcoin is still worth the same. No one, including the government, can print more of it (hard asset). They have no way to crack the Bitcoin network to change the Bitcoin monetary policy or the Bitcoin algorithm (secure). So, your wealth stays secure or even increases in value during a crisis. Even if they are printing fiat money, they cannot print more of the valuable hard assets of Bitcoin. As a result, the value of Bitcoin will rise in relation to the fiat measuring stick.

- Another trick that governments can try is seizure. Governments throughout history have crumbled into chaos. And as they did, they tried to tax, then trick, and then eventually outright steal people's money. This is a common event. Just look at any empire, and you will see it. During Roman times, the government would take the gold and silver coins in circulation, and they would clip off the edges of them. Then, they would melt the metal down to get more desperately needed money for their next war or other corruption. Why do you think there are ridges on the edges of coins? It was an indicator of coin clipping. There were many tricks like this.

- In our case in the USA, we have the case of Executive Order 6102, issued in 1932 at the height of government policies that caused and perpetuated the Great Depression. President Franklin Roosevelt used the pretext of an economic crisis to confiscate the gold of law-abiding American citizens. Yes, he paid them a "fair price" according to his mandate for it, $26 per ounce of gold. If you didn't sell it, you were subject to 10 years in prison and the complete confiscation of your gold anyway. If you did "voluntarily" turn in your gold, you would get $26 of worthless paper. Then, after Roosevelt took everyone's gold, he proceeded to reprice gold at the actual fair market rate of $35 an ounce. Basically, stealing $9 per ounce from Americans and performing the first actual default of the US economy. The second default of the US economy was the Nixon Shock in 1971, which we talked about earlier. Turns out that $26 wasn't such a fair price for their gold.

Un-Confiscatable And Un-Censorable.
But with Bitcoin, they cannot confiscate your Bitcoin (secure). In fact, Bitcoin is pseudonymous, meaning it is private and is not readily apparent which individual owns which Bitcoin (safe), at least not without a lot of investigation. On top of this, Bitcoin is distributed and decentralized, meaning they cannot just go and pick up each share of Bitcoin even if they wanted to because it would be too hard.

There are currently about 200,000,000 separate Bitcoin wallets worldwide. Can you imagine finding, and then going to each wallet holder with a gang of government thugs and putting a gun to each person's head and forcing them to give up their keys? It's much easier to confiscate people's centralized bank accounts or centralized 401(k) accounts.

Bitcoin is decentralized in private wallets all around the world, not in one place, not stationary or vulnerable (portable). In the network security business, we have a name for centralized banks, centralized 401(k)s, and centralized brokerage accounts. We call it a honey pot. This is where the hackers and desperate government officials go to take a concentrated amount of wealth. Gold faces the same vulnerability. It requires special buildings, security systems, and armed guards to protect it. Bitcoin is easily protected by cryptography, and only the owner of the keys can access it.

Even if governments issue confiscation orders (as Roosevelt did with gold), they can't actually enforce them without your cooperation. China has banned Bitcoin 13 different times. Why did they have to ban it 13 times? Why not just one time? Because it didn't work. Just that simple. And this is from a country that has massive capital controls on its population. Remember the strength of Bitcoin's multi-layered security? It is a powerful deterrent to confiscation and interference. We will discuss this again soon.

How Do You Protect Your Bitcoin?

The "how" is relatively straightforward. Your actual Bitcoin does not sit in your pocket, or in your safe, or even in your Bitcoin wallet. It sits on the Bitcoin ledger. Just like your bank balance. If you go to an ATM now or to your bank teller, yes, you can pick up a few hundred dollars of paper or even a few thousand dollars before they start to ask you questions. But the real money in your bank, your brokerage account, your 401(k), or your ETF account, is in a bank ledger somewhere. Not in actual cash because most transactions today are electronic already.

Yes, banks have a little bit of cash on hand in the bank vault. But not much. An infinitesimally small amount. It's estimated at around 2%, but of course, this is a lie also. The total US money supply is around $300 trillion. At 2%, that would be $6 trillion. There is no way they have $6 trillion in paper circulating currency. The vast majority of money you have, use, and earn is just simple accounting entries. Debiting and crediting between different bank balances.

Bitcoin works the same way, except it cuts out the middleman entirely.

How To Get Bitcoin?

There are three primary ways to acquire Bitcoin: buy it, earn it, or mine it. But you have to offer some type of value to acquire it. This is called **proof of work,** which we will talk about later. But for now, understand that you cannot get Bitcoin without providing value. This proof of work makes Bitcoin real. It makes Bitcoin have value. It does not exist at the whim of some faceless politician.

The most common way that people acquire Bitcoin is to purchase it, usually from an exchange. A Bitcoin exchange is similar to an exchange where you buy stocks, ETFs, or other investments. You open an account. You link the account to your bank account so you can transfer fiat dollars into the exchange. Then you transfer the fiat dollars to your new account on your Bitcoin exchange. Then you select an amount of Bitcoin to purchase, just like you were buying a stock or bond. There are trading pairs, limit orders, market orders, and rolling quotations. It looks just like a normal stock trading or currency trading application.

When your account is opened on the Bitcoin exchange, they assign you a wallet address that is affiliated with their Bitcoin exchange, whether it's Swan Bitcoin, River, or Strike. This is your wallet on the exchange, but it is really just your account. It is not really a wallet. I do not consider it secure. Look at it like a temporary holding place for your Bitcoin after you buy it.

At the same time that you make this purchase, you should set up a Bitcoin wallet that belongs only to you. No one else has access to this personal wallet. As you may recall, there are two categories of wallets: a hot wallet, which is a wallet on your phone or computer. It's less secure. And a cold wallet. This is a hardware device that stays offline most of the time and does not connect to the internet. It's more secure. As soon as possible after you purchase Bitcoin on the exchange, you should transfer your Bitcoin to your personal wallet.

Recall that when you set up a Bitcoin wallet, it will generate the encrypted keys to your Bitcoin. And once you transfer your Bitcoin from your account on the Bitcoin exchange to this Bitcoin wallet, you are in complete 100% control of what happens to this Bitcoin. For example, it's the same as the difference between having $100 in your bank account and seeing it on the bank's app, versus actually withdrawing the $100 bill from your bank account and putting it in your leather wallet in your pocket. The latter is that you have actual ownership; the former is that the bank actually owns it.

No one anywhere on Earth can move your Bitcoin without access to this Bitcoin wallet (remember, your seed phrase is your keys, which is your wallet). So, you need to keep this wallet safe. This is the device or software that contains that powerful, military-grade encryption that we have been talking about. This encryption is what protects your Bitcoin forever. And when I say forever, I mean forever. There are many Bitcoin on the Bitcoin network where people have lost the keys to their wallets and have no way of recovering their Bitcoin. So be careful.

If you don't want people stealing your Bitcoin or the government confiscating your Bitcoin. If you want your Bitcoin to be secure for all time. This is how it's done. There are no do-overs. There is no customer service to call to recover your keys once they are lost and give you your Bitcoin back. It's strictly up to you for its safety. But you are now an adult protecting your family's wealth forever. This is the tradeoff. And we are going to help you with effective procedures and practices to keep it safe. We will help you to harden your Bitcoin holdings so it will be safer than the fragile fiat investment world.

Bitcoin Will Catch This On-Ramp. Will You Be On It Or Under It?

Christine Lagarde, head of the European Central Bank, once called Bitcoin "the escape hatch." Escape from what? From the fiat money system. Why do we need to escape? As we have talked about, it is obvious. But I like to see it in a more positive way. I like to see it as an on-ramp. An on-ramp to prosperity and safety.

Or imagine you are on a highway, and the highway is rickety and old. Full of potholes, failing bridges, and overpasses. Cliffside mountain curves are collapsing. At one time, it was strong and sleek and fast and efficient. But over the years, many tons of freight and many passengers have worn this road. Worse, the highway never gets any routine maintenance, and it's only repaired when there is a crash. And the crashes are getting bigger and bigger every time. More cars are piling up, and more people are dying. But the owners of the highway don't do anything about it. They just blame everyone else. Or make up excuses and lies.

Then someone comes along and builds a new superhighway parallel

Bitcoin Bit.
Did you know that Bitcoin is not just money, it is not just an investment, it isn't just a ledger, it's also a network. In fact, Bitcoin is the largest computer network in the world. There is no other network worldwide that even comes close. Not Google, not Facebook, not JP Morgan Chase or Visa. You can combine all of those networks and it would not even be close to the Bitcoin network. And it is growing every day. You can measure it anytime you like just look at the "hash rate" this is the number of calculations per second. Currently it is 599.2 exa-hashes per second. That is 599.2 quintillion hashes per second.

to the old one, capable of supporting 1000 times as many passengers and traffic, at 10 times the speed. It is safe and easy to ride on. It costs almost nothing to use. And you know that it's a better way to go. But the managers of the old highway constantly criticize and fearmonger about the new, sleek, fast, efficient, safe superhighway. Instead of fixing their own, they tell you how dangerous the new road is.

Every day, new on-ramps make things easy and simple to move over to it. But you're not sure. It's new. And while the new superhighway on-ramps are being built, the managers of the old highway are tearing them down. It is obvious they will continue to tear them down, making it more and more difficult to get on the new superhighway. Eventually, there may not be any on-ramps left.

What are you going to do? Are you going to wait until the inevitable happens? Either they will close all of the on-ramps blocking the exit, or the old highway will collapse completely, consuming you and your family in the process. Right now, the transition to the new system is fairly easy. But in the future, it may get more and more difficult to accomplish.

Once again, there is effort involved. And you must decide in which areas you will make the effort. You managed a career. You built a family. You've navigated real complexity — travel, finances, health scares, maybe even personal loss. You can do this, too.

The on-ramp is right in front of you.

Bitcoin Exercise.
- Try adding 1% or 5% or 10% Bitcoin to your portfolio on paper.
- Do a five-year or ten-year projection to see how this could affect your portfolio. This exercise is going to help you visualize what a small percentage of Bitcoin will do to your current investment portfolio (short-term visualization is not valuable; we are investors and savers, not traders).
- One spreadsheet calculator you can find online was developed by Michael Saylor. You can find it on GitHub at https://github.com/bitcoin-

model/bitcoin model/blob/main/Bitcoin24%20v1.0.xls m . (You will have to download the spreadsheet into Excel and follow the instructions.)

- Another valuable tool I recommend using is called the Nakamoto Portfolio. This tool allows you to visualize different percentages of Bitcoin inserted into your portfolio without having to do all of the calculations yourself. Be conservative at first. And see how your world can change. Here is the link: https://nakamotoportfolio.com/nakamoto/start.

- Finally, after seeing the advantages compared to other assets. Try simulating a crash. The results will be startling.

PART III: IMPLEMENTATION AND FUTURE PLANNING

In Part II, we saw that Bitcoin is more than just another investment. It's your solution. We learned how it works, why it's secure, and why it protects your savings better than anything else. Now it's time to act. In Part III, we'll walk through how to buy Bitcoin, secure it in your own custody, and use it with confidence. Every step you take here moves you further from the risks of the failing fiat system and closer to true financial sovereignty. The sooner you start, the more control you'll have over your future.

Chapter 11

Ten Rules For Ten Times The Benefit

"Short cuts make long delays."

J.R.R. Tolkien

There is this story about a young tech executive who got into Bitcoin early. He was smart, well-positioned, and already seeing serious gains. Excited by Bitcoin's potential, he was happy to share this wonderful new technology with others. So, he started to talk about it in social circles and on social media. Eventually, he started writing about his successes on Facebook and Twitter. And answering questions and telling anecdotes, and stories about his wealth and his clever moves. It was a considerable amount of money. You see, that's how we have learned to use social media in this day and age. Share everything with everyone, and even post it online.

Unfortunately, someone else was reading his social media posts, and they were very interested. It was a computer hacker. This hacker followed his posts and pieced together the details. He figured out what this young tech exec looked like, where he lived, what phone he used, and even his mobile carrier. He learned that his target kept a hot wallet on his phone. But the hacker didn't have access to the Bitcoin investor's phone. So, he followed the individual to his known locations, and once he was in physical contact with him, he was able to clone his phone and his phone number.

Once the hacker had this, he contacted the victim's phone company and claimed to be him. He told them that he had lost his phone and wanted to transfer his number to his new phone. Now the hacker had full access to the victim's phone. He was then able to do password recovery with the phone as verification and drain the victim's phone wallet of all of his Bitcoin.

How many security violations and mistakes can you spot in this story? What should he do differently? How can we learn from his mistakes and misfortune?

Learn As Much As You Can About Bitcoin.

If you intend to get involved in Bitcoin, and I sincerely believe you should, you will need to learn. And keep learning. There are more resources available today than ever before for the new Bitcoiner. A great place to start is *The Bitcoin Standard* by Saifedean Ammous. This is considered the best book on the fundamentals of Bitcoin, what it is, and what it will become. For video tutorials, the absolute best series is by Andreas Antonopoulos. He is masterful at explaining all the facets of Bitcoin, and he is fun to watch. His series on "Introduction to Bitcoin" and "Bitcoin for Beginners" is excellent. Robert Breedlove's interviews with Michael Saylor, a Fortune 500 CEO and prominent Bitcoiner, explore the subject of "What is Money." It's very good and goes into great depth. Also, any interview featuring Michael Saylor is worth your time. If you're looking for practical help, check out Ben Perrin, known as BTC Sessions. He gives very professional and comprehensive tutorials on how to set up a Bitcoin wallet and which wallet to use when. He also describes how to run your own Bitcoin node and many other subjects.

Here are a few suggestions as you travel down this Bitcoin path that many in this space call a rabbit hole (an ode to Alice in Wonderland and her never-ending journey). Don't get too caught up in the minutiae, unless you like minutiae. Don't get too technical, unless you like tech. And, don't spend hours studying financial charts and economic anomalies unless that's your thing. Because Bitcoin can let you go there. Try to get the basics, and then move forward. But

BITCOIN BIT: GOVERNMENTS AROUND THE WORLD USE A PARTICULARLY INSIDIOUS STRATEGY TO HURT THEIR POLITICAL ENEMIES. PARTICULARLY IN THE USA. THEY DE-BANK PEOPLE. SOMETIMES VERY WEALTHY PEOPLE. NO DUE PROCESS AND NO LAW IS FOLLOWED FOR THIS. THEY JUST PRESSURE THE BANK. AND YOUR BANK ACCOUNT GETS CLOSED. FORCING YOU TO FIND OTHER WAYS OF SAVING YOUR WEALTH. DO YOU KNOW WHAT DOESN'T DEPEND ON A BANK TO KEEP YOUR WEALTH? THAT'S RIGHT BITCOIN.

keep learning. This book is a learning tool. It is here to take your special needs, the needs of a Baby Boomer, and introduce you to the issues that are a challenge for Baby Boomers, and give you direction and ideas on how to remove yourself from the confusion. But the learning is all up to you. You will need to learn and keep learning.

Bitcoin is deep and wide. It will swallow the best technology gurus and academics and have them studying for years. That's not our purpose, here. Our purpose is to get our financial lives and our family's fortune in order as quickly and simply as possible. But in order to do this, we need to learn. And we need to continue learning while we keep our eye on the ball. What is the ball? What is our prize? We know what it is because we have already identified our goals. Now we just need to learn how to take those first steps.

Technology Is To Serve Us.

We hear a lot of scary things about Bitcoin and crypto. We also get a lot of fearmongering about technology in general. And since Bitcoin doesn't have an owner or a CEO or a board of directors or a marketing department, many of these lies go uncontested and take hold for a very long time. When that happens, it prevents people from gaining the benefits of Bitcoin and seeing their lives change for the better.

Hopefully, this book will help you understand that there is nothing to be afraid of if you take the time to learn about it. Technology is here to serve us all. Technology is the great equalizer. It does not cause prices to go up. In fact, technology follows a concept called "Moore's Law," which states that the number of transistors on a chip doubles approximately every two years without an increase in cost. This is what keeps technology improving while prices decrease. This results in deflation. Simply put, deflation is the consistent drop in prices. This is something we all should want. But why don't we see this? Because at the same time, the deflation is causing prices to drop, the government is moving in the other direction, inflating the currency. When you enter the Bitcoin economy, you will be able to benefit from these dropping prices. So don't be afraid of technology. It is your friend. And Bitcoin is an innovation of technology, the likes of which we have never seen.

It's Not Just About Money.

It's about survival and freedom. I don't want this to be all about esoteric subjects. But without a free and functioning monetary system, we will not survive as a wealthy and prosperous country. We will be just another dying empire. So yes, you are protecting your money, your economy that you depend on for so many of the products and services that you use every day. But you're also protecting your family's wealth. Your children's inheritance, their future, and your grandchildren. None of this is possible without a functioning and usable financial system.

Don't Talk About Your Bitcoin With Strangers. In that classic book and film, *Fight Club*, there is the line where the main character says, "The first rule of Fight Club is you don't talk about Fight Club. The second rule of Fight Club is you don't talk about Fight Club."
At first, this may seem limiting and frustrating, but it is a fundamental of any cybersecurity posture. The cornerstone of security is privacy. It has been said that Bitcoin is anonymous. It is not. It is pseudonymous. There is an important distinction, and you need to understand this. Bitcoin can be traced and observed via tools known as chain analysis as it is transferred across the Bitcoin network. And from this chain analysis, your IP address can be tied to your identity. However, it's not easy, and it takes considerable effort and technical skill.

On the other hand, if you remain quiet about your Bitcoin holdings to strangers and prying eyes on social media, you have a much better chance of staying anonymous and keeping your Bitcoin off anyone's radar who you don't want to know. Now, if you are discussing it with a trusted friend, you may want to mention you are looking into Bitcoin. Or with your family, who know your financial position, that is okay. But I wouldn't recommend talking about your Bitcoin holdings and your investment strategy at a cocktail party full of people. Treat it like you would your bank account. Don't share the details or even that you have this cash. Never tell people about your Bitcoin holdings. No specifics.

Hold On For Dear Life.

There is a phrase in the Bitcoin community called HODL. It stands for "hold on for dear life." And it is quite appropriate when you understand Bitcoin's volatility and how it can take you on quite a rollercoaster ride. Once you have lived through one full four-year cycle of Bitcoin, you will understand this well, and you will mature to the point of staying with your strategy. Bitcoin is volatile, and it takes fortitude and temperance to stick with it. It requires us to learn and maintain adult values.

The legendary investor and Bitcoin advocate, Paul Tudor Jones, noticed with amazement that during a major 70% drawdown in the Bitcoin price, most of the Bitcoin holders did not sell. They stuck with it or even bought more Bitcoin. This blew his mind. He euphemistically called these HODLers "psychopaths" because they never sell. Bitcoin is that good. It was a teaching moment for him and helped him focus his attention on Bitcoin.

Don't Trade Bitcoin.

Bitcoin is not for trading. It is for investing. It is for HODLing or DCAing (dollar cost averaging). But not for trading. If you are a trader, you are in the wrong place. The sheer billions of dollars that have been wiped out of traders' accounts, whether from short or long positions, is mind-boggling.

Bitcoin's radical moves in the short term are face-melting, eye-bleeding changes. It will wreck you again and again if you try trading it. They call it in the industry getting rugged. And the best traders who thought they could master Bitcoin's moves and trade it up or down have lost and suffered.

I used to run a Bitcoin meetup group, and it had some lively discussions. During one of Bitcoin's fantastic bull runs, when it was making huge gains and everyone was talking about it, in came the altcoin scammers and traders to join my group, trying to attach themselves to this wave, like remoras on a giant fish. One of the members of my group posted a message on the group chat offering to help people trade highly volatile altcoins and crypto, playing altcoins like a casino. All the members had to do was just follow him to another site, he beckoned. Not only did this gentleman have little knowledge about Bitcoin and money, but he knew even less about investing in the altcoins he was promoting. I keep the group open so they could debate and explore, and I let him talk. But I did challenge him. I mentioned how dangerous this was and showed him proof. I asked him how he was going to account for taxes as he moved in and out of these unheard-of altcoins. He said he trades through an outfit in Dubai. So apparently, he didn't understand US tax obligations either. And the danger of not reporting foreign-held gains to the IRS (please always report your tax obligations). Finally, his defense was that he needed to make money before he could then invest it in Bitcoin. He gave an example of investing $100 in altcoins and quickly growing it. This was a man who had four children and was in his fifties. His goal was to make a quick score and then exit, dragging others down with him. This strategy almost never works out. Ninety-five percent of these traders lose money. Please don't go this route.

We are investors and savers. We buy and hold. Let me ask you something: What do you gain by trading Bitcoin if you actually did successfully trade it? Bitcoin's annual gains are massive. Why risk your capital if you almost certainly lose? And by the off chance you get lucky and win, then you have fees and taxes to deal with. And every time you enter and exit an asset, you incur a taxable event, which means a new round of taxes and record keeping. Why not just hold it and watch your wealth grow? Sleep easy at night, feel the grass outside, and play with your kids or grandkids. If you want excitement, go to Las Vegas. You have better odds there than "**trading**" Bitcoin and altcoins.

Keep Bitcoin Close And Safe (custody).

We have talked about the importance of custody quite a bit. But it's one of our basic rules. You need to keep your Bitcoin safe and close. Do you have a list of trusted advisors? A group of reliable and safe family members? Or a small group of professional advisors who can help you implement your Bitcoin plan?

You will need to know who you trust. So, you know who not to trust. Don't get too elaborate. On the other hand, if you have multiple wallets where you keep your Bitcoin in cold storage, you want to do the opposite. Don't put them in one place. Separate them and compartmentalize them. Also, if it's not necessary, do not tell one trusted member of your team about the other members (Remember, compartmentalize). If someone has a need to know, tell them. If not, then don't. For example, if you store a wallet at a sister's house in another city, do you need to tell her that you stored another wallet with a friend in a different location? It may not be necessary. It protects you, your Bitcoin, and even your sister from exposure.

Get Help. (ETFs, Managed Custody, and Service Providers).

Now, at the same time that you are keeping things quiet, you might need to carefully get help at some point, depending on your level of knowledge and learning. But that is the only reason you are sharing any information about your Bitcoin with anyone else. If you don't need their help, be careful what you say and who you tell. And even when you do start to talk with professionals, experts, and service providers, do not tell them anything they don't need to know.

ETFs. Bitcoin ETFs (Exchange-Traded Funds) are like other ETFs except for one, simple distinction. The underlying asset held in Bitcoin ETFs makes them the highest-performing ETFs of all time. And they did this in the first few months of their release. Bitcoin ETFs are a viable option for gaining Bitcoin price exposure in your portfolio. It may be how you want to start. You can simply push a button and let the EFT provider maintain custody of your Bitcoin. But it is not the preferred way. While this is certainly not what I would recommend, it is an option. It may be your only option, depending on your ability to custody Bitcoin. If you have doubts about your ability to custody Bitcoin, this can be a reasonable consideration.

Managed Custody. Bringing in a third party to manage your custody is akin to leaving your Bitcoin in your account on an exchange. We will probably see this industry develop more in the near future. However, at this time, the main custodian for many of the ETF companies is Coinbase, a large exchange operator. And they have a terrible record of security and an even worse record for network downtime. I do not recommend this option for anyone at this time.

Still, it's better to place at least part of your portfolio into a managed Bitcoin account than to leave everything in the fiat system. I expect established financial entities like Schwab and Ameritrade to develop custodial products in the near future.

Having said that, your best option would probably be Fidelity. They are a large Bitcoin ETF player; they reside in the traditional financial world; and they custody their own Bitcoin. So, Fidelity is likely a logical approach, but I don't know enough about the company's services to recommend them. There has been special permission given to BNY Mellon to offer custody, and I expect to see more banks expanding their services to include Bitcoin custody in the future.

Service providers. We discussed service providers earlier, and I recommend you investigate this carefully. This is a real option for many Baby Boomers. There is going to be a certain segment of us who are either not inclined or not technical enough to do full self-custody. A service provider such as Casa, Unchained Capital, or The Bitcoin Adviser are good options, as is a planning service called Sound Advisory. You can also classify technology service providers such as The Bitcoin Way and The Bitcoin Adviser. I am not endorsing any of these organizations, nor am I sponsored by them. And as usual, I am not giving you personal financial or legal advice. I am simply giving you options on how to pursue this route.

Tax advisors. This one may be a challenge. Because not only do you need tax advice, you need tax advice from someone who knows Bitcoin and how it relates to US tax laws. I know that Swan Bitcoin and Unchained Capital have a Bitcoin IRA service, and they offer some type of "white glove" or concierge service with consulting. However, you will need to quiz them to see how much they know. And how much they can help you.

Uncle Jim. The "Uncle Jim" concept has been developed in the Bitcoin world as a workable alternative for some people and some families. This option is essentially a hybrid of the other options. Simply put, many families or even close friendship circles usually have a person who is more technically savvy than the rest of the group. This person is relied on for technical advice and assistance. Often, the assistance can be quite extensive and safe.

You may have or may even be an "Uncle Jim" in your family or clan. This can be a good option if you and other members of your group feel comfortable with it. If it is a possible option, you would need to decide how far you want to go with it. For instance, maybe you have a group of golfing buddies, and one of them is a good Uncle Jim. He may be an excellent resource to partner with to help you set up Bitcoin wallets, subscribe to Bitcoin exchange accounts, and work on security solutions for your phone and your computers. But he may not be the person with whom you share your financial details or share where you hide your seed phrase. Or even what your portfolio mix is.

Another type of Uncle Jim can be a family member with whom you have close ties, someone like a son, sister, or brother. In these cases, you may have accumulated more trust, which can make it easier to share personal financial and security information — perhaps even locations of certain wallets.

Your circle may come down to a small network of friends and family whom you trust to some extent. And maybe you've set up reciprocal agreements to hold one of each other's wallets in a personal multi-signature arrangement. For example, you each have a two-of-three multi-signature set-up. You hold two keys, and Uncle Jim holds one of yours in a safe place, while you hold one of his. The wallets are available on demand or to an authorized successor. This kind of arrangement can work out very well, and it greatly increases your security.

Self-Custody. Can You Do It?

The critical questions are: Can you do it? Even if you can do it, are you willing to do it? If you feel you can do it, how much responsibility should you take on? I am sixty-four, and I know others in my age group who handle this task on their own. It takes study and a bit of determination, but it certainly can be done. But I am in no means sitting here pretending to know if your situation allows you to take on this responsibility. I am merely suggesting that leaving the current responsibility up to others, as we do in our crumbling fiat system, is not a very wise choice, regardless of your skill level.

Trust Is Critical

Regardless of how you structure these arrangements, be it an Uncle Jim, a family member, or a reciprocal custody arrangement, this is the critical question you need to ask: Do you trust this organization or this person with your life savings? Or if it is partial custody or knowledge, do you trust this person or organization with partial access to your life savings? Would you hand them the keys to your life savings or one of the keys to your life savings?

Learn What Rich People Do With Their Assets.

What do rich people do? Well, for one thing, they have lots of help. Lawyers, accountants, tax advisors, personal investment desks, and many have their own "family office" to manage their money. You probably don't have this type of help. This is where service providers can come in handy. But you will need to do some research on your own. It is beyond the scope of this book to give you this instruction. But Bitcoin provides you with a critical piece of this puzzle. Bitcoin is an asset. Rich people stay rich and grow their wealth by putting their money into assets, not into investments or trades. They are saving their money in assets: real estate, gold, treasury assets, commodities, art. You now have two distinct advantages with Bitcoin that they don't.

First, Bitcoin is an easy asset to understand from an investment and savings point of view. You do not have to become an expert in real estate or real estate laws in your area. Or an art expert in how the vagaries of the art market work. You just invest in Bitcoin. This is simplicity. Your other advantage is that you will be saving in the most pristine and superior asset on the planet. So, while others are struggling with tenant law changes in real estate, or what's the latest vagaries of the wheat commodities market, you will be safe and secure in Bitcoin. This is a wonderful peace of mind.

Bitcoin Exercise.

- Select at least two, but not too many, service providers or managed custodians that match your criteria for management.
- Have your criteria spelled out. Remember the list we started in Chapter One? Our list of challenges? This will come in handy now.
- Use this book and other resources I've talked about to make your own list. Do they provide the level of service you are looking for? Are they offering you help right off the bat, or are they just trying to hit you with fees right away?
- Do they have a deep security offering in addition to their financial knowledge? Ask them a security question, such as: "How do you handle a client if his account gets hacked?" or "What would you do if a person calls and their identity cannot be verified?" or "If I need help configuring my router, what would you say?" "Or what wallets do you recommend and why?" or "Who is the service provider's Bitcoin custodian?"
- See what they say. Test them, challenge them. Do they take the time to talk? Do they explain things clearly to you? See who shows promise.

- Once you have these service providers selected, then you are ready to use one or both (for diversity and safety) when the time is right.
- Do a similar exercise with trusted individuals, family members, or friends. Figure out who you can trust. Discuss your Bitcoin ideas with them.
- Then rank them in order, from highest to lowest, based on competency and trust level.
- Quiz tax professionals, too. One thing that has worked for me is using lawyers and CPAs to find other lawyers and CPAs. I will hire one lawyer to give me advice on whom they recommend as a specialization for another lawyer. Also, use this first lawyer to draft questions and items to quiz the new expert. Use the other advisors on this bullet list to give you items to quiz the potential lawyers and CPAs about. I have hired many lawyers. Believe me, they are not the same. You really have to dig to find a good one. For instance, what is the lawyer's reputation within his own community? Will he talk to you without charging you a bunch of money? When he hasn't offered you anything? Is that the way to start a business relationship? Is there any value here? Is that someone you can trust? Important questions.

We now understand some rules to help us plan for a Bitcoin implementation in our own lives. Now let's start to work on some of the specifics. How do we get this ball rolling?

Chapter 12

Can I *Really* Do Bitcoin?

"Good decisions come from experience; experience comes from making bad decisions."

Mark Twain

When I first started in Bitcoin, it was a different time period. The world was still reeling from the aftershocks of the Great Financial Crisis of 2008. I was ensconced in my career in the world of technology and the internet as an engineer building intranets and the wider internet, as well as keeping up with security challenges. I could see what a lot of people could, but most would not admit it. There was something seriously wrong with our current, rigged economic paradigm.

I had tried my hand at multiple investments and was still not able to significantly get ahead. I heard about a so-called "expert" in crypto and Bitcoin. He professed to have the answers and would show me the way for a fee. I paid the price first in his fees, then in disappointment, and eventually in losses. I swallowed my losses in a variety of ways. They basically fell into three categories: fees, poor security hygiene, and chasing altcoins. But, if you follow the ideas in this book and others I have recommended, you can avoid many of the pitfalls that I and many others experienced. I am not saying you will never see losses, just that you can avoid these traps.

First, I paid plenty to this "expert" in fees. That's a loss I will never get back. He was right on a few things, but wrong on most, and intentionally misleading on others, all for the purpose of lining his own pockets.

The second loss was not following the technology and not practicing good security hygiene. This cost me early holdings in Bitcoin that I had acquired at a low price. I simply didn't know what I had and how important it was. I got sloppy and literally lost some Bitcoin.

The third set of losses was related to the first two, but basically, I was chasing after altcoins. Altcoins or crypto are what most people hear about or get tempted by soon after they get into Bitcoin. They hear about coins branded as "newer," "better," and "faster" than Bitcoin. I fell for it, too. Yes, Bitcoin was interesting, but altcoins or crypto just seemed better from my inexperienced point of view. I was going to beat the market. At least that is what I was told by relentless marketing.

A market that I didn't even understand yet. I paid, and I lost. And when I was done, I had learned my lesson. I never turned back. You will discover, as you meet many Bitcoiners, that many had a crypto phase early on. The smart ones, the honest ones, survived and learned from this phase. Others are still trapped in this endless hell of promises, half-truths, outright lies, manipulation, and self-deception. It becomes a gambler's kind of journey for many. They never learn.

I urge you not to go down this road. Learn from others' mistakes. Bitcoin is a different world today. The tools are better; the learning is more concise and productive. It is much easier than it used to be. Stick with your plan, and you will be leagues ahead of the others in the game.

When Your Vision Is Clear, The Decision Is Obvious.

If you just wake up one day and say, "Hey, these folks on the news keep talking about Bitcoin, and there are huge returns to be had. I think I am going to take some money and invest in Bitcoin." I would not recommend this. You will not be clear about what you want. And you will not be clear about how to get it. Your expectations are unknown or unrealistic at this point.

Simply making a plan will sharpen your clarity about what you want. It may tell you that you do not want to do certain functions recommended in this book. For that, you will need to alter your plan. For instance, you may determine that you just don't have the skill or desire to maintain multiple wallets on your own. It's just too much for you. This will, in turn, affect your overall decisions about how to move forward with Bitcoin. These types of choices will be revealed many times as you go through this planning process.

Start the planning process early, and keep planning. Write things down, take notes, make decisions. Reevaluate your decisions and plans frequently. Discuss with trusted advisors as you move forward. Hopefully, you have a spouse or maybe some adult children that you can discuss these plans with. On the technical side, maybe you can talk with other members of a Bitcoin meetup group, or you have identified an "Uncle Jim" in your family and friends circle that you can ask questions about technical issues. Even if you hire a Bitcoin advisor who will give you more knowledge and options to look at, use these resources and continue to refine your knowledge or change your plan, further growing your Bitcoin muscles. Never stop this process.

Set A Budget. Set An Allocation. As you become familiar with Bitcoin and gain your confidence, you will want to consider how much you want to spend. This will require you to start an exercise in budgeting. I want you to think about what you feel about Bitcoin. Think long and hard. Don't make this decision haphazardly. Give careful consideration to your overall budget. If you have been doing the exercises so far, then you will be more comfortable with this next step. This is your choice; however, I categorically do not recommend a large early allocation of Bitcoin. At least, certainly not at this stage of the game. Later, as you become better informed through experience and knowledge, you'll be in a better position to make that kind of move.

The first step is budgeting. Use your own budgeting standards, but some things to look at are current living expenses, current investment allocations, and what you have chosen as your short-term and long-term goals. This will give you an idea of what direction to go and how much to start with. For instance, do you have a typical 60/40 portfolio? If so, how is that working for you?

Be realistic. What is it really returning? Including fees? Do you have

BITCOIN BIT:

DID YOU KNOW BITCOIN MINING IS DONE ON EVERY CONTINENET AROUND THE WORLD? CURRENTLY 40% IS DONE IN THE USA. 17% IS DONE IN CHINA. AROUND 10% IN RUSSIA. AND AROUND 7% IN IRAN. THE REST IS DONE IN OTHER PARTS OF THE WORLD. THIS IS TRUE DECENTRALIZATION.

money tied up in a friend's investment idea, and it won't be available for a while? Are you committed to some real estate for the next 5 or 10 years? Be honest. It's okay if you have something that is losing money. The important thing is to be brutally honest with yourself. These are the kinds of issues that will inform your decisions.

Once you have an idea of a budget you want to start with, I still do not recommend a full allocation of your money into Bitcoin. Take your time. What's your allocation? Where do you want to be in one year, two years, five years? This is important. You want to know your progression to getting there. Bitcoin is volatile, so to treat it like an all-or-nothing investment is a mistake. It could ruin your peace of mind and your ability to make the most prudent decisions. Once you have decided on these variables, then it's time to work backwards into how you want to start.

Start Small.

The next step is to start small. Getting in a hurry is the path to making mistakes, particularly with Bitcoin, where you are still learning. So, give yourself ample runway, and then get your toe in the water. What do I mean by this? Let me give some examples.

You decide to get your first wallet. Don't buy and install several wallets right away. Just get one or two, and practice with them a bit.

When you decide to do business with a Bitcoin exchange, select one at first. When you start to locate physical storage locations for your Bitcoin wallets or seed words, don't go and tell twenty people. Start with one or two people and discuss your basic ideas with them discreetly. See if they are receptive and possibly willing to work with you.

When it's time to buy Bitcoin, don't buy a lot of Bitcoin. Maybe start with a $100 or $500 purchase. Remember, you can buy as large or as small as you want, but the beginning is not the time to buy large amounts.

Take notes. Rank the different products and services by your criteria to help you understand which is the better choice. Later, this will come in very handy when you need to make a large purchase. At that point, you will be glad you took these notes, as they will assist you in making very big decisions.

Start By Doing… But Carefully.

The best way to learn Bitcoin is by doing Bitcoin. But like the recommendation above, you need to start small. For instance, let's say you want to buy some Bitcoin. You decide to buy a whole Bitcoin at first. You don't even have a wallet yet. So, you spend the $115,000 plus on one Bitcoin and leave it on the Bitcoin exchange. You are not sure if the Bitcoin is yours. You lack confidence at first. You don't know the terminology well yet.

Then you read some report about Bitcoin taking a huge price loss because of some crazy news story. Next thing you know, there is an investigation of the exchange and you are not even sure if your Bitcoin is still yours. You try calling the exchange, but customer service does not get back to you. So, you email them, and a week later, there is a lame email about how everything is fine and there's no need to worry. This is a very, very scary thing to go through.

Let's look at a different progression. You decided on an allocation, and now you're ready to buy some Bitcoin. You buy a small amount, about $500. You have researched several Bitcoin exchanges and decided on one to try. You open an account and only transfer to the exchange the amount of money needed to buy the Bitcoin. You have set up a wallet for testing, and you have studied your new wallet. You have written down your seed phrase, deleted the wallet, reinstalled it, and recovered it. You have now verified that your seed phrase is working correctly before you put Bitcoin on it.

Every step of the way, you are feeling more comfortable and more at ease. You are learning, and when you come to something you don't understand, you research the issue or ask for help on a discussion board or in your Bitcoin meetup group. Now it's time to make the purchase. You make the buy on the exchange and notice it goes through quickly. You verify that the Bitcoin is in your exchange wallet (this is just your account on the exchange's ledger).

At this point, you immediately transfer a little bit, $50, to your personal wallet. You verify that the Bitcoin gets transferred; it takes about an hour, but it's done. You once again delete the wallet and reinstall it with the seed phrase, proving to yourself that you still have your Bitcoin after recovery. Then you transfer the rest of the Bitcoin off the exchange to your tested wallet.

Again, you read some news about Bitcoin with a huge price loss. You are concerned, of course, but you can see you still have the same amount of Bitcoin on your personal wallet. The exchange you are using is under investigation, but you don't have to worry because your Bitcoin is now stored safely in your own wallet. No need to call customer service or wait for lame emails from the exchange. You own Bitcoin, and this is not going to change. The price going down because of the bad news has no impact on your wallet. After about a week, you discover that the negative Bitcoin story in the news was false. They usually are. And the price simply rises back to where it was.

Every step of the way, you are learning more and more about Bitcoin and what you want to do with it. You are gaining confidence and competence. Did you like the exchange? Did they do what they said? How were their fees? How about their support? What about the wallet? Did it work out well for you? Or maybe you want to try a different wallet? Maybe you want to install a different wallet and transfer your Bitcoin to it. So, you practice this. And see how easy it is to make this change. No intermediaries involved. No need for permission to make the change. You are in complete control. Life is good.

Dollar Cost Averaging.

One of the most effective ways of saving in Bitcoin is to utilize a simple strategy of Dollar Cost Averaging (DCA). Basically, with this technique, you buy a specific amount of bitcoin at regular time intervals. Say, $100 every week, or $500 per month. This can be whatever amount or interval you choose. Whatever fits into your budget and into your plan. What many people do with their investments is they try to time the market based on different metrics. It could be based on news about the asset, or chart information, or personal information. Many of these ways are emotion-based and leave the investor worse off than they started. With Bitcoin, this problem is multiplied by the volatility and unpredictability of Bitcoin.

Bitcoin is not a good asset to try to time the market. It will leave you in shambles, financially, and should never be tried. A much better way is to take the emotion out of it completely. There is a tendency to follow the Bitcoin price action carefully, day by day or hour by hour, riding these changes like a wild ocean of emotionality. This is not recommended.

Decide your strategy and follow it with a plan that removes emotion from the process. Like the plan we are helping you build here. Dollar Cost Averaging helps you implement this plan. Bitcoin goes up, and you buy your normal allocation of Bitcoin. When the Bitcoin price goes down, you still do the same, not worried about the price swings. Think about it. Your house is a long-term investment. If you own it outright, are you going to sell it if the price suddenly drops, or buy another one if the price suddenly goes up? Or vice versa? No, you are committed for the long term. The same with Bitcoin. The difference is that when you enter it, you do it in a regimented, emotion-free method.

Bitcoin Not Crypto. Bitcoin Not ETFs.
As you investigate Bitcoin, something will become very apparent very quickly. And that is the phenomenon of "crypto" or "cryptocurrency." Strictly speaking, by definition, Bitcoin is a cryptocurrency. Bitcoin, however, is completely different from the other 100,000 cryptocurrencies that have been created by basically copying Bitcoin. Bitcoin was the original and the only one like it. Never think that any of the others are even close. They are not. They will claim similarity or superiority; this is false.

You will hear a lot of stories about bigger and better gains, more elaborate and fancier technologies. Don't fall for it. Zoom out and look at a chart of nearly every crypto over a longer period of time, more than two years. You will see a common pattern repeated time and again. Copycats go up in price early, then drop and never recover, eventually going to zero. The vast majority are outright scams. Some may be interesting and even have some nice or cute innovation; however, none of them are Bitcoin and cannot be Bitcoin. The goal of most of these cryptos is to get your Bitcoin, which tells you all you need to know. Their developers know where the value is.

This book is not about a debate on Bitcoin vs Crypto. This has been done in many other places. But understand, money is a technology that needs stability, security, and immutability. And it is simply not possible to get this anywhere else but Bitcoin. If you want to explore altcoins, I just can't help you. I had my crypto phase at the beginning, so I understand. But my experience is like most. I lost money. Luckily, I recognized the scam early enough and got out. I learned more about Bitcoin and moved on. I am happy I did.

Bitcoin ETFs are a little better. They are legitimate investments, but they don't give you the value and sovereignty of actually owning Bitcoin. They will give you exposure to Bitcoin's price, but they don't actually give you ownership. It is strictly a dollar-denominated vehicle. You use dollars to get into the ETF and dollars to get out, giving you all the exposure to the dangers of fiat currency without any of the protections of owning actual Bitcoin. Sure, you can lock in price appreciation with Bitcoin ETFs, and this may need to be an option in certain cases, but only if you cannot properly take custody of the real Bitcoin.

On top of this, many of the so-called experts in traditional finance know very little about Bitcoin. It is not in their wheelhouse, and they aren't really taking the time to learn. In fact, the most difficult people to educate on Bitcoin are financial people. They reflexively resist it. There was a recent interview with the head of the Goldman Sachs Wealth Management Unit. And she said in an interview for the whole world to see, "You can hold gold in your hand, but you can't hold Bitcoin." As if this showed gold as an advantage over Bitcoin.

This was an amazing display of ignorance. I can guarantee you this woman has never had a Bitcoin wallet, and she does not seem to be interested in ever changing that. Do you think she has ever held an S&P stock certificate in her hands? Has she ever held a US Treasury bill in her hands? Do you think her company is a legitimate advisor on the options of Bitcoin vs other investments? You'd think she might want to learn a bit about the fifth-largest asset in the world before she pontificates on it to the media?

Let me tell you who else can hold your gold in their hands, criminals and robbers. You know who else? Big banks and other scammers. And of course, the biggest entity that can hold your gold in its hands is the government. And if they can hold your gold, they can also hold your stocks, your dollars, and your real estate. The one asset they cannot get their hands on is your Bitcoin in your custody.

Not Just An Investment, It's A Savings Technology.

A lot of what we cover in this book is specific, hands-on, practical things. Other parts are more conceptual, ideas and concepts that require a deeper understanding. But there's a third category that's just as important: how you *think* about Bitcoin —your mindset and your attitude. And this is critical. It's more than, go get some Bitcoin, and here's how you do it. Or Bitcoin is great and here's why. Yes, those things are important, and it's all a part of it. But it's bigger than this. You also need to think about Bitcoin in the proper way; otherwise, you will have difficulty along the way.

For example, if you were going to buy a piece of real estate and your mindset was, *I am going to buy this real estate to create immediate cash flow*; that is a specific mindset. So, you research your real estate market, and you learn about deal-making and financing of properties. You understand the tax advantages, then you go buy a piece of unimproved property in a good section of town with imminent development.

You have made a mistake. Your mindset was for immediate cash flow. But you bought property that will probably increase in capital value in the next few years. But it is unlikely to generate cash flow for you. With expenses and taxes, it is actually going to be cash-flow negative from the start, and it will violate your intentions because your mindset was not clear. If you were clearer about your mindset or intentions, you would have selected an income-earning commercial property or rental properties.

It's the same with Bitcoin. We have talked a lot about the advantages of Bitcoin as a good investment. And it is. But where Bitcoin really shines is as a savings technology. And when you look at it this way, your understanding will become much clearer.

I will give you an example of this misconception playing out recently. Bitcoin has solidly proven itself to be a far superior investment than just about anything that I can think of. And the world and Wall Street are slowly starting to realize this. It has grown to a very large asset with a market capitalization of over $2 trillion in value. And as we have discussed, Bitcoin is volatile, with occasionally wide daily price swings. But still, people don't fully understand its properties.

Recently, there was an event in the world that was very war-like and concerned many people. It was on the weekend when markets were closed. However, Bitcoin trades 24/7. There is no closed market since Bitcoin is incredibly liquid and universally available. If you have Bitcoin, you can sell it anytime you like. This is a feature, not a bug. It's called superior liquidity. So, people affected by this event can buy Bitcoin, and they can sell Bitcoin at a moment's notice. They can move it anywhere in the world without needing permission. This would be impossible with most other assets.

There have been many investors who have entered the Bitcoin space with very little knowledge and understanding of what is going on with Bitcoin. Their mindset is not correct. How could it be? They have not studied it. A major event happens, and they are scared for whatever reason. They have only one asset out of their entire portfolio that is completely available to sell, and they rush out and panic-sell it, forcing the price to fall in the short term.

Smart investors, knowledgeable investors, immediately scoop up this lower-priced Bitcoin at a bargain. A day or so later, the weekend is over, and the market stabilizes. A week or two after this, the price bounces back up to where it was or even higher. This is looking at Bitcoin not as a savings technology, but as a liquid account to be dumped. These "inexperienced investors" almost always lose money on these trades. And they have a new tax bill to contend with. Research will show that the wallets that sold Bitcoin were those of short-term holders. In other words, people or entities who had been in Bitcoin for less than a year, many for less than a month.

Instead, the experienced investor, with a savings approach, is in a different place. He has done his research; he knows that investing in Bitcoin is a long-term prospect with many advantages over saving. He gives himself plenty of room for volatile price shifts, using a strategy he already has in place to stay on his path. So, when something crazy happens, he is confident in his current plan. Maybe if the price dips a lot, and he has a few extra dollars in cash, he buys a bit more.

This mindset, this shift in thinking about how Bitcoin should be treated, will give you many restful nights when other investors or traders will be panicking in some type of mania following Bitcoin price swings.

Make Informed Decisions.
As you start to get more experience with Bitcoin and practice the exercises, you will make more informed decisions. The exercise tools are designed to specifically compel you to become educated in a variety of ways. These informed decisions will, in turn, give you the confidence to make progressively bigger decisions.

This is why, throughout this book, I have urged you to practice and use small amounts of Bitcoin. Start by reading and watching videos before committing large amounts of your money. Interview different service providers before transferring money to them. This will put you in the position where you know what to do before you are fully committed.

Compare this to going to a financial advisor. How does this work?

Maybe you go to a seminar, or the financial advisor sends you some brochures that you may or may not read. He shows you some colorful, glossy investment "strategies" broken down into a few minor categories. Maybe you have a follow-up meeting or two, or a couple of hours of discussion. Then, the next step is to deposit tens or hundreds of thousands or even millions of dollars. Talk about taking a risk. But will an investment advisor take $150 from you and start making it work for you? Proving how effective he is? If you asked him to do this for you, he would laugh at you. But with Bitcoin, this is relatively easy to do. And a strategy that I recommend.

Levels Of Bitcoin Adoption.

Type of Investor	Allocation	Emotional State
Phase 1. Trader	Under 5%	Non-committal.
Phase 2. Short-term.	5 to 10%	Educated investor
Phase 3. Long-term.	10% to 15%	Study 100 hours
Phase 4. Saver.	20% plus.	200+hours,study,

Fail Early, And Don't Lose Alone.

The technology company I used to work for was not only a pioneer and a leader in technology; they were also an innovator and a leader in business. And some of the things they taught us were just plain common sense and discipline. But one of the most valuable things they taught us was "fail early, and don't lose alone."

They knew about failure, and they knew that it happens whether you want it to or not. So don't be afraid to challenge your own abilities and knowledge. Be able to take some risks, meaning there will inevitably be failure. This is the same with Bitcoin. You must learn and progress, and as you progress, you will make some mistakes. If you don't, it is doubtful you will learn anything or that you will ever gain any confidence.

As for "don't lose alone," it's about recognizing when you need help. The important thing is not to lose alone; otherwise, you haven't really brought all the necessary resources to bear on your loss. For instance, when you encounter a serious challenge, if you are determined to tough it out, and you don't ask for help or research an issue or maybe bring it up with a service provider or a Bitcoin meetup group, then you are just wasting time and creating frustration. Realize you need help. And get the right help at the right time.

Don't Use Leverage.

As we have talked about before, Bitcoin is volatile. Actually, it is highly volatile, and using leverage to buy and sell Bitcoin is a mistake. Just like the name says, leverage is a multiplier of your ability to buy and sell Bitcoin. With this multiplier, you multiply your risk of liquidation and loss of your own Bitcoin. Long or short, futures trading or Bitcoin spot market. Do not use leverage.

An example to help you understand how this happens: you are new to the Bitcoin market. You are impressed and excited about your newfound profits in Bitcoin. You may get greedy and decide to increase your gains. Let's lever this sucker up a bit. So, you go long with a leveraged position. Then, in the middle of the night, the price of Bitcoin rips violently down. Remember, Bitcoin trades 24x7, every day of the year. You are asleep. There is a notification on your phone. You immediately need to put in more capital, or your Bitcoin will be liquidated (meaning your collateral will be forfeited). Of course, you don't see this until the next morning, when it's too late. All your Bitcoin has been taken from your account to cover your levered position. And, as this is happening, countless other levered investors with even deeper, out-of-money positions are liquidated. I have seen hundreds of millions in levered contracts evaporate in a matter of hours. Please do not do this. We are not traders. We are not gamblers. We are savers. Don't turn a superior investment like Bitcoin into a high-risk gamble.

Develop Good Habits

To be successful with Bitcoin, it's important to develop good practices and habits. These are basic behaviors that will ensure you are able to apply all the necessary teachings we have been talking about.

- **Study Bitcoin**. Do I mean you need to start a new graduate degree program to study Bitcoin? No, I don't, unless, of course, you want to go that deep. But you should develop some good, consistent study habits to get through your first 100 hours and to continue ongoing study of Bitcoin as you evolve. There is no way to apply a competent level of Bitcoin knowledge without a certain degree of study. As usual, your mileage may vary depending on your level of interest and involvement in Bitcoin. You will not gain confidence with Bitcoin without a certain level of study.

- **Build a team**. We have talked about your need to seek help from other sources. Whether it is friends, family, a Bitcoin meetup group, or a hired advisory service, build a team around you. People you can trust. People with knowledge. Maybe for security, you compartmentalize these team members but use their knowledge to help you with your goals. For instance, you may want to interact heavily with your Bitcoin meetup group. That's great, but it doesn't mean they need to know your level of Bitcoin investments, what wallets you use, and your investment strategy. Actually, they don't need to know if you own any Bitcoin at all or that you have decided to include three family members in your Bitcoin team. Do they really need to know about what the others know?

- **Practice**. One of the things I've noticed in my own journey is that as soon as I learned a particular issue, I would tuck it away, store it, and forget about it, sometimes for a long time. This is a bad habit. A better habit is to continue to practice these newly learned activities on a regular basis. Not just read about them. But try them and verify balances and recovery procedures. Walk through succession plans with relatives. Show peers how to set up a wallet or use an exchange. This keeps you sharp and up to date. I can't tell you how often I change or adjust something because of this ongoing practice. You will, too.

- **Contemplate**. Spend time, at a strategic level, reviewing your plans, the knowledge you have, and make adjustments to where you are. Apply this knowledge, and see it in action. It's not enough to just read an article; you should think about how you want to include it in your plan. You have the time, so contemplate. Set up regular meetings with successors to discuss your ideas and keep them in the loop, if it helps you to visualize how you will make the handoff.

Plan Your Taxes Like You Plan Your Bitcoin.

It's important that you look at tax strategies for all investments. And with Bitcoin investments, it's no different. Like rich people and our desire to live like rich people, we need to know how to treat taxes like they do. Rich people understand this game. They are treated by the tax system completely differently from regular people. And they use that to their advantage.

There are almost two parallel tax systems in the United States. And if you are in one system, the traditional system, you will not do very well. Taxes will appear as your largest expense item. In the other system, taxes can be minimal at worst and sometimes not at all.

Luckily for us, Bitcoin lends itself to some very nice tax advantages if you pay careful attention and get some professional help. As usual, this is not tax or financial advice, and I am not a tax advisor or financial advisor. Please discuss with your trusted tax advisor or financial advisor. This is strictly information about some areas that you can research to help you keep your wealth.

First, understand the two systems. One system is for regular people. You do it yourself or get minimal help from the tax service down the street. You know, the guy standing in a funny suit on the street corner, offering to help you file your taxes for a couple of hundred dollars. Or you can be extremely careful and seek out professional advice that can cost four or even five figures to set up and prepare.

The Two Worlds

There are two tax systems in this country—and they are *very* different, serving two different communities.

The first will almost certainly leave money on the table for Uncle Sam to scoop up.

The first system is for wage earners. The second system is for owners of assets, businesses, and rich people. Even if we are not rich yet, we do anticipate impressive gains with our Bitcoin journey. And we need to be prepared when we get there. So, we need to understand these two very different categories.

A wage earner might make a good income of $300,000 per year or more, receive a paycheck with a W-2 form, own a big house, have a family, two nice cars, and lots of bills. This is the category that pays the most taxes, and it's brutal to think about. He is probably easily paying 40% to 50% or more of his income in taxes when it's all done — think income tax, FICA, Social Security, Medicare, state and local income taxes, and other things you can't even define.

Now, let's contrast this with the wealthy the second system. A rich person is different. He lives in a different world. He has a high net worth (assets!) but not necessarily a high income. And the **assets** are not necessarily taxed in the income tax system. If a rich person owns a $20 million office building, and rent on this building just covers his expenses, those expenses could include many things, such as cars for him and his family, trips, office space, lunches, dinners, hiring his kids and his wife and paying them a salary, as well as usual real estate expenses. When he is done tallying all these expenses, he has very little net profit left over. So, while he is a multi-millionaire and his family all have jobs, he is not realizing any income. Thus, he is paying very little income tax. I won't go into the details, but you can see how this would be advantageous compared to the wage earner.

Another example of how wealth can be structured involves the use of trusts. For instance, a wealthy individual might hold assets, including Bitcoin, within a trust. In some cases, this can offer protection from certain income taxes. Now, I cannot give you details on this. I am not a lawyer or a tax accountant or an expert in trusts. But it's important to recognize that trusts are legal vehicles designed to shield assets from certain claims or taxes, and to preserve them for the benefit of a designated beneficiary. Bitcoin can absolutely be held in a trust for tax planning, estate purposes, or other reasons. This is where advice from a qualified tax attorney or accountant is essential. Talk to one.

The point of this is: let's say it costs $10,000 in tax and legal advice to set up your protections. But in doing so, you save $8,000 per year in taxes. Over ten years, that's $80,000 saved, more than worth the initial investment and effort. Do not overlook this area. Bitcoin lends itself very well to some of these strategies.

Bitcoin Exercise. Practice The Basics.
- A big part of learning about Bitcoin and understanding it better is to use it. Use the tools and start practicing the basics. This will give you confidence and help you make better decisions.
- You have your Bitcoin wallets. Practice sending between your wallets, second round. Practice sending a little bit of Bitcoin to a friend or family member.
- Try sending bitcoin to someone and having them send it back to you.

- Use small amounts, so if you make a mistake, you don't lose a lot of money.
- Find a restaurant or store and buy something with Bitcoin. You can find them on this site **https://www.coinmap.org**.
- Delete a wallet with no Bitcoin on it. Then recover the wallet with your recovery or backup seed.
- Then delete the wallet with a little Bitcoin on it. Then recover that wallet with your recovery or backup seed, proving to yourself that you can always recover your Bitcoin if you take the proper precautions.
- Assist a family member or friend in installing a wallet. Teaching someone else helps you to learn better.
- Use a Lightning wallet to send a Lightning transaction. Good Lightning wallets to try are **Strike, Aqua,** and **Alby** (advanced exercise).
- Send from Lightning to Bitcoin and back again (advanced exercise).
- Convert some Bitcoin to Lightning. **Boltz** is a good tool for this (advanced exercise).
- **Bonus exercise**. Read or watch YouTube videos on how to install your own node. You may be surprised that it may be within your capability. (advanced exercise).

Now we have seen some practical ideas on how to make Bitcoin more of a reality in our own lives. And we are feeling like we have the confidence and the tools. Let's look at the next chapter on some things to be aware of.

Chapter 13

Beware Of The Shiny Object

"Wall Street's favorite scam is pretending that luck is skill."

Ronald Ross

During the late 19th century, America saw the rise of a wealthy class of industrialists, bankers, and speculators, often lumped together and derisively called "robber barons." Somewhat similar to today's oligarchs, most of them made their money via graft, inheritance, or rent-seeking, the economic term for leveraging powerful government connections for special government favors.

They are best described as Cantillionaires, discussed in an earlier chapter, as those reaping enormous rewards by positioning themselves close to the monetary spigot and benefiting from the Cantillon Effect. But some of these early entrepreneurs were actually building, producing things, and creating new industries, and on rare exception, they actually built new industries that we still benefit from today, such as steel, oil, electrification, and transportation. One of the most interesting was a man by the name of Jay Gould. Considered a wizard of Wall Street, he was a talented strategist. Long before the days of quants, programmatic trading systems, or special government favors allowing Wall Street traders to have an advantage over regular people, Gould played the markets with cunning and precision.

This was a time of mind-blowing changes in technology and commerce. It was referred to as the Gilded Age, and we have not seen anything like it since. Sure, we have cool technologies today, neat gadgets. But most of what we see today is just better versions of existing technologies. They are not fundamentally new technologies. Think about electrification. For centuries, people lived and toiled in subsistence conditions. Now, any type of device can be powered or lit, and light shines brightly in nearly every home.

It's hard to imagine a more monumental breakthrough in technology. People watched with fascination and excited curiosity. People also watched the machinations and competition among the robber barons. It was almost like some kind of sport for everyone to marvel at. And there were some entertaining grappling matches. Jay Gould did not disappoint.

Gould brought a different approach that amazed his contemporaries. He was also an innovator and consolidator in the railroad industry, which at that time was a patchwork of diverse ownership and quality. A handful of honest and effective railroad operators existed, but the majority were corrupt, rent-seeking operators who got government concessions and just milked their routes, while angling for cheap land grants. Despite deep public demand, route safety and efficiency were not a priority. Along comes Gould, and he starts to consolidate these different railroad ventures into a more unified system run with efficiency and safety. Naturally, this didn't sit well with the entrenched players. In region after region, local rail barons fought tooth and nail to keep Gould out of their territory. But Gould persevered and eventually built the Union Pacific railway system, controlling 10,000 miles of track.

At one point, Gould famously entered into a war with another oligarch, Cornelius Vanderbilt, who owned the New York Central. The two were competing for a lucrative route running to upstate New York, carrying a large number of beef cattle to this populous region of the country. Using typical competitive techniques, they both eventually slashed the rates on transporting cattle on this route. The war raged on for some time. Vanderbilt vowed to ruin Gould, as both kept slashing prices to below their own operating costs. Eventually, the prices got so low that Vanderbilt cut his prices to just $1 per head of cattle to transport on his New York Central line.

 Certain that this would finally do in Jay Gould, as he could see the massive amount of cattle freight increasing on his New York Central rail line, Vanderbilt could feel victory in his grasp. The amount of freight on Gould's line dropped to a trickle. Then all of a sudden, Vanderbilt received news that stunned him to the core. Gould had been quietly purchasing all the cattle at the railhead in Chicago at steep discounts because transportation prices were so low, driven down by Vanderbilt. And Gould was now transporting the cattle on Vanderbilt's own line, profiting handsomely because of the discounted $1 per head Vanderbilt was offering. Vanderbilt was apoplectic. And he was beaten. Beaten at his own dirty little game. It was a simple strategy but ingeniously clever and outside the grasp of most business people.

Nothing has changed in the investment and banking industry since the Gilded Age. If you think you are going to beat these guys at their own game with some new technique, then I suggest you do some more study about what you are up against. We, as regular investors, have never had an edge before, but we do now. We have talked about an edge outside the system that allows us to front-run Wall Street. Bitcoin is simple and direct. No special fancy maneuvers or tricks. The time is still ripe for your ability to exploit that edge. But it won't last for much longer.

Bitcoin Keeps It Simple.
Please keep it simple. Don't try to complicate things. How much time and money do you have to study, learn, strategize, and hire people to help you? Sure, I recommend some strategy and hired help, but only in a limited, specific area where you can see definite, measurable results. Seeking help must be specifically defined, investigated carefully, and designed to help you acquire and save with Bitcoin. How long can you keep it up, trying to compete against Wall Street and professional traders? How much can you do, or how much do you want to do? If by some huge stretch of your imagination you do get a win or two under your belt, how long

will you be able to keep it up before there is an inevitable loss? If you do get that win, then how will you protect those winnings? Where will you put it?

These are questions that you must consider carefully. Fortunately, these are issues you do not have to deal with if you follow some basic rules with Bitcoin. As I've noted several times, this is not investing advice. And I am not an investment advisor. Nor is this legal advice, and I am not offering any legal advice. But I am recommending you do learn and study for yourself in a focused and goal-oriented way. Studying traditional investment strategies, books, and techniques is an unlimited endeavor that will completely consume you. Is this what you want for your retirement? Is this how you want to spend your time? Even if you say yes, and you do want to go this route, I still recommend considering putting a small amount of your portfolio into Bitcoin anyway. Use the Nakamoto Portfolio tool or Michael Saylor's Excel calculator, which I highlighted earlier, for this planning. I think you will come to the conclusion that it is the only successful winning strategy available to normal people.

Learning and implementing the ideas and strategies in this book will require some effort. I am not denying this. Ownership and sovereignty certainly require your attention. But the good news is, the effort is limited and time-bound. I recommend starting with a minimum of 100 hours of study. Begin with this book, then move on to the other resources I have shared. Use that time to absorb and start implementing the ideas of this book that you think are right for you.

These ideas do not come only from me. They are the culmination of experiences and hard-won lessons over several years with thousands of hours of study and dedication. Once you put in those first 100 hours and start to implement these ideas, I firmly believe you will see the value. At that point, I believe you will be ready to move into a second and more advanced phase of Bitcoin learning. And I would then recommend another 100 hours of study and practice. But if you choose a different investment direction, even after 200 hours, you will be nowhere near the study and mastery required to get through that investment path. If you choose another path, you will always be behind and trying to play catch-up.

Remember The Two And Twenty?

Remember in a previous chapter when we talked about the financial services industry and how they fleece you with their fees? This is a very real thing. To understand this, let's go over a very real scenario. Financial services run a very effective confidence game with the average consumer. It looks like this. They tell you that you cannot just invest in a good product, such as Apple, Google, or some other super-equity investment. "It's not safe. It's scary," they explain. You don't have the appropriate knowledge. This scam is FUD (fear, uncertainty, and doubt). It's a common sales tactic designed to funnel you into their own products. FUD is a fear-based tactic that doesn't require the salesman to prove anything. He just has to get you worrying about the alternative. Then you will turn to him for a solution.

What the advisor is not telling you is that the S&P 500 Index's performance is overwhelmingly driven by just a handful of stocks. Nearly all its gains come from an average of only seven of the top stocks. The other 493 make virtually nothing! It's so well known that it has a name in the community. But I doubt most consumers know this name. Wall Street calls them the "Magnificent Seven" — Apple, Microsoft, Amazon, NVIDIA, Meta, Tesla, and Alphabet. So, it is relatively easy to just choose one or two of these or all seven. But then, why do you need a financial advisor? For the Two and Twenty, of course. For his commission and fees.

What does this look like in practice? You invest $100,000, and you actually make a 10% return on it. You must pay the "expert" 2% of your total investment, that's $2,000, and then you must pay them 20% of your gain. That's another $2,000. So, what has just happened here? You were supposed to make $10,000 on your $100,000 investment, but instead, you made $6,000. Wow, that doesn't seem like such a good deal. You have literally given up 40%

of your gain. Not a very good deal. Even if you wanted to go this way, investing in a good stock like Microsoft or NVIDIA, you could have done that yourself instead of getting beaten up with these fees.

Bitcoin, on the other hand, is a buy-and-hold strategy, with no percentage of your wealth evaporating in maintenance fees (2%) or huge fees (20%) on the gain. You buy it, and you take custody of it. Sure, you may pay a little bit to a consultant, or even an annual fee to a multi-signature custodian, but they are actually providing a service. The fees in that case are minimal and not based on a percentage of the principal.

What would the same $100,000 investment in Bitcoin look like using a simple buy-and-hold strategy? The total fees for a $100,000 investment in Bitcoin might be a few hundred dollars for the wallet and about $25 in transaction fees. If held in multi-signature, you could expect another $200 per year. A fair price for iron-clad security.

Now, let's assume the gain is 10%—just to make an apples-to-apples comparison. This is a big assumption, since Bitcoin has far greater gains than typical fiat investments. But we are just comparing fees. On $10,000 gain, you would have approximately $225 in fees the first year, 2.2% of your gain or 0.22% of your principal. In the second year, you would not have to pay a purchase fee on the exchange, only the $200 fee for multi-signature. Now, your second year in fees would be 2% of your gain or 0.2% of your principal. This is a huge difference. No comparison: 40% vs 2.2% or .2%.

That's only looking at the fees. It is not even looking at the realistic gains you can receive in Bitcoin over the long term. And if you have been following along with the exercises, I have given you, you will have seen there is no comparison. For example, use the Nakamoto Portfolio investment tool and compare Bitcoin's performance to the S&P 500 or whatever your favorite investment has been. You

223

will get some more practice, and you will be shocked at how much more your portfolio will be worth with Bitcoin exposure.

Allocation Control

Careful how much you allocate to Bitcoin. We talked about starting small, and this applies in an ongoing manner. Not that you should always continue small, but you should be aware of your allocation percentage and how it fits into your plan. We talked about dollar cost averaging into Bitcoin if you have a steady income. But how much to allocate? This is something you have to decide for yourself, using help from trusted advisors and your own research. However, I do not recommend going too deeply into Bitcoin or too quickly. What is too deep? And what is too quick? These are decisions for you and your family. I will give you some of the tools to help make this decision, but you are the ultimate decision-maker.

There is a good chance that when you start to experience the mind-blowing benefits of Bitcoin, you will feel excitement and elation as you see your wealth growing rapidly. It's possible you've never experienced gains like this. The next natural thought is, well, if I invest more, I will gain more. I urge caution in this phase of your acceptance of Bitcoin. Step carefully. It's okay to alter your plan, but make it incremental. Are you a Boomer with a steady income? If so, how much of your income do you get from employment or business sources vs your investments?

Are you on a fixed income? If so, how is your living situation? Keep all of these things in mind. Make sure you have other assets available, and it's not all in Bitcoin. Use a three-layer model (we will discuss in a later chapter), which is a system balancing short-term, medium-term, and long-term investment strategies, just like you did with your wallets. All people should have a certain amount in cash, another amount in liquid investments you're willing to convert to cash relatively quickly, and a third category not to be touched for a long time. What are these amounts? Only you can decide this.

For example, let's say you have a lot of money allocated into Bitcoin, and we are in a bear market. You have learned by now that

Bitcoin experiences very deep drawdowns at times. This is part of volatility, and volatility is okay (and expected) in an asset that is trending up. But since it's a long-term savings technology, this is not necessarily an immediate problem. Jack Mallers of Strike said, "Volatility is life. Nothing happens without volatility. Imagine going into a high-rise building, and you need to get to the top floor. How are you going to get up there without volatility? You will never leave the first-floor lobby."

Consider These Scenarios:

- One day, your family faces a medical catastrophe, and you need $50,000 cash within the next 30 days. What would you do? If you don't have liquid cash reserves, you may have to sell some Bitcoin, perhaps at a loss, to raise the cash. This is not something you want to do. If done at the wrong time, it could wipe out your Bitcoin gains. So, plan carefully. Have a cushion of liquidity in some other short-term vehicle, such as a money market or an ETF.

- Another example is the volatility of Bitcoin. You allocate a large amount of your life's savings to Bitcoin, and you are loving the returns you are receiving. But what happens when there are volatility events? Are you going to sleep ok at night when the Bitcoin price is down 30%, 40%, or more? If you have invested 5% or 10% or 15% or your life's savings in Bitcoin, it may not be so bad. But what if you have invested 90% of your assets in Bitcoin? How are you going to sleep at night? Because drawdowns like this can and will most likely happen. Remember, volatility is life, and Bitcoin is busy bringing life to our dying financial system. Does this mean you are losing 30% or 40% of your money? Not if you don't sell it. It always goes back up over time. But if the volatility is too much for you, you may find yourself not sleeping at night and selling at the worst time. Allocation control is critical. Follow your plan. Keep the emotion out of it. Easier said than done.

To ETF Or Not To ETF?

The issue of a Bitcoin ETF is going to come up again and again, so it's worth considering this option carefully. It's a tempting one. A Bitcoin ETF gives you price exposure to Bitcoin, the most pristine savings asset in the world. But don't mistake that for true ownership. In reality, you hold an IOU for the asset being held in custody by a third party of the ETF company.

The advantages of a Bitcoin ETF are its ease of purchase, its support from a large company, and its regulation by the US government. I would add one other hidden benefit. Since the large Cantillionaires are involved in Bitcoin ETFs, it creates a bit of political cover if other political interests try to overregulate or stop Bitcoin adoption. The Cantillionaires will help protect it. Guys like Larry Fink and mega-corporations like Fidelity or Goldman Sachs have a lot of power in Washington, DC.

Despite the convenience of an ETF, the disadvantages are real and considerable. So much so that if you can own Bitcoin for yourself, you should. Once you own your Bitcoin, you are not required to pay anyone any fees to hold the asset for you, maybe a tiny ongoing fee for multi-signature service, but it is not a requirement to hold the asset. Remember what the original J.P. Morgan said years ago? "Gold [Bitcoin] is money. Everything else is a credit."

- **Trust.** As big and powerful and convenient as these ETF companies are, there is also the issue of trust. How much do you trust them? If you think they are trustworthy, that's okay. But you might take a look at how often these companies violate the law. And what recourse do you have if something is lost or stolen? Remember, the government is not there to protect you. It is there to protect them. And when push comes to shove, you see this time and again. Were you bailed out during the Great Financial Crisis? Or were the big banks on Wall Street bailed out? Did you receive huge bonuses after the 2008 GFC was contained? I never received mine. But the big Wall Street banks did.

- **Fees.** So, do you want to pay ongoing fees for an IOU when you can actually own the asset yourself? Plus, once you own it, no one can take it away from you.

- **Portability.** How about portability and immutability? We now know that you can take Bitcoin with you anywhere in the world with relative ease. Can you take your Bitcoin ETF with you anywhere in the world? Is it usable when you take it with you? You may say yes. But maybe, no? What if there are sanctions on the country where you want to take it? Which countries will be subject to sanctions in the future? How do you know? How could you know when some country loses favor with a politician in the USA? And this seems to happen a lot. What control do you have over this process? Remember, we are trying to preserve our wealth for decades and generations. Not for the next few years. This is how rich people think.

- **Risk.** You may think these big companies are risk-free, but are you familiar with the concept of counterparty risk? That's the risk that the other party in a transaction fails to deliver, or worse, takes your money and disappears. Who are the counterparties of BlackRock's Bitcoin ETF? Well, there is Blackrock. But Blackrock does not actually hold the Bitcoin asset; it relies on a custodian, in this case an exchange custodian called Coinbase. Coinbase has suffered many successful hacks. They have always recovered the client's money. But still, the counterparty risk is there. Are there other players in there? Other intermediaries? Banks and financial institutions that are responsible for transferring funds? What happens when one of these counterparties loses something? When analyzing risk, consider points of failure. You must be prepared in times of crisis.

Only you can decide if a Bitcoin ETF is right for you. You will have to come up with your own decision-making process. But I recommend that if you are on the fence about this issue, learn more about Bitcoin. Try to see how far you can get. You may be surprised. Maybe you even buy a bit of a Bitcoin ETF just to get some exposure. Even if you determine that you do not want to own Bitcoin itself, talk to some of the Bitcoin advisors or custodians previously mentioned. You will be surprised by how much these professionals know about Bitcoin, and how easy they can make the process for you. If none of this works, you always have the option

Bitcoin Bit.

Did you know that the Bitcoin network can handle a peak number of 684,000 transactions per day. We are told this is not a lot of transactions because the Visa network handles 707 million transactions per day. This is much larger however Visa is a payment processing network and not a final settlement network. In fact, it can take days for merchants to get paid on Visa and months to settle the transactions between banking entities. Because it must go through multiple banks and then through Fedwire. And the Fedwire network handles 800,000 transactions per day but can take days or even weeks to finalize transactions, sometimes involving multiple telephone calls and verifications and repeated attempts. Whereas in the Bitcoin network you get final settlement and the money is transmitted and received in minutes usually or sometimes hours if urgency is not needed.

of buying into the Bitcoin ETF. It's still going to be there as a last resort.

It's Very Easy To Recognize A Scam Altcoin.

At some point, you're going to be pitched the idea of "crypto" or "altcoins." Their marketing is fierce and determined. They are looking for your money, more importantly, they want your Bitcoin. They know if they can get your Bitcoin, they will be very, very rich. Take EOS, a popular altcoin, a few years ago, for example. Its team made many promises and claims. It was going to make customers rich. Of course, none of this happened, and it went the way of almost all altcoins. It had a huge mania phase at the beginning, and people bought into it, trading their money and a lot of their Bitcoin for it.

Predictably, it peaked then descended to almost nothing. Its price peaked years ago at over $20 per token, then it dropped like a rock and has been riding the bottom at under a dollar for years. This is typical. Just look at the charts of these tokens over the years.

The pattern is unmistakable. So, EOS never developed anything, and the only people who got rich were the scammers who started it. But they do have something that keeps them afloat — a lot of Bitcoin. You see, they were collecting investors' Bitcoin, telling them that EOS was better than Bitcoin. So now they have 164,000 Bitcoin from poor unsuspecting suckers. The current value of this massive stash of Bitcoin is worth about $11,480,000,000. If EOS is so great, why are they holding all of this Bitcoin? They seem to be short EOS and long Bitcoin. Don't fall for these tricks. You will be sorry.

How about Dogecoin, the altcoin that Elon Musk talked about on *Saturday Night Live*? The hype around his appearance made the price spike to $0.70 per coin. That's the highest in its 9-year history. Now it rides the bottom at around $0.17. Or Shiba Inu coin? It spiked to $0.00008 per coin. Then has settled on $0.000028 for years now. Or maybe a big one like Cardano, pushed by crypto venture capitalists. It peaked at $3 and then fell to $0.45, despite regular network failure and no meaningful development. Somehow, they convince people to continue to buy and hold it.

What Are The Ways To Recognize An Altcoin Scam?

- **"It's like Bitcoin, but better."** This is called an affinity scam or a bait-and-switch. They know you have heard of Bitcoin, and they play off this name recognition to attract you. Then, with fancy words and slick marketing, they tell you how theirs is better. It's very common to see scammers post a Bitcoin logo on their YouTube video thumbnails. Then, when you click on the video and start to watch it, they shill all kinds of scam altcoins and not Bitcoin.
- **They offer free tokens or "airdrops."** Free giveaways are bait. "Airdrops" are basically just an incentive to buy their new scam altcoin. Or they have some way of sending you more of their scam altcoin to get your friends into it. If they are offering to pay you directly or to send you Bitcoin, then maybe they are serious and not a scam. But this will never happen. Why? Because what they really want is *your* Bitcoin.
- **They ask for your Bitcoin.** If they ask you to send Bitcoin, stake it, lock it, or deposit it in their system for any reason— walk away. This is for sure a scam. They know your Bitcoin is very, very valuable, and they want to get it from you any way they can. And once you send it, you will never get it back. Remember not your keys, not your Bitcoin.
- **They promise "yield."** This one fools a lot of people. "Earn interest on your Bitcoin." "Get 8%, 10%, even 20% yield." Sounds great until it collapses. There is an adage in social media: "If it's free, then you are the product." The same with yield: "If you cannot figure out where the yield is coming from, then you are the yield." This is a typical Ponzi scheme. What did they produce to give you yield? If you cannot figure out what they produced to give you a yield, then you have just been scammed. I know these offers are tempting, but don't be swayed. It's not a good

feeling to be involved in the next FTX, Celsius, or another scam.

Not Your Keys, Not Your Bitcoin.

Let this be your mantra: "**Not your keys, not your coins.**" Repeat it. Imprint it. Live by it. This simple phrase may be the single most important rule for protecting your Bitcoin.

In the world of security, effective practices matter more than any device or app. And the most essential practice is protecting your private keys, the 12 or 24 words known as your *seed phrase* or *backup phrase*. If someone else has access to those words, *they* control your Bitcoin, not you.

Let's Look At Some Common Traps:

- **Leaving Bitcoin on an Exchange.** If you buy Bitcoin on a Bitcoin exchange and leave the Bitcoin on the exchange because it's "safely" in your account, is this your Bitcoin? **No!** These are not your keys. The exchange holds the keys in their Bitcoin wallet, which means it's theirs. Until you transfer Bitcoin from that account to your own personal wallet where you hold the keys, it is not your Bitcoin. I don't care who they are or how honest they seem to be. They have your Bitcoin. You should immediately remove your Bitcoin from these exchanges and transfer it to your wallet as quickly as it can be done safely.
- **Giving Your Seed Phrase to Someone You Trust.** If you write down your seed phrase and give it to your business partner or lawyer to hold for you, is this Bitcoin exclusively yours? **No!** It is now shared Bitcoin. Not your keys, not your coins. Think of this as if you had a $1 million bar of gold. Who would you give it to for safekeeping?
- **Storing Your Seed Phrase Electronically.** If you install your new wallet, copy the seed phrase down, and then email it to yourself, snap a photo, store it on your phone or laptop, or print it out. Is this your Bitcoin? **No**, it is available for any hacker who has broken into your phone

or laptop. Not your keys, not your coins. And most computers and phones have been compromised already.

- **Printer Hacks.** If you print out your keys on your printer and then delete the file from your computer so no one can see your seed phrase, is this your Bitcoin? **No.** Any hacker can scrape information from deleted files or even information saved on the printer itself. Never use any electronic device to record your seed phrase. Not a printer, not a scanner, not a camera. Never store your seed phrase digitally. Ever. Not your keys, not your coins.

- **"Customer Support" Requests Your Seed Phrase.** You may or may not be having problems with some type of Bitcoin software or a Bitcoin wallet. You are contacted by customer service to fix the problem. They ask you for your seed phrase so they can troubleshoot your problem. You give them the seed phrase because he is a trusted expert. But you are worried that you could potentially lose your Bitcoin. Is this your Bitcoin? **No.** It is the customer service agent's Bitcoin now. Stop talking to them immediately, the moment they ask for your seed phrase. And then change your passwords. Technical support agents should never ask for your seed phrase; if they do, stop all communication with them. Not your keys, not your coins.

- **Trusted Setup Services Ask for Your Keys.** You have hired a "trusted" company to help set up your Bitcoin wallets and security plan. They ask you for your seed phrase to help you back up your Bitcoin. Is this your Bitcoin? **No.** Also, you have not hired a trusted company. You hired a scammer and thief. A trusted security-oriented company will never ask for your seed phrase or passwords. They don't need it to do their work. I don't care what they say. And the more they try to convince you of this, the more dishonest they are. Not your keys, not your coins.

- **You Suspect Your Keys Are Compromised.** Act fast! If you think someone has received a copy of your seed phrase or has your Bitcoin keys in any way, stop everything you are doing. Do not contact that person. Immediately move all of your Bitcoin to a safe wallet, one that has not been compromised. Then destroy the wallet that has been compromised. Don't try to reset it or install a new seed phrase. Get rid of it. It's not worth the risk. Don't try to outsmart a hacker over a $150 Bitcoin wallet. Separate your valuable Bitcoin from this person at all costs.

Some Bitcoin Tax Ideas (Consult A Pro!)

As you start building your Bitcoin investment strategy, you also need to consider how to handle taxes. Here are a few ideas to explore. But *always* consult a tax advisor or attorney before taking action.

Be a Borrower, Not an Earner. Wealthy families have used this strategy for generations. Instead of selling valuable, appreciating assets (which triggers taxes), they borrow against them. They never sell the assets, even if the asset has income, because the income goes into a trust. And grows the trust in value year after year, for decades. Such as a family that owns a wealthy mine, or an oil property, or a valuable piece of real estate, and others. So how do they get the income from this?

They borrow money from the trust, and this money is now a loan obligation that they must pay back. This is not considered income to the IRS. And because of this, it is not taxable. So how do they pay off this borrowed money if they don't have any income? They use an additional loan from the trust to pay off the previous loan. How is this possible?

Will they run out of money eventually? Yes, that is possible. But if it's a valuable asset like prime real estate in a major city, or an oil well, or Bitcoin, these assets appreciate constantly over time. This means the percentage of the asset being borrowed in every subsequent borrowing round is shrinking smaller and smaller. It's a brilliant strategy and has been used for centuries. Not something the average wage earner is going to know about or know how to implement.

Set Up a CRUT. Capital gains taxes can take a serious bite out of your wealth, especially if you're holding highly appreciated assets like Bitcoin. That's why it's essential to explore structures that can help you reduce or eliminate these taxes—while also generating income. One such vehicle is called a CRUT, a Charitable Remainder Unitrust. It's a well-established, perfectly legal strategy that's been used for decades by families looking to reduce tax liability and protect assets. **Important:** Do **not** try to set up a CRUT on your own. You'll need an experienced estate or tax attorney who understands charitable structures and the complexities of Bitcoin. Also note that this is not something your neighborhood tax preparer is equipped to handle, either. So, seek true experts.

Here's how it works: You donate your Bitcoin to the CRUT. In return, you receive:

- **A partial tax deduction,**
- **Lifetime income** from the trust (based on a fixed percentage of its annual value), and
- The satisfaction of knowing that whatever remains in the trust when you pass away will go to a charitable organization of your choice.

You can continue to invest and reinvest the trust assets without triggering capital gains taxes, and the entire trust is **asset-protected,** meaning creditors can't touch it.

The Roth Reworked. Do you have significant funds sitting in an IRA or 401(k)? How many folks reading this book have six or seven figures sitting in an IRA and don't know what to do with it? Consider rolling it into a self-directed Roth IRA that allows for Bitcoin investments. Once inside the Roth, your Bitcoin can grow **tax-free**. There are custodians and services that specialize in managing the complicated conversion to Bitcoin IRAs. This is a highly effective way to allocate retirement funds toward long-term Bitcoin exposure. But again, seek professional guidance.

Bitcoin Exercise: Your Wills And Trusts.

This is a fairly straightforward exercise, but you would be surprised by how many people have never done this or have not kept their estate documents updated.

- Make sure you have a will, a trust, and any associated succession documents drafted and up to date. These should be completed by a trusted legal professional licensed in your state or jurisdiction. I am not a lawyer, and this is not legal advice, but these operating documents must be in place and include your Bitcoin assets as a line item in your estate plan. Presently, the IRS classifies Bitcoin as property, not a currency, so make certain your attorney knows how to properly include it in your will and trust. You should review these documents annually.

- If you are using any Bitcoin custody services or multi-signature services, make sure that they have the proper legal documentation to hand over your Bitcoin keys or custody to your appointed successor. This is similar to the succession setup at a traditional bank or brokerage firm.

- Investigate different tax strategies and how they fit into your Bitcoin investment plan. This means talking to high-quality lawyers and accountants. Do not skimp on price or the vetting process.

- Start researching IRAs. I recommend a website called www.directedira.com.

- For instance, in the USA, a bank or an investor custodian like Fidelity or Schwab has a specific form you fill out documenting your successor or beneficiary in case you die. Same with your bank or credit union. Usually, this just requires a personal visit and a signature, but sometimes it can be done exclusively online. Check with each and get this done.

- Once you have done these steps, be sure you review this with your successors as soon as possible to make sure they understand these steps.

The shiny objects will keep coming. The new schemes, "better than Bitcoin" pitches, and clever Wall Street traps are endless. Ignore them. The game is still rigged.

Your edge is Bitcoin. Keep it simple. Stay disciplined. Protect it.

The real story is about the financial shift Bitcoin offers. The future of Bitcoin will be the future you live in.

Chapter 14

The Future of Bitcoin is Your Future

"The revolution is always impossible until it happens."

Leon Trotsky

In New York City during the 19th century, the primary mode of transportation for moving freight and people throughout the city was via horses and horse-drawn wagons and carts. Unfortunately, NYC had a scaling problem, and it was quite serious. These horses each deposited about 22 pounds of manure per day every day, and no one was there to clean it up from the stone streets and gutters. Horses did not live forever, and when a horse died, many horse owners would just leave the horse in the street to rot, not having the strength, money, or inclination to move a 1500-pound dead animal. This created a traffic and health problem that was unsustainable.

At the peak, there were around 200,000 horses in New York City, leaving hundreds of thousands of tons of putrid waste everywhere. If you notice pictures from this time, you will see everyone wearing long boots. There was an obvious reason for this. In some places, the dung would pile up to almost knee height. This was not just a few piles of horse poo here and there; this was a massive problem. When it rained, it created a slurry of soaking wet mud-like filth that was nauseating.

When it was dry, the manure would turn to light fibrous dust and fly through the air for people to breathe this pestilence into their lungs, constantly attacking their immune system. Remember this is 19th-century New York City, where it gets very hot in the summer, and no one could close their windows and turn on the air conditioner. AC did not exist then. There was no escape, no refuge from this oppression. Then came the diseases of cholera and typhus, causing massive epidemics and infant mortality, especially among the poor. There was a thriving business of thousands of laborers who would shovel and remove manure from street crossings or from in front of your shop. They'd even cart off a dead horse that was clogging your street and filling your life with the miserable stench. It was disgusting, and it was dangerous to public health, making our current public health concerns pale by comparison.

Now this description sounds frightening, I know. But just imagine this for a moment: fast forward to a modern American home, and you have to take your dog for a walk. You are admonished to clean up after your little poodle when walking on a public street. Why? Because over the millennia of our evolution, we have been designed to associate this issue with the danger of disease and sickness, and even death.

Imagine how overwhelming and oppressive this environment would be to you? How would this environment attack your sense of calm and safety, knowing that you are literally right there in the middle of this imminent danger? What would you do? How would you deal with this problem? You would do anything you could to solve it. And rich people did just that. During the summer months, they left the city if they could. Or at least sent their families to live outside the city in places like upstate New York, Long Island, or the Hamptons to flee the filth and danger.

Ultimately, city leaders found a solution, and it was the modern New York City "underground" sewer system. This solution would greatly mitigate this problem, making the streets clean and pleasant and modern, as well as preventing disease and death. But it was blocked for years by the manure removal workers, their companies, and their labor unions. This protectionist behavior is called "rent-seeking."

The workers didn't want to lose their business or jobs cleaning the streets. And the rent-seeking went on for years, as those fearful of losing control fought for votes using graft and bribes. Eventually, as the disease and suffering became too much, the city finally relented and started building the new sewer system. So today, we have the modern New York City sewer system that we take for granted.

Two decades after the sewer system began to improve the city landscape, a second innovation in technology came into being, and that was the automobile. I think that most people would be surprised to know that the car was actually a solution to pollution, not a cause of it at the time. If you want to experience real pollution, take a walk in a city with 200,000 horses in its confines. The sewer system cleaned up the pollution, and the automobile removed its cause. By 1915, almost all horse traffic had been removed from the streets of New York - about 30 years later than it could have been because of the rent-seeking and corruption at the time. Almost no one at the time would have recognized these ideas as revolutionary as they were. Only someone like Henry Ford truly understood what was about to happen. The same is with Bitcoin today.

An Idea Ahead Of Its Time.

Every major technological innovation is opposed by someone, usually an incumbent business or a business competitor supported by their willing cronies in the government. They use their power to corrupt the natural progress of technology to easily and efficiently find solutions to problems. This is what humans have done throughout history; it's unfortunate but common.

The oil industry successfully fought the clean, safe, and efficient energy production of nuclear energy for many decades, terrifying people into thinking there was going to be some kind of nuclear disaster. Today, nuclear remains the safest, cleanest, and best source of energy available. Steamship ferry companies used to fight railroads from building bridges across their waterways, forcing trains to stop, unload, and use the ferry to get across a river. Phone monopolies fought the construction of the internet. I could go on and on. But new technologies are just solving problems, and those problems have value to someone. When there is enough value, people pay for it. Or they put their money into it like Bitcoin. It may take some time to recognize its value. It may be disparaged by incumbent competitors such as Jamie Dimon, CEO of JPMorgan Chase, who needs to keep charging exorbitant fees while offering almost no value. Eventually, people will get it. But while the amazing innovation of Bitcoin is blocked, people will continue to suffer. The large banking institutions blocking Bitcoin are no different from the manure disposal workers in New York City years ago, blocking progress to maintain their own privilege.

Bitcoin is that idea that is ahead of its time, for our time. It is an idea so big and beautiful that it's very difficult for most people to understand. We cannot imagine that something this wonderful could be available to us. This idea solves the problem that we as Baby Boomers need to solve: the problem of losing control of our financial future. This is what we need to focus on. And focus like a laser beam. Because if we don't, our investments and our life savings will go the way of the horse-drawn wagon. And one day, people will forget about us and the ridiculous hoops we jumped through by the current predatory financial system. They will take for granted that we had to ask permission to send our own money electronically anywhere in the world. That if someone needed to send money to someone, they had to wait a week or more, even when an email took seconds. They will laugh at us.

Finance Is A Progression.

The history of finance is like the history of anything else. It must be seen as a progression, and it must be seen through the eyes of the contemporaries at that time. You cannot look at the congested streets of modern New York City, with all of its gas-guzzling cars and trucks spewing noxious gases, and say this is awful. Whoever thought this was a good idea? You must see where we came from.

Go back to 1870 New York City. It was a modern marvel, a progression of what came before it. A place that integrated dozens of languages and ethnicities into one massive modern center of commerce and finance. Where people came from all parts of the world, with only pennies in their pockets or maybe nothing at all. Under all these influences, the city grew into success in a short time. This was never heard of before in Europe or Asia.

A guy from impoverished Italy could come to New York from Sicily as a small boy infested with Small Pox and not only not speak the language, but also rarely speak at all. And in a few years, he could have a thriving business and a growing, happy family. This story is told beautifully in Mario Puzo's book and Francis Ford Coppola's masterpiece movie, *The Godfather Part II*. The cinematography and the richness of this story set against the backdrop of historical accuracy in Sicily and America is a real joy. Set aside the character Vito Corleone's turn toward crime, this story is told millions of times in New York, as immigrants entered and assimilated into the new world. Into a life that their ancestors could not dream of.

This is just part of the natural progression. New York didn't stay locked in its original design. Over time, it eventually became a city of laws and regulations beyond its configuration and modernization. It built great bridges and infrastructure, like the Brooklyn Bridge. It overhauled its health and wellness systems. Then came the era of the skyscrapers, and this shot New York forward again. All of these progressions could not have been imagined, but they came true because of the unique juxtaposition of New York in history, and its conditions allowed people to flourish there. You could step into any of these eras, and you will find criticisms about the way they solved problems, but they were solving them from the context of their own unique time in history, not ours.

The same is true of Bitcoin. It is impossible to understand how important Bitcoin is to our future without being able to clearly see it. It's ahead of its time, and we can't predict its exact evolution. We have to look beyond our current perspective of how things have always been.

We have a current electronic payment system that works very well compared to the rest of the world. We can go down and open a bank account. If we don't like that bank, we can go to another bank. Even today, in many countries, you cannot even walk into the bank, let alone open a bank account. Our paychecks get deposited faithfully and easily into our bank accounts. We use our ATM cards and credit cards without a second thought. So, it's sometimes difficult to see the future and how much better it can be. It's certainly hard to see what we are missing. But there is so much more to be done. These systems were built bit by bit over time, by men. And they are being dismantled bit by bit by our power institutions. And this is exactly why Bitcoin will replace it.

Why Don't They Get It?

If you happen to talk to a financial advisor, or an RIA, or even Wall Street insiders or bankers about Bitcoin, you will quickly notice something interesting.

1. You get the look, like their brain has just been shut off.
2. They aren't really well-informed about Bitcoin.
3. They see Bitcoin as a threat. They usually spout FUD and other ill-informed criticisms that make no sense.

Why is this? The reason is simple. They don't make any money from Bitcoin. And their primary incentive is to make money through the system that they are already a part of. They are committed to this system, and they are incentivized by this system. Bitcoin does not bring them anything they think they want.

In reality, though, it brings them all of the things they purport to want. But they just don't see it yet. They will. But like the deregulation of the telecommunications world, and its subsequent fall from primacy with the advent of the internet, they are not going to get it until they have to. And they make too much money right now on their two and twenty from you. So, they will ride this horse until they cannot ride it anymore.

They have invested a lot in learning about their current technologies and systems. They are not going to leave all of this behind just for a new idea. They will eventually, when they have to, but they will be late.

The Future Is Bright. Join Us. The Water Is Fine.

As we move into a Bitcoin future, it gets brighter and brighter every day. Companies are now starting to add Bitcoin to their treasuries to maintain a stable protection of their cash balances. Young people, who cannot even conceive of buying a house now because of exorbitant real estate prices way above their utility value, are saving in Bitcoin so they can have a future. Many are learning about strategies to get paid in Bitcoin, bypassing the usurious and oppressive fiat system that robs them at every turn. China, which previously banned Bitcoin and Bitcoin mining, is realizing that it made a big mistake and is now changing its tune slowly and quietly. China is now the second-largest government Bitcoin holder in the world. There are several firms in Hong Kong that offer their own Bitcoin ETFs to support their massive financial markets. The demand is simply too large to resist.

Around the world, real people use Bitcoin every day to survive, to protect their savings, and to send money across borders without middlemen or government interference. In countries plagued by corruption, currency collapse, or financial exclusion, Bitcoin offers a fair playing field. Let's take a closer look at how Bitcoin is quietly transforming lives, from the unbanked in Nigeria to anyone seeking portability, privacy, and financial control.

- **Helping the unbanked**. People in third-world countries are using Bitcoin to protect their wealth and to transfer money peer-to-peer without government interference. Here is an example from Alex Gladstein of the Human Rights Foundation. Alex travels the world and meets

243

people who are victims of brutal human rights violations and oppression. He gives the example of Nigeria. A big part of income in Nigeria is remittances from foreign countries with a stable currency. The Nigerian Naira is terribly debased and losing value all of the time. It gets reset lower every year or two. There are two rates of exchange in Nigeria, the official rate, which is about 1000 Nigerian naira to one USD, and the unofficial rate, which is about double that, around 2000 NGD to USD. If someone sends 100 US dollars to someone in Nigeria through a service like Western Union, the Western Union branch is going to follow the official exchange rate, and the person is going to receive about 100,000 Naira. And then he will pay steep fees to Western Union out of that, possibly up to 30% of the amount. This leaves the recipient about $35 ($50 minus the 30% fee of $15). The same person could send the 100 US dollars' worth of Bitcoin and receive 200,000 Nira, with minimal fees as low as a few cents to a few dollars. So, with Bitcoin, the recipient would receive a full $100 minus a few dollars in fees. What do you think that $65 means to that poor Nigerian? It means a whole lot. The difference between feeding his kids and sending them to school.

- **Transferability**. As you can see, the transfer would be massively valuable for the user. It could mean the difference between one month's income and three months' income. And it will only take a few minutes. They do not have to go to another city and stand in line at a Western Union office. And then the recipient can walk out of his house and find a money changer anywhere and get spendable cash for his Bitcoin, or he can keep it in Bitcoin as savings indefinitely, and protect himself from the next impending currency devaluation. The choice is simple and is being done millions of times every day on every continent already.

- **Beneficial for everyone.** Every day, more and more of these stories are being told, and you can be a part of this new world too. Protection of your assets, massive reduction in usurious fees from financial institutions, privacy, peace of mind, safety, portability, and instant settlement of your transactions.

- **Portability**. Imagine that you live in a safe and prosperous Western country. Not a big stretch. But what if something happens to your financial system? What are you going to do? How are you going to move your wealth to a new and safer location? If it's real estate, forget it. You can't take land with you. If it's stocks, and you need to liquidate during a time of panic, this will cost you a big part of your wealth. Then, if capital controls are implemented, what will you do? You may not be able to move your money at all. If it's Bitcoin, you don't have to move it. You already have it. It's a bearer asset. You may not think this scenario is a real possibility. Maybe not, or maybe so. The question is, do you want to gamble on it? Or do you want to be prepared? How do rich people look at these things? They are prepared. They have an edge. They stay informed. They can and do pass on all of their wealth to their family for generations to come.

- **Accessibility**. There are currently over 100 million known active Bitcoin wallets. This number is growing every day. The growth rate is expected to be around 16% per year. There are around 35,000 Bitcoin ATMs worldwide, a growth of 4800% since counting started in 2013. There are approximately 500,000 Bitcoin transactions processed every day. The market capitalization of Bitcoin is $2.4 trillion, making it the 5th largest asset in the world, right above Amazon. And all of this is growing rapidly. The time is right.

Starting Strategies.

There's no perfect way to begin, but there are plenty of good ones. What matters most is that you *do* begin. Everyone's path into Bitcoin looks a little different, but the patterns are often the same: curiosity, hesitation, a small first step… and then a growing sense of conviction. Below are some common strategies to help you get started. None of them requires perfection, just that step.

- **You can't play if you're on zero**. First, you must get off zero. If you are on the sidelines and not in the game, you will never fully, truly understand Bitcoin. You must give yourself exposure. This means getting off zero. Get your toe in the water. Put some skin in the game. Take the first step. Once you actually put some money on the table, your perspective changes immediately. You feel the emotion of gain and loss; even if it's at a small level, you will feel it. And your attention to what you are doing also changes. Your focus sharpens. Your concern grows. Your desire to learn and absorb information changes from that moment on. So, you must get off zero.

- **3% to save your portfolio**. Okay, so you have decided to make a move to do something. What are your options? There are many, but let's look at two. One option is what I have discussed in this book. If I am correct, the massive problems with the economy are coming, and there will be a huge correction. Well, if this is the case, a small allocation of 3% could shield your portfolio. If, on the other hand, I am wrong, and nothing happens, you've only committed 3% to Bitcoin. Hardly a threat to your family's wealth. If, in the most unlikely scenario, Bitcoin drops and stays down forever, your loss is limited to that 3%. Pretty easy decision. And if you are skeptical about 3%, take a look at the Nakamoto Portfolio, and see how it will affect your own personal portfolio. You will be quite pleased.

- **Don't dive into the deep end**. Do not go all in at the beginning. Start small, like we talked about earlier. If you go in hard with a lot of your portfolio at the beginning, Bitcoin's volatility can force you out, creating massive losses in the short term. Get used to owning Bitcoin first. Spend some time. Think about it. Measure your performance. Compare it to your plan. Compare it to the models I have previously recommended. Review how things are turning out.

- **Get on the ladder**. The ladder is simple. Get off zero. That's the first step. Figure out your initial trial allocation, 3% or maybe even less. Maybe a few hundred dollars' worth of Bitcoin to play with and to learn. Or maybe a few thousand dollars. The beauty is you decide how much and when. You select your own progression on the ladder. You determine when to go to the next rung by allocation and by the method of ownership. The options are limitless. Then maybe you decide that buying and holding Bitcoin is too much for you right away. You are still learning. So, you do the easy thing. You put your 3% into a Bitcoin ETF and keep learning and studying, listening to podcasts, and watching videos. But then you will notice the benefits of Bitcoin as it grows your portfolio rapidly while you are not having to do anything. At this point, you will take the next step. A fuller allocation will come.

- **Become sovereign**. If you have a Bitcoin ETF, you will start to realize that you don't really own the Bitcoin that is in your Bitcoin ETF. It's just an IOU, and you need to gain greater sovereignty. You will start to shift your capital to personal ownership and control of your Bitcoin. Or, if you own Bitcoin, you will start to feel a greater sense of control and independence. This is the building of your own personal sovereignty. This will grow over time. In turn, this will make you stronger and better able to weather financial bad weather.

The Top Five Myths.

Let us tackle some myths about Bitcoin. There are a lot of them. But we'll focus on the big ones. Otherwise, we would fill this book with Bitcoin myths.

- **Bitcoin is for criminals, drug dealers, and terrorists**. Factually not true. Actually, if you want to break the law, the easiest way to get caught is to have Bitcoin. Remember in previous chapters when we talked about triple-entry accounting? You literally can trace every transaction ever done on the Bitcoin ledger. Only dumb criminals and criminals who want to get caught use a system like this. Criminals prefer the US dollar in cash form. The really large criminal cartels use the big, well-known banks to launder their money. Chase has paid many fines for money laundering, again and again. TD Bank just paid a $3 billion fine for laundering criminal drug gang money. There are many stories about this in the news. Even larger terrorist organizations use the US government to launder their money. None of these are using Bitcoin. If you are breaking the law, avoid Bitcoin. Then avoid my book. We pay our taxes, and we obey the law.

- **Bitcoin uses so much energy; it is an environmental disaster**. This is patently false and has been proven wrong many times. Bitcoin mining currently uses a lot of energy. This is true. However, this energy is for a specific reason that we discussed earlier. This is proof of work. This is the energy used to power the Bitcoin network, and it provides the protection and security of the network. In 17 years, Bitcoin's network has never been hacked. No other network can claim this. Money and electricity are well spent to protect the 6th largest asset in the world. Christmas lights use more electricity than Bitcoin. Computer games use more energy than Bitcoin. Is that a good way to use electricity? Why is no one complaining about these uses?

- **Bitcoin is not backed by anything**. Not true. It's your government's fiat currency that is not backed by anything. The same people who tell you that Bitcoin is wasting energy do not realize that Bitcoin is backed by energy. Energy is the fundamental building block of the universe. Brilliant minds such as Thomas Edison, Buckminster Fuller, and Henry Ford talked of the need for a form of money backed by energy. When you send money to someone, you are sending your human energy. It's just being converted to electrical energy. The electrical energy in Bitcoin is just another way of protecting this. Actually, it is fiat money that is not backed by anything except violence and war. As we explained in early chapters, paper money used to be backed by gold, but now it's not. That's why it's called fiat money. I was once told by my very smart and successful financial advisor, "Sure, the American dollar is not backed by anything. But there are 11 US aircraft carriers sailing the world's oceans, and they are what is backing the US dollar." The sad thing is, he is almost correct; the US dollar is backed by violence and terror. The dollar is backed by proof of war. Frankly, I don't want to be a part of this. This is talked about extensively by OG Bitcoiner Simon Dixon. He calls it the "proof of weapons network."

- **Bitcoin is difficult to understand**. While Bitcoin does take a bit of learning, most of the learning is trying to unlearn all the false things we have been taught about money. Conversely, and more difficult to study and learn, are the 15,000 different stocks listed in the USA, or even more in the international markets. Then add on to this learning about different commodities, different currencies, and topping it off with multiple trading strategies. If you are a dentist or a farmer or an engineer, you want to learn and practice your profession. You do not want to spend all of your time trying to beat the market with its dizzying array of options and strategies. Bitcoin is much easier. Learn the basics as discussed in this book. Maintain a baseline of ongoing learning to stay sharp with security. Hold onto it. And then go outside, and play golf, or go fishing, or play with your grandkids.

- **Bitcoin is too volatile and risky**. Yes, it is volatile, but this is not risky. Risk is a different issue. The volatility from Bitcoin comes primarily from the radical changes being made in the traditional economy by government and central bankers' machinations of their debased and wildly fluctuating fiat currencies. And if you are keeping your Bitcoin safe, and not trading Bitcoin and using it properly as a savings technology, then it will not exhibit risk. If you try to enter and exit Bitcoin multiple times, yes, you will experience risk. It's not recommended. You must look at Bitcoin as a savings technology and not as a short-term investment or a trading strategy. If you decide to go the short-term route, this book cannot help you. You must go into Bitcoin with a long-term savings perspective of a minimum of five to ten years. Or even better is 20 years. There's no need to chase anything. Hold steady, time does the heavy lifting.

Your Three-Layer Model

As you start to get more familiar with Bitcoin and develop more strategies for buying, holding, and disposing of Bitcoin, you are going to want some type of guide. I like to talk about a three-layer model for this strategy. And it fits in with other strategies and models we have discussed. It is the next step in bringing it all together into a unified system.

Remember how we talked about how managing Bitcoin is like being your own bank? Well, this is one of the ways we want to act like a bank. Banks separate money into time frames. For our use, we will separate into three buckets or time frames. Short-term, medium-term, and long-term, just like we did with our custody strategy. The idea is to think of our money in a different way. Just like you wouldn't walk around with $100,000 in your pocket, you probably don't need to keep $100,000 worth of Bitcoin on a custodial single-signature wallet on your iPhone. The chance of something happening to this Bitcoin is high and unnecessary, as we talked about earlier.

Let's Use An Example To Illustrate This.

1. First, you will have your deepest and most secure cold storage, most likely a hardware wallet with a multi-signature protection scheme. This is where you keep the bulk of your Bitcoin. You know that it is unlikely that you are going to spend or send this Bitcoin to anyone in the foreseeable

future. So, you want it locked away safely, and it's ok if it's hard to get at it instantly. Some rules with this layer:

  a. Don't do transfers from outside your possession, to or from this cold storage wallet directly. If you need to transfer to or from this wallet, go through your medium-term wallet. Then transfer to the long-term wallet. Always use this intermediary for security and protection.

  b. Always use a fresh receive address. Never, ever reuse a receive address; that's just bad Bitcoin security hygiene.

  c. Next, keep the wallet and the backup phrase in separate locations. Never store your wallet and your keys (seed phrase) together.

  d. Even though this cold storage wallet is considered long-term, do regular key checks on the wallets to make sure they are up-to-date and have the proper balances and firmware versions. Minimum twice per year.

2. The medium-term wallet is where you will do most of your work. This is where you would keep larger amounts than short-term, but not large amounts.

  a. For instance, you may be getting paid in Bitcoin for some work in your business. You would receive the Bitcoin payments in your medium-term wallet. You can send large amounts to it safely.

  b. Or you are doing a DCA in Bitcoin monthly, and the exchange automatically sends you the Bitcoin at the end of the month. This is the wallet to receive that. It is a wallet that is secure but also has lots of functionality.

  c. This wallet is where you make transactions, consolidate UTXOs, and do other management.

  d. This wallet is for movement and consolidation of Bitcoin, not for storage. Use your cold storage wallet once any work has been done, or if you don't plan on spending the Bitcoin for a while.

3. The short-term wallet can be a hardware wallet, but it is very convenient as a hot wallet on your phone. The choice is yours. Just don't keep large amounts on it. See our guidelines on amounts and match this up with these layers.

   a. This is where you would pay for dinner, make a purchase, or keep some Bitcoin for traveling.

   b. Generally, under $1000, you must decide. But a good rule of thumb is what you would walk around with in your pocket.

Use This Model Daily.

Don't veer from this model. Use it to plan your Bitcoin purchases and sales. Use it to save with. Use it in the context of your security plan that we discussed earlier. Use it in your investment plan. This three-layer model is just an outline. Add to it and refine it, and grow it over time. When working with advisors and security consultants, refer to it. And don't break its rules. The rules are what keep you secure.

As you grow and learn, you will make it more real. Don't give it to anyone to look at. They don't need to see it. Unless it's someone you can trust. And by trust, I mean trust with your Bitcoin, such as maybe close family members.

Bitcoin is Patient.

This brings us to our next area, patience. Rome was not built in a day, and the Bitcoin network is not built overnight. Yes, amazing growth and accomplishments have been made in the past 16 years. More innovation and growth than I could have predicted. But we have a long way to go. Unfortunately, Americans are accustomed to instantaneous gratification and quick, easy results. This is not the way to think of Bitcoin.

You need to have a bit of patience because Bitcoin is patient. It doesn't care what you want right now. It doesn't alter its release schedule because you want more Bitcoin on the market. It doesn't give up its information without a bit of study. One of the structures of this book is the way that I build a series of exercises to help you gain a slow, steady progression of knowledge, one idea built on top of another. This is how the Bitcoin network is progressing and being built. One brick at a time. Warren Buffett famously said about investing, "You make money in the waiting."

This describes Bitcoin perfectly. Wait, learn, watch, and try out different technologies and systems bit by bit. Do the 100 hours of study, practice the exercises in this book, then build a position, do the next 100 hours of study, discuss Bitcoin issues with others like a meetup group, a trusted advisor, or a mentor, and then build and invest some more. By the time you get to the 200 hours, you will start to get and understand Bitcoin. You will grow your skills based on study and the exercises in this book. You will recognize and

Bitcoin Bit.
A recent comment by the great Michael Saylor arguably the largest individual and corporate investor in Bitcoin worldwide. This is what he had to say about Bitcoin Volatility; "People think Bitcoin is risky because its volatile, but actually its volatile because it's not risky. It's the lowest risk thing in the world. You can own it because it's the thing that has the most risk stripped away."

understand your risk tolerance as you become more self-aware and understand more about the technology.

You will not have mastery. But you will be on your way. You will be able to combine your skills with your risk tolerance and your studies to determine how much Bitcoin you should have. As you add to this mix, you will be able to move your level of Bitcoin holdings up safely.

As you get better with Bitcoin, you will also be learning about security. You will be discussing new ideas and strategies with trusted advisors and your meetup group. Learning from your peers and from forums. This will build and build. As your wealth and confidence build. Eventually, you will start to get stronger in your skills. Maybe even teaching family members and friends about Bitcoin.

Confluence of Practices

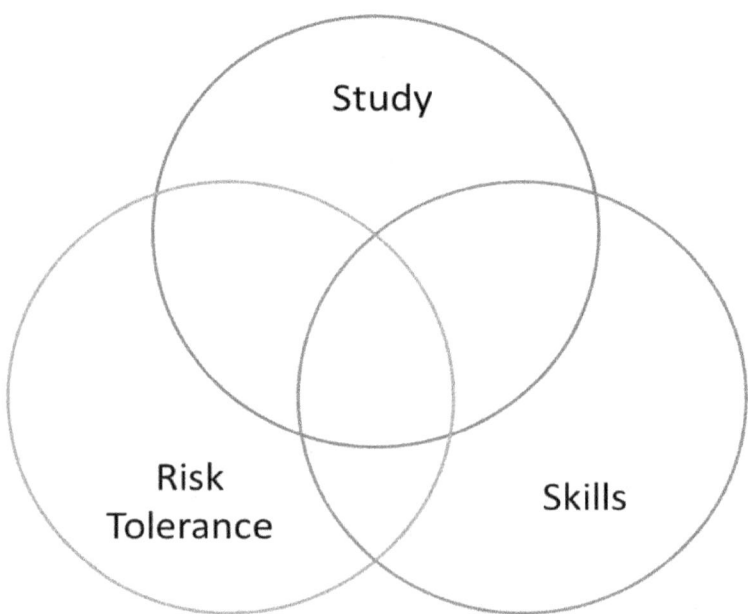

The sweet spot will be where these circles meet.

Bitcoin Exercise. Develop A Succession Plan.

In this next exercise, I want you to try your hand at creating a succession plan for your Bitcoin holdings. Like a lot of these exercises, this may seem like too much to take on, and you may be right. But that is not the purpose. The purpose is to get practice and prepare yourself for succession planning. Even if you have decided to use a professional to help you with this area, I still recommend going through the process.

Below is a rough outline to get you started. This should grow from here at your discretion.

1. Go through the steps. Make them part of your thought process.
    a. Start by reviewing previous plans.
    b. Read your plan out loud to see if it sounds sensible.
    c. Careful not to make it too complex.
    d. Think about your timeline. How far into the future do you want to go?
2. Decide who your successors are and their roles in your succession.
    a. Family or friends.
    b. Select a number of successors and then approach them to see how they feel about participation.
    c. Identify them as technical successors and financial successors.
    d. Compartmentalize. Decide how much to tell each one.
    e. Hierarchy. Should you have tiers of successors to deal with disagreements?
3. Decide which professionals or executors will be involved in your succession plan and their roles.
    a. Compartmentalization. For instance, does your attorney need to know your Bitcoin holdings? If he doesn't, then don't tell him.
    b. Decide who is technical and who is financial.

      c. You may need backups for this process in case someone cannot or will not perform.
4. Decide how you want to integrate it with your will or trust.
      a. Make sure your will is already in order.
      b. Study your scenario to see where succession should fit.
5. Include your custody strategy from previous chapters.
      a. This previous custody strategy should fit in nicely with this plan.
6. Set up an implementation of your succession plan.
      a. How long will it take to implement?
      b. Set meetings, times, dates, and an implementation schedule.
7. Decide on the maintenance schedule of your succession plan.
      a. How often do you review your plans?
      b. What are the maintenance items?
      c. Meet with successors and professionals how often?
8. Meet with successors and professionals to train them.
      a. Do you want to meet individually?
      b. As a group or two groups?
      c. Who gets what information?

Chapter 15

Bitcoin Is The Baby Boomer's Lifeboat

"Bitcoin is hope…"

Michael Saylor

When President Nayib Bukele took office in El Salvador in 2019, his country was in chaos. It was a failed nation by every measure. Because of America's exporting of its violent, rapacious, drug-fueled gangs back to El Salvador, it had become the murder capital of the Western hemisphere. The official crime rate was 106 murders per 100,000 people, a staggering number. It was comparable to Chicago, murder-central of the USA. Violent gangs caused by America's war on drugs had turned the country into a madhouse of death and mayhem. One of the first things President Bukele did was to implement changes to the economy. He enthusiastically supported Bitcoin and even made it legal tender, which meant that businesses and banks had to accept Bitcoin as payment if someone wanted to pay with it. They still had the US dollar, but now they had an alternative. A lifeline. An "escape hatch," as European Central Bank chair and convicted felon Christine Lagarde once called Bitcoin. (She accidentally said the quiet part out loud. As a key figure in the international banking cartel, she knows exactly what bitcoin represents, even if she doesn't like it.)

As president, Bukele instituted multiple reforms, most controversially an aggressive crackdown on violent gangs, jailing thousands of offenders. Western media outlets criticize Bukele's reforms as extreme or harsh. The same media sources that didn't seem to care at all when innocent, poor people in El Salvador were dying by the thousands and lived in sheer terror on a daily basis from extortion, rape, and robbery. Nor did they seem to care about all the death and destruction wrought on the global South by the USA and its endless wars. He also instituted economic reforms, breaking the stranglehold the rich oligarchs and the International Monetary Fund (IMF) had on the country. He allowed poor citizens to get bank accounts, and he instituted a plan to build massive Bitcoin mining facilities powered by cheap, clean geothermal energy from volcanoes, which El Salvador has in huge supply. To solidify the nation's turnaround, Bukele invited Western tech professionals supporting the Bitcoin network to come there and work. And for a small donation of 2 bitcoin, they could gain citizenship and a passport.

Now, a few short years later, El Salvador is a new country with a new lease on life. The murder rate has dropped all the way down to 2.4 per 100,000. The mood in the streets is totally different. There is a rebirth, as people are able to live and breathe again. They can walk with their children and not worry about violence and crime. You see, El Salvador is now the safest country in the Western hemisphere. Is this all because of Bitcoin? Of course not. But it's part of the solution. When Bukele adopted these reforms with Bitcoin, the economic hitmen at the IMF, who are well known for spreading much of the poverty in the Third World, howled pitifully about how this would be terrible for El Salvador. Just like the media whined about the poor criminal murderers in the gangs getting arrested.

The IMF complained in panic because it cannot manipulate El Salvador if it's not using the US dollar. The IMF urged El Salvador to stop using Bitcoin. And cited "significant risks" for "consumer protection." But they couldn't specify any risks or how those risks would come about. But if we go back and look at the IMF, we see a trail of broken economies, dead bodies, and devastation. There is plenty of proof of the IMF's death and destruction. With advisors like the IMF, who needs enemies?

BITCOIN BIT:

DID YOU KNOW THAT THE TINY KINGODM OF BHUTAN HAS BEEN BUYING AND STORING AND MINING BITCOIN FOR YEARS? IN FACT, THEY CURRENTLY OWN AROUND 13,000 BITCOIN IN THEIR TREASURY. WITH AN ESTIMATED VALUE OF AROUND THREE QUARTERS OF A BILLION DOLLARS. MAKING THEM THE FOURTH LARGEST GOVERNMENT HOLDER OF BITCOIN. HOW MANY TINY COUNTRIES HAVE THIS KIND OF SAVINGS IN THEIR TREASURY? ANY? JUST THINK EVERY SMALL COUNTRY ON EARTH COULD DO WHAT BHUTAN IS DOING AND FRONT RUN THE BIG BOYS EASILY.

In 2019, El Salvador's debt-to-GDP was a staggering 95%; by 2024, this had dropped to 49.5% and is still falling. For comparison, the USA has a debt-to-GDP of 134% (lower is better). El Salvador's GDP growth is the highest in the Western Hemisphere, going from -7.6% in 2020 to 3.5% today, and may soon explode to the double digits. This is a startling turnaround. Can we attribute all of this to Bitcoin? I don't think so. But hard money that is honest and does not inflate away encourages economic development. And the proof of this is easy to see. Just look at how loudly the financial media and NGOs such as the IMF whine about the perils of Bitcoin. This tells us all we need to know.

Bitcoin Will Change You.

The evolution of your Bitcoin journey is going to make changes in your life in ways you cannot yet imagine. I know this sounds hyperbolic, but I really believe this. This is why I have only recommended two 100-hour study tracks of Bitcoin. By the time you get through the first and certainly the second, I believe that many of you will start to feel this change in your life. And not just at a financial level, but at the psychological, moral, and even philosophical level. Your sovereignty will be increased and altered forever. And it will be occurring at just the right time. Because in the next few years, we are going to see a loss of sovereignty like we have never seen in our lifetimes.

This change will not be noticeable at first. But it will become quite evident soon enough. People will tell you so. Family members may get exasperated at discussions of Bitcoin at the Thanksgiving table. Once you start to explain to them what you see, believe, and can prove. But once you see it, you will not unsee it. And it will not stop you.

I will point to one simple example to give you an idea of this. Larry Fink is one of the most powerful men in finance. He is the CEO of BlackRock. This behemoth has around $10 trillion of value under management. Several years ago, he called Bitcoin "An index of money laundering." He couldn't criticize it enough. Now he says, "It could revolutionize finance." He himself admitted that he didn't expect to be so surprised by Bitcoin and to have this turnaround. He says it's the best way to protect your wealth. What happened? Well, Fink would have to tell you this. But for me, it's simple. Bitcoin changed him. He took the time to study it and to learn. He got through the first 100 hours, and now he runs the biggest and most successful ETF in Wall Street history, and that is a Bitcoin ETF. And it accomplished this startling success in a matter of months.

And like Bitcoin changed Larry Fink, you should expect to be changed also. It certainly changed me. The time is right. It is not too late. It is actually early in the game. But the time is not unlimited. Think of Microsoft in 1992, or Amazon in 1998. Wouldn't you have liked to have been a part of these revolutions? But this time, you don't have to stand in line behind pre-IPO sales or other special privileges of Wall Street, getting scammed and front-run by the slick suits in these investment banks. This time, you are ahead of Wall Street. They are the ones catching up for once. Now is the time.

You Cannot Help But Be an Optimist.

When you think of Bitcoin and you understand it, I mean you *really* understand it, you realize it's more than a passing fancy to make a bit of money. And it's more than just an investment in your future. But what it really is a revolutionary technology that is changing how we humans communicate with each other. Once you see this, you cannot help but be an optimist.

Just think for a minute that I asked you to build a network. Let's assume that you are a very skilled engineer. The top of your field. You have been working in information technology and engineering, designing and constructing computer networks all over the world. You have access to a massive budget, all of the latest equipment, and a top-notch team of experts. You have everything you need. You have the time to plan this network out, utilizing the latest technologies and design techniques. You have the best project planners and a blueprint for building the network. Now I asked you to build a network that was larger than any other network, more efficient, more secure, it never gets hacked, it never goes down. Could you do it? Could anyone do it? I worked in this field for decades, and I don't see how.

Now, let me add a wrinkle to this little mind exercise. Take away the budget, take away the management team with fat stock options, take away the top shelf highly paid engineers, and the best technicians. Take away the specific project plan, or a blueprint to follow. Could it be done?

How can we look at Bitcoin as anything but a modern miracle? How can we not be optimistic when we see such a wonder growing before our eyes? Living and breathing, taking its first stumbling baby steps, falling and getting up, getting stronger every day. Growing and protecting itself as it crawls and then walks. Being attacked and maligned and victimized every step of the way by people who simply do not understand it. And this lack of understanding actually contributes to its protection. When I see Bitcoin and what it's done in 16 short years, I am optimistic for the world and for humanity. I feel elated and excited to be a part of it. And if you can get past your own few baby steps at the beginning and get through the first 100 or 200 hours, you also will feel this optimism. I can almost guarantee it.

Another Word About Risk.

There are all kinds of warnings about Bitcoin, and "crypto," and risk. Detractors say it's just a risky, speculative investment. I say that you are bringing on unnecessary risk if you don't include Bitcoin. Let's talk about some of the inherent risks you are faced with every day. Risks that you don't readily think about.

- **Counterparty risk**. This is a big one. Every time you include another party in your financial decisions or custody, you are taking on counterparty risk. This is something you always want to reduce as much as possible. With Bitcoin, you can own the actual asset itself and keep it in your own custody, eliminating counterparty risk.
- **Liquidity risk.** What do you do to get your cash out of your investment in a moment's notice? Let's say there is a situation where you need a large amount of your money quickly. Do you think you will get it immediately? Will there be intermediaries asking questions? How about snooping regulators? What about holidays and weekends? Remember, the hardest times are when you will most need your money. With Bitcoin, this is not a problem. It trades in every country 24 hours a day, 7 days a week. It is the most liquid.

- **Currency risk**. When you invest in an asset denominated in a fiat currency, you are now exposed to the risk of that fiat currency. For example, if you buy a stock in the S&P 500, you are now exposed to US dollar risk. If you invest in a bond in England, you are exposed to British pound risk. With Bitcoin, it is the money that you are investing in. And you don't have to worry about its risk. It has never been debased or compromised. At the same time, all fiat currencies are going to zero compared to Bitcoin.

- **Management risk**. Whatever the investment vehicle you are looking at, it has a management team. A company CEO, a money manager, a bank manager, and board members, all of these human beings are fallible. Each one of them is a risk, and the more of them there are, the more risk. What if a CEO gets caught in a scandal? What if a CFO embezzles and absconds with your money? What if someone steals the trade secrets of a company you invest in? These and many others destroy your investment in the blink of an eye. There is no management team with Bitcoin. It is you. Risk eliminated.

- **Political risk**. What happens when the political environment changes in your investment's jurisdiction? For instance, your company may be favored by one political party, and the other party comes into power. What do you do now? How will you adjust? Will you be the first out the door? This is not a problem with Bitcoin. It is liquid and mobile and is not subject to the whims of any political party.

- **Mobility risk**. Can you move your money when you want to and how you want to? Is it possible to get on a plan with your life savings in a moment's notice? Many very wealthy people in China cannot just take their millions and move away. These are called currency controls. They even exist in the USA to a certain extent. It's called an exit tax. This is not an issue with Bitcoin. I am not recommending that you not pay your taxes. But you certainly can take your Bitcoin with you at any time and from any place.

- **Technology risk.** What if your investments are tied up in a technology that is becoming obsolete? What do you do now? Where is the value of your investment if you invested in DVDs or video stores? Were you able to get your value out quickly enough? How about an investment in digital cameras before smartphones? Or Kodak or Xerox. There are numerous examples of technology risk. Bitcoin has been a technology for a millennium. No worries there.

We spoke of risk before but risk is literally as important as gain. It cannot be separated from any investment. So, we should discuss a bit more. There are many other risk factors. Hundreds of them. Do you know which ones you are exposed to? You should at least be aware of these, and others, that may affect you.

Taking Care Of Your Family

I live far from my family, so I don't see them every day. But I make it a point to schedule and see them for social and family events. But also, once a year, I make sure to schedule and meet with family and friends specifically to discuss Bitcoin issues. We talk about the latest Bitcoin trends and the newest consumer technology for Bitcoin. We discuss succession planning, tax strategies, storage, and wallets. We compare strategies for saving vs other investment ideas.

This meeting is, of course, a social and family event. But it's also a Bitcoin and business event. It is a time for learning. I admit I am the lead of this. But I also learn a lot from other members. Like many Boomers, my kids are grown, and they are busy with their own lives and careers. But this is a nice break for me and gives me a good excuse to see them more often. It's something none of us can miss. It's something we all need. And I recommend you do this also. And build some structure around it. Here are some ideas to put some meat on the bone, so to speak.

- Have a meeting agenda with actual points of discussion. And leave enough time for each person to have input, regardless of what they want to say. This is important, and their participation is critical. Ask for agenda items in advance, and include them for all to see. Email is great for this.

- Include technical discussions as well as money topics. It doesn't have to be all about Bitcoin. But I feel that as you do include money topics about other products or services, you will soon see the value of Bitcoin more and more over time.

- Suggest learning exercises before or during the meeting. This will instill a small amount of discipline. Things such as a good article or video work for this.

- If you receive pushback on learning exercises, you can also create fun things to do. Have it at a fun location, or assign members to handle part of the agenda items. Or have games and contests along the way. Make it fun. This will encourage buy-in. Remember, this is friends and family. You have the added benefit of actually enjoying being with these people.

- Include an advisor if needed. You will be talking about legal issues such as succession planning, tax advice, financial advice, or technical advice. If you are going to have these meetings, it wouldn't be too difficult to include a lawyer or technical advisor to join in on a Zoom call during one of the meetings. You can even invite a guest speaker, such as a technical engineer, to do a demo or present a new product. Many times, this can be done for free or as part of their ongoing service.

- Don't try to do this all-in-one sitting. Plan to have multiple or at least two meetings to cover everything. You are only doing this once a year. Try to spread it out so ideas and issues can be hashed out. Remember, you are now your own bank. How does a bank behave with a lot of money? How does one of these rich, multimillion-dollar family offices handle these issues? This is exactly how they do it.

Advanced Exercises.

At this point in your Bitcoin journey, you are getting pretty good. You have a plan, you have tried out several wallets, and you have started investing some of your capital in Bitcoin. You are studying and you're learning. And more importantly, you are taking control of your life. This is a feeling of freedom and sovereignty. You also feel a bit of that optimism that I have referred to above. What do you do next? Where do you take this?

Well, you are probably going to reach a fork in the road. You can take the steps I have outlined in this book, along with the help of some other recommended resources, books, and videos. And you can stop right there. And the beautiful thing is, you can hold on to your Bitcoin and keep it going forever. It will be there for you, for your kids, for your grandchildren, and beyond. Or you can take the other fork in the road and advance in your Bitcoin journey. These steps are beyond the scope of this book. Consider those extra credit exercises. This is the stuff you do to reach greater heights. Let's take a brief look at where you can go.

- Attend a Bitcoin conference. One of the most rewarding experiences I have had in my Bitcoin journey is meeting, learning, and commiserating with other Bitcoiners. This is a beautiful feeling to talk and commune with like-minded individuals who understand what you are doing and where you have been. Learn from their trials and challenges. It was not always easy for any of us. The additional treat of learning from experts, who have gone further down the rabbit hole, is even better. These folks can give you insights and communicate at a level that sometimes is way more advanced. It's fun and you get to learn more.

- Start your own Bitcoin meetup group. Similar to attending the Bitcoin conference or joining a Bitcoin meetup group, starting your own Meetup has a few nice payoffs. First, there is the issue of some Bitcoin meetup groups not always going in the direction that you want to go, such as interference by altcoiners or salespeople trying to scam a group (very common problems). If you are starting your own group, you can control this part of the group. Another benefit is the ability to teach and tutor other new budding Bitcoiners. When you do this, the payoff is extra special. The sparkle in other people's eyes when they get introduced to this fabulous new technology is truly rewarding. And of course, there is the benefit of bringing Bitcoin to the rest of the world. And remember the old Confucius quote, "You teach best what you need to learn the most."

- Run your own Bitcoin node. This is a more advanced technical endeavor, but it's not as difficult as you might think. There is a lot you have learned up to this point, and running your own Bitcoin node is just the next step. You only need an old laptop or even a microcomputer such as a Raspberry Pi with at least one terabyte of disk space. The software is free. But there are other custom software builds you can buy that have support built in with them, such as Start9, Umbrel, and Raspiblitz. The benefit of running your own node means greater privacy for your transactions, greater control over your own destiny, and helping to support the overall Bitcoin network. It's a nice set of payoffs.

- Make a list of your risk factors for all of your different buckets of wealth. It can be a very sobering exercise.

- Be Uncle Jim. We have talked about Uncle Jim before. He or she is the person within a specific group of friends and family who is a trusted advisor. There to help answer questions and lend a helping hand to folks when they get stuck. It's another rewarding way to get you further down the Bitcoin path. Helping the folks in your circle will bring its own intrinsic rewards down the road for many years to come.

As you can see, Bitcoin is a family matter. And should be viewed in the context of how you and your family work together with finances. Next, we want to see how Bitcoin affects the world around us.

Chapter 16

How To Build A Better World…one Satoshi At A Time.

"You may never know the results of your actions. But if you do nothing, there will be no result."

Mahatma Gandhi

I remember when I was working in the early days of building the Internet. What an exciting time it was. If you were a consumer, it was interesting, maybe even an oddity. But if you were a young engineer like me, it was a time of dazzling fascination and innovation. A time of breathtaking new discoveries and daunting challenges to be overcome. A never-ending cascade of newness and possibility.

It lifted my colleagues and me out of our mundane world of sameness and commonality. We were confronted by constant change as we built a new world brick by brick. Only our bricks were not made of clay or masonry but of bits and bytes, routers and switches, and hubs and firewalls. Instead of hand tools, we worked with computers and complex drawings, scanners, and Time Domain Reflectometers, running command lines and scripts. Linked by endless miles of cables carrying a diverse rainbow spectrum of light signals and radio waves, it was confusing and brutally humbling but so much fun. We felt that we could do anything. And that anything was possible. I am still in awe of the process and what the Internet has brought to the world. It was confusing, uplifting, and absolutely exhilarating.

Let's imagine a world where you went to school, a very hard school, maybe an advanced graduate school. And you learned totally new and foreign concepts and procedures and processes. You built on these and made them work and overcame great obstacles. It took you a couple of years to accomplish. But in the end, you had effectuated a great deal. And you proudly looked upon your accomplishments as the best work you have ever done. Happy and satisfied with what you have done. This describes a five-year cycle in my field of network engineering. At the beginning of each cycle, we started over completely with newer, bigger, more complex tasks. Many times, the previous work was either made obsolete or just shrunk down to a few lines of code, or a piece of silicon to be stamped out by the millions in some cavernous factory for pennies. Our prior accomplishments were now superfluous, just an afterthought hidden in a cramped, dark closet somewhere. Never to be seen by anyone. Not supposed to be seen by anyone.

Now, as the consumer, you did not have to deal with this ongoing cycle. We were building the systems to make it easier and more understandable for you along the way. That is why we were there. To get us to the next cycle, so the technicians behind us could learn and standardize it more and more, until it could be reduced to a simple piece of software or a plug-and-play box available at your local electronics store or even run as an app on your phone or laptop.

Fast forward, twenty or thirty years down the road. The inevitable march of this progression continues. More innovation, newer tools, greater discoveries built on the recent technology, this gets automated, shrunk down, price reduced, pushed to the background of convenience and anonymity. Making our lives better and better every day. Only to see the cycle continue. On and on and on.

This is all a normal progression. It's the way technology evolves, and Bitcoin is going through this progression. And it still has a long way to go. The great gains we see now will continue at least for the near future, and most likely for a long time. This is part of two processes: one is the evolution of a new technology; the second is the evolution of a new way for humans to communicate securely and safely. The evolution of a new kind of money. And that second one is a big one. Its evolution will require a huge, almost inestimable amount of propellant. And that fuel, that burning propellant, is the Bitcoin price appreciation. The more price appreciation, the faster and more efficiently Bitcoin will evolve. But make no mistake about its future. It will evolve. It will happen. Just like Spring follows Winter. There is no choice in this. Adopt it or be left behind in poverty.

One day, Bitcoin will not appreciate in price by 10X or 20X in a cycle. It will be more realistic. It will appreciate by maybe 40% in a year, and then 25%, and then 15%. When will this happen? No one knows for sure. And I certainly can't forecast this. But what I do know is that we are very early. And it is still in the very high growth stages. And will continue this way for the near future. So maybe we should get on board while this continues to happen.

If You Think Bitcoin Is Just About Investing, Then You Need To Look Closer.

As you start to go through your Bitcoin discovery, you are going to notice many things. You are going to feel more empowered, more active, and have more peace of mind. You will notice there is a different sense of purpose in your life, especially as you help friends and family join you on this intriguing journey. You are going to feel a closeness and comfort with your family that you didn't have before. All of you will feel safer and more secure.

You will notice a different way of looking at the world. And a different way of looking at yourself. You will feel strong and capable. More in charge. Just think of your current state... so disempowered, so manipulated, and so lied to. So battered by this crisis and that disaster. Constantly living in a fog of uncertainty and crisis. We are like an exhausted and beat-up boxer, our knees wobbly, our head confused and clouded. Who knows what's going to happen next? The fear and stress that are incorporated into our daily routine are like a heavy blanket that we can never seem to shake off. It smothers us with the oppressive weight of the state and the worldwide banking cartel. Fleecing us at every turn. Chipping away at our savings and whittling down our hard-earned wealth to a brittle, little stick.

How many pieces of junk mail do you get every day? Do you still have a landline telephone? How many scam calls do you get every day? How many solicitors come to your door to sell you something you don't need? How many times have you been ripped off in the past year by unscrupulous vendors? How many hidden charges and taxes show up on your bills, like your cell phone or your cable bill or your utility bills? How many of these fees and charges are actually optional, but no one ever bothered to get your permission? Many times, these vendors are actual companies you already do business with. And they are still preying on you at every opportunity.

Just think of it. The oppression of the next terrorist attack or pandemic or financial or food disaster. The next political threat or foreign war. All constantly thrust upon us from distant, uncontrolled, and uncontrollable sources expertly fed to us by social media and traditional media. The fear that comes from all of this constant haranguing and harassment. All paid for by the massive fiat financial system.

You will start to see through this more and more and not take it so seriously. At least if you don't want to. Of course, if you want to pay attention to it all and keep feeling threatened by it, you can. If you don't, you will now see a path out of this morass, this incessant maze filled with labyrinths of anguish and fear. Or you can stay in it. Some people choose this path. But it is your choice.

One of the things you'll discover about Bitcoin over time is something I and other Bitcoiners have learned. Gigi, a well-known Bitcoiner, noticed that just trying to explain what you learned about Bitcoin is not an easy question to answer because you will start to notice how it affects so many different parts of your life, for the better.

Balaji, an influential technologist and venture capitalist, said, "Bitcoin is a game designed to teach you about…ethics of money, history of central banking and gold, adversarial system design, commodities markets, distributed system engineering and the software lifecycle, securities law." That's quite a lot. Luckily, we don't have to go into all of these. But these are all areas that Bitcoin will affect and improve. As Baby Boomers, we can easily learn to save with Bitcoin and leave these other disciplines to others.

Marty Bent, another Bitcoiner and thought leader who runs a very good podcast called *"Tales From The Crypt,"* wrote, "Bitcoin changes you more than you change it."

Gigi continues, "Bitcoin will completely change your worldview." And it will be for the better. A clean, pleasant, capable view of the world.

I can personally vouch for these insightful points. I have noticed in myself a constant learning that goes on every day that I am in Bitcoin. This is exciting and challenging at times. Much of it seems almost automatic, as if I am a wilted plant absorbing sunlight after years of neglect in the dark. Yes, there are specific things that I learn intentionally. And we talk about many of them here. But there seem to be so many other ideas that are almost osmotic in their change of my knowledge and attitude. Giving me a greater breadth of my view of the world. The constancy, serenity, and security are warm and comforting. Making my world easier, and making it more of my world and not anyone else's world. Not a victim but an individual sovereign human being.

Make Bitcoin Part Of Your Daily Routine

It's much more productive, as you get used to Bitcoin, to start to make Bitcoin part of your daily routine. What do you do every day? Maybe you eat three meals. What do they cost you? What would it cost you if you didn't have a Bitcoin strategy? How much does your trip to the store cost? Are the things you are buying necessary, or could these extra spending items partially go toward more Bitcoin? I know this seems extreme, but it won't once you start to understand what wasting money on the next air fryer or the next $100,000 pickup truck is really costing you.

Money Is Energy.

Please remember, money is energy at the end of the day. It is simply a representation of your energy in every sense of the word. From the physical energy you exert to the mental energy of solving a problem. Or the creative energy of your soul used in building a new product with the concomitant skill. Or even the massive release of energy when inventing something totally new. It's all energy. And energy is the fundamental building block of the universe.

Without energy, nothing we say or do or even think is possible. And there is only one productive way to communicate and move this energy around from person to another or from entity to entity. And that is via the exchange of money. This is why governments covet it so much. Why do they steal it, manipulate it, control it, and always want to have more of it? They need this energy. They will never stop doing this. It's what they are; it is their basic purpose. But with custody of your own Bitcoin, this process of theft stops.

Give this energy to another, and they benefit. Take this energy from another, and you will benefit but not as much. But the important thing is that no other asset in history has the ability to transport this energy through time and space like Bitcoin. It is a phenomenon never seen before. If you are sitting on your couch on a Saturday evening, and for some reason, you need to send $1,000 or even $1 million of Bitcoin to someone in Tokyo, you can do it. And for very little cost. Reliably and quickly. If you want to take $1 million of Bitcoin and store it for your great-great-grandchildren 100 years from now, you can do that, too. And for very little cost. These concepts were unheard of before. This ability to move your energy through time and space is unprecedented.

A World Where Everyone Is Equal.

One of the ways that law enforcement tries to trick and trap innocent people into seizing their cash is to use "drug sniffing dogs." Essentially, what they do is search your belongings or your car, and if the dog wags its tail, that's considered "probable cause" to seize your cash. Usually targeting large amounts of cash. The little trick they are not telling you is that virtually every US dollar in currency has been touched by drug dealers. Remember, money is meant to be circulated. So, of course, the dog's sensitive nose smells

BITCOIN BIT:

IN THE EARLY DAYS OF BITCOIN WALLETS USED TO BE KEPT ON PAPER. AND BITCOIN WAS ACTUALLY GIVEN AWAY TO ENCOURAGE PEOPLE TO START ADOPTING IT. ONE OF THE EARLIEST SCHEMES WAS A WEBSITE WHERE YOU COULD GO AND PUSH AN ONLINE BUTTON AND GET A FREE BITCOIN SENT TO YOUR WALLET. OR PEOPLE WOULD HAND OUT FREE BITCOIN AT PARTIES TO ENCOURAGE DISTRIBUTION.

drugs on the money, manufacturing the false probable cause for the seizure. This practice is called "civil asset forfeiture," and it's a real thing. Done many times a day. Something that would never happen with Bitcoin.

There was a recent attempt to track and blacklist certain bitcoin addresses and pressure miners to reject transactions involving those coins, essentially, to control the bitcoin system by targeting people the government didn't like. No law authorized this; it was just a rogue agency trying to bend bitcoin to its will. It was ridiculous and failed. Some miners, including large corporate mining companies in the USA, actually did try to follow this insane mandate. But Bitcoin mining is an extremely cutthroat and competitive business. And there were 10 miners happy to process the transactions to replace every one of the government collaborators. So eventually they gave up on this gambit.

One of the richest men in the world, Elon Musk, owns quite a bit of Bitcoin in his companies Tesla and SpaceX. However, he bought his Bitcoin the same way you and I buy Bitcoin. There is no special benefit that Musk or dozens of other billionaires receive from their Bitcoin. They receive the same ability to store and move their wealth in Bitcoin that you and I do. Bitcoin is highly egalitarian, and there is nothing anyone can do about this, either.

There is no central authority, special group, or government that can make your Bitcoin any different than anyone else's. It is all 100% equal and fair. One Bitcoin is worth 1 Bitcoin, regardless of who owns it or where you are or how it is sold. And this will never change.

You're Not A Financial Expert And Don't Have To Be.

You're not a financial expert, and you never will be. What is your profession if you are a boomer and still working? Or if you are a retired boomer, you spent your life not only accumulating wealth and abundance for you and your family, but you also gained a skill. If you have any wealth to show for it, you probably got good at your profession. Are you a dentist or a doctor? Are you a technical engineer or in IT? Maybe you are really technical? Or maybe you are a financial expert working in corporate finance or accounting? Or, like many of you, you started and owned a successful small business. Maybe in construction, or retail, or manufacturing? Or a hundred different other professions. But most likely, you are not an expert in investing, saving, and growing the money that you earn. And here lies the problem. Do you know financial trading strategies? How about international currency arbitrage? Do you know the best commodities to trade in and understand futures markets? No. And you shouldn't need to.

There are 500 different companies in the S&P 500. There are 2000 leading companies in the Russell 2000, and there are 3108 ETFs traded in the USA alone. There are 68 different commodities traded in the US, and there are thousands more internationally. And multiply this by hundreds of investing and trading strategies. Don't forget to select experts or specialists in each area and each strategy. And you have the unenviable task of trying to figure out which of these to protect and save in. Where do you start? Where do you find the time? Which expert do you trust?

Let's say you are a veterinarian. You have struggled, worked, and sacrificed to build a successful veterinary practice. You have seven employees and hundreds of patients. You are reliable and respected in your community. You can look at a horse and know what's wrong with her almost instantly because of your years of practice and expertise. But put just 25 different investment options in front of you, and you would not know where to start.

When would you have the time? You spent the last 40 years building your career. Are you going to take time out each week to study investment trends, stock indexes, or charting strategies? How about trading? Are you going to become a technical trader in your spare time? Or how about a FOREX trader, trading currencies in the international markets? Of course not. But if you are to stand any chance of keeping any of that hard-earned money after taxes, you had better figure out a way. Do you think your RIA or financial advisor is going to do it for you? Guess again.

But you can focus on Bitcoin. Do the 100 or 200 hours of study and get to a possible place of security and safety for your money. It was never meant to be the fiat way. You were never meant to be in this type of conundrum. And you will never get out of it by using the traditional finance world. And this problem multiplies when there is a major financial crash, which is an inevitability in our future.

Bitcoin Is A Force Pulling Everything Into It.

Bitcoin will pull you in. It will pull everyone in. It is just a matter of time. Our goal as Baby Boomers is to be at the front of this wave, not at the end of it. To lead ourselves, our family, and our friends into this inevitable force from the beginning, we need to be organized and have a plan. Giving ourselves the ability to not only avoid the calamity of the coming economic collapse, but to actually be protected from it and to benefit from it. Potentially at a very high level.

First, we see early adopters. Then we see intelligent systems and AI that want to participate and will make decisions that move them toward Bitcoin systems. Then there will be the folks who believe in Bitcoin, or more importantly, people who really need Bitcoin like us. From this will come the masses. But they will come. This is not a question of who or how many. It's just a question of when. As referred to earlier when talking about economic movements, it will probably happen slowly and then suddenly. This is a symptom of the human psyche and its herd mentality, particularly in financial realities. But it will all collapse into the Bitcoin network eventually, like an enormous financial black hole. Pulling us in inexorably. And when it does, I want to be safe and secure knowing where my nest egg is and be able to get to it at any time. I want to know how to use it, protect it, and exploit it.

Onboarding Another. The Final Exercise.

Your final exercise, if you choose to accept it, can be the most important one: onboarding another individual into the Bitcoin world. This is not necessarily an easy exercise and can actually be a significant challenge. But the personal reward is fabulous.

There are several things you will learn by onboarding someone else. First, you will learn about the other person. And second, you will learn about yourself. Have you really accomplished these previous exercises so well? Do you really know? How do you know? It's kind of like your final exam. And of course, you will learn even more about Bitcoin. You will find out more about what you didn't know when you have to articulate it to another.

Don't get too ambitious, unless you want to make it into a bigger project. As you go through the onboarding process, it will force you to face up to your previous exercises and see exactly how well you did. No one is watching. Just you and your new student. But now you will know for sure. It will build some discipline. If you want to think like rich people do, you need some discipline.

Onboarding will also show you how other people think about money, technology, and Bitcoin. You will need to fill in the holes that you think are self-evident, that are really not so intuitive to other people.

Onboarding another person gives you even greater buy-in. Responsibility for helping another person helps guide your own fate by guiding theirs. Having no selfish desire to get anything. Only to help. And this process can engender a good feeling. How often do we get the gratifying opportunity to give another human being something of real value?

Wow, what a tremendous benefit. Life is truly beautiful.

Glossary of Terms

Advanced lending. The ability to lend products to preferred customers.

Alternative Coin. Commonly known as an Alt Coin. Is a token issued by a company or institution or individual to raise capital to avoid SEC and other government regulations. Also known as a unregistered security. Commonly used in different types of scams.

AML/KYC. Anti money laundering, and know your customer. This is an arcane and oppressive set of regulations ostensibly designed to prevent money laundering. When in reality they are specifically designed to spy on their customers and citizens. It is actually one of the most serious erosions of personal privacy.

Bank. A form of business that has the ability or privileges of storing and lending money and other financial services. Banks are the primary source of capricious adding of money into the system without stop.

Bitcoin. A unique form of money defined by the Bitcoin Whitepaper authored by Satoshi Nakamoto. Giving a new form of electronic currency, and a supporting network. It has been called digital gold.

Blockchain. A form of primitive database that when combined the centralization of Bitcoin and Bitcoin's monetary policy creates a safe and reliable way to see all transactions in the network.

Block Reward. The reward in Bitcoin that is given to the winning miner when they discover a new Block and then they get to process the transactions in this winning block. The current block reward is 3.125 Bitcoin worth about $380,000.

Cantillon Effect. This is the economic theory that states that when fiat money is produced it contains incentives that reward the intermediaries who are closest to the source of the issued money. At the expense of the mass of people further downstream. This then results in a greater diversity of the distribution of wealth.

Centralization. The continuous moving of resources and money and power into fewer and fewer hands resulting in the concentration of power. And the resulting declining levels of freedom and autonomy for the rest of the population. And decentralization is the distribution of power across space, and time, and many people or institutions. This always results in greater freedom and benefit for everyone.

Central Bank. I special bank for other banks. That exerts control and monetary policy on member banks and the citizens within its system.

Commodity. A basic input to an economic system that does not originate within a company or government entity. Corn or Gold or Bitcoin are commodities. A phone or a refined steel bar or a corn souffle' are not commodities.

Custody. The possession of financial assets by a specific party. There can be self-custody and centralized custody. Whoever has custody of the asset actually owns the asset.

Bitcoin Network Confirmation. The procedure of a Bitcoin transaction going through Bitcoin miner processing. And the block getting forwarded and transaction getting confirmed. This will then be stacked upon other transaction consecutively meaning 2 confirmations, and then three confirmations, ad infinitum.

Consumer Price Index. Also known as the CPI is a measurement of a basket of goods. Purportedly a way to measure the rate of inflation. However, this statistic like GDP has been highly falsified and manipulated for years. Its ok for measuring a month to month or year to year comparison but is not good for really measuring inflation overall. A good general measure is to use "shadowstats" or the S&P500 annual growth rate.

Encryption. The obscuring of data on a network or computing system using multiple cipher and scrambling techniques. Virtually all financial systems today use encryption techniques. Bitcoin uses a variety of techniques, such as SHA-256, Ripemd-160, and ECDSA.

ETF. Exchange traded fund. An investment device certified by the state that closely follows another investment vehicle. Such as a gold ETF, or a S&P500 ETF. If you have a gold ETF it is going to own the underlying asset. And it will closely follow the price action of the underlying asset.

Equity Market. Essentially the stock market, expressed in ownership of a company using the trading of stocks.

Fiat Money. Money that is made by decree. It has nothing to do with any type of effort or value. It is just ordered into existence. It rewards the fiat money issuer tremendously at the expense of the common user. Please see proof of work vs proof of stake. As a secondary effect it also rewards the parties immediately downstream of the money printer. Please see Cantillon Effect.

Firewall. A piece of network technology that detects and filters and blocks security threats from your network.

Fixed income market. Consisting of fixed income investment vehicles, such as coupon bonds, dividend paying stocks, cash flow real estate.

Generational Wealth. Wealth that is saved or invested in a sufficiently large enough mass to be able to span multiple generations of your family.

GDP. Gross Domestic Product. This is defined by the measurement of the total goods and services within a nation's economy for one year. However, this number like many statistics has been altered to make things look better for the incumbent politicians in office. So please be careful with this number just like inflation statistics.

Gold Standard. The monetary standard based on the metal gold which has superior characteristics in immutability, scarcity, and fungibility. Was the de-facto monetary standard of the 19th and twentieth century.

Hash Rate. I method of measuring and recording the total amount of processing and power utilized to maintain Bitcoin network.

Hypothecation. The taking of monetary savings and lending it out, and then relending that money out again, and again. Resulting in something called re-hypothecation. Typical of a phenomenon called fractional reserve banking.

Inflation. Expansion of the money supply due to central bank and government debasement of the currency. Hyperinflation is officially defined as 50% per month. This is an extreme late state of an inflationary spiral.

Keynesian Economics. A study of economics that follows John Maynard Keynes that is the dominant school of economics today. It is highly supportive of constant government and central bank interference in the system.

Margin. Lending technique used to further your investments. Borrowing money to support an investment position. Highly risky.

Miner. A Bitcoin miner is a piece of computer hardware that performs calculations specifically to win a Bitcoin lottery. In order to bring out the next block of Bitcoin transactions. This will then result in a block reward to the owner of the miner. These miners evolve into newer and faster technologies, to compete to win more Block rewards. This then results in a stronger and safter Bitcoin network. Protecting everyone's Bitcoin in the network.

Money. A technology that allows the exchange of value between two parties. It has one or more properties of store of value, medium of exchange, unit of account, and system of control.

Node. A Bitcoin node is a fundamental feature of the Bitcoin network that is run with a piece of software called Bitcoin Core. Its basic functions are to verify and validate transactions in a public way. And to provide a public audit trail for Bitcoin blockchain. And to vote on changes to the Bitcoin network.

Password Manager. A piece of software that requires you to enter one master password for the software. Then it generates strong passwords for all of your other applications. Keeping them up to date and making changes to keep them hardened. A highly recommended tool for good security.

Privacy. Computer privacy is the obscuring of your identity from other entities in order to protect yourself. This is a fundamental building block of computer security. All forms of privacy physical and computer are encouraged to enhance your security of your assets.

Proof of Work. A concept used in crypto currency to define its monetary policy. It simply means work or some other effort or value has to be expended in order to bring more of a monetary unit on the market. In the case of Bitcoin work is performed by expending energy to run the miners that bring the Bitcoin into the market. This is opposed to proof of stake which requires no work or expression of value to issue the money.

Redundancy. The concept of reducing failure in a network or system by creating multiple devices or paths within a network or a computing system.

RIA. Registered investment advisor. These are professionals hired by investors with specific expertise and registered with the state to assist in building investment portfolios and provide investment advice.

Risk. The opportunity for failure and loss of a specific investment or transaction. Usually measured in comparison to other systems.

Reserve Currency. Refers to the default or preferred currency in a system. This is usually the currency that is most fungible within a system. Currently it is the US dollar. Before this it was the British Pound.

Scarcity. A critical expression of the value of money. The scarcer an item I the more value it has. Gold is very scarce so it retains value very well. There is only about 2% new gold every year. So, it takes 50 years for gold's value to go in half. Bitcoin has absolute scarcity, so it retains value better than other commodities or money.

Security. 1. This is a method of maintaining safety, privacy and protection of resources for you and your systems. 2. Also known as "A security," is a financial instrument that is issued by a bank or corporation and under their control. To raise capital for the issuing institution. Stocks and bonds are examples of securities.

Self-Custody. This is possession of an asset as opposed to centralized custody. This gives the putative owner of the asset actual true ownership as opposed to centralized custody. Examples of self-custody are owning gold in a safe, or Bitcoin in your own personal wallet where only you have the keys.

Settlement. Or final transaction settlement is the process of going through multiple intermediaries with your transaction. And the central intermediaries settle the transaction to both parties' satisfaction. For instance, your credit card charges go through your bank and the credit cards bank and the merchants bank and possibly a central bank taking over 90 days to reach final settlement.

SHA-256. This is an encryption scheme that defines how to achieve 256 bits of encryption into a data packet. This 256-bit hash value is extremely secure. The important thing to understand is how difficult this is to crack. Currently there is not enough computing power on earth to crack a SHA-256 hash value.

Treasury Securities. These are a mix of financial instruments that the US government uses to borrow money from their people, other governments, banks, and even themselves. T-Bills, T-Bonds, Savings Bonds. They are usually assumed to be guaranteed by the US government however they have defaulted on them several times.

Trustless system. Typical monetary systems Rely on specific institutions of trust to ensure the safety of storage of monetary transactions. A trustless system does not require these "trusted intermediaries." A particular value of Bitcoin. Since it has been discovered throughout history that these intermediaries cannot provide trust or safety. A trustless system is always superior.

Two Factor Authentication. This is an extended authentication method to harden your security of electronic access. In a normal scenario you log into a system with username and password. In two factor you add a second method such as texting a code to your phone, or using a two-factor authenticator such as Google Authenticator. Highly recommended for all important transactions.

Volatility. The variability of the price of a financial instrument over time. Volatility is sometimes confused with Risk. However, this is not always the case.

VPN. Virtual Private Network, this is a security technology that allows you to protect network communications by building an encrypted tunnel between your device and the destination device. VPNs greatly enhance your security. Particularly when you are running on an untrusted or public network.

Wallet. A piece of software or hardware that contains a set of keys. These keys are encrypted and protected from theft by military grade encryption. The purpose of the wallet is to maintain a user's ownership of his share of Bitcoin on the ledger. Wallets come in two primary forms. Hot wallets run on a computing device. Hot means the wallet has electricity through it. Hot wallets provide good protection. And a cold wallet which is a separate piece of hardware that provide very strong protection. Contrary to popular belief the wallet does not contain the Bitcoin it only contains the keys, to access the owner's Bitcoin on the network.

Zero Confirmation. A Bitcoin transaction that has not been confirmed yet. Meaning the block has not been processed by a Bitcoin miner.

Interested in buying 10 or more copies? Call us for our discount schedule.

Phone Number: 321-244-4988
Email: JH@JERRYHUTCHESON.COM

10-50 Copies: $12 plus shipping.
50-100 Copies: $10 plus shipping.
100-500 Copies: $8.50 plus shipping.
500 + Copies: $7 plus shipping.